Encyclopedia
of
Hardy
Plants

Annuals, Bulbs, Herbs, Perennials, Shrubs, Trees, Vegetables, Fruits & Nuts

Derek Fell

Firefly Books

A FIREFLY BOOK

Published by Firefly Books Ltd. 2007

Copyright © 2007 Derek Fell and David Bateman Ltd

First printing

Publisher Cataloging-in-Publication Data (U.S.)

Fell, Derek.
    Encyclopedia of hardy plants: annuals, bulbs, herbs, perennials, shrubs, trees, vegetables, fruits & nuts/ Derek Fell.
[224] p. : col. photos. ; cm.
Includes index.
Summary: Reference to over 1,000 cold-hardy plants. Included annuals, perennials, woody plants, herbs, fruits and vegetabls that can survive severe winters, especially where the ground freezes.
ISBN-13:978-1-55407-240-8
ISBN-10: 1-55407-240-9
1. Cold-tolerant plants—Encyclopedias. I. Title.
632.11 dc22   SB454.3.W43.F455 2007

Library and Archives Canada Cataloguing in Publication

Fell, Derek
    Encyclopedia of hardy plants : annuals, bulbs, herbs, perennials, shrubs, trees, vegetables, fruits & nuts / Derek Fell.
Includes index.
ISBN 1-55407-240-9
    1. Cold-tolerant plants--Encyclopedias. I. Title. II. Title: Hardy plants.
SB450.95.F44 2007   635.9'0912   C2006-905101-1

Published in the United States by
Firefly Books (U.S.) Inc.
P.O. Box 1338, Ellicott Station
Buffalo, New York 14205

Published in Canada by
Firefly Books Ltd.
66 Leek Crescent
Richmond Hill, Ontario L4B 1H1

Designed by Intesa Group, Auckland, New Zealand
Printed in China through Colorcraft Ltd, Hong Kong

RIGHT: Pansy planting at Cedaridge Farm, Pennsylvania, U.S.A.

Contents

Introduction
What is a hardy plant?

In my experience of growing and writing about plants for 45 years, the first question people in temperate climates ask about an unfamiliar plant is whether it is hardy. They wish to know if it will survive severe frosts and frozen soil even though hardiness in its broadest sense can mean drought resistance, heat tolerance and survival in poor soil. To most people, therefore, hardiness among plants means COLD HARDINESS.

But even the term cold hardiness can be confusing because some plants will tolerate light frost (such as Chilean gunnera and New Zealand flax), but they are killed by prolonged freezing weather and especially frozen soil. There is also the common practice in books and catalogs to refer to plants as hardy, half-hardy and tender: hardy meaning a plant will tolerate heavy frost; half-hardy meaning a plant will tolerate light frost; and tender meaning that a plant is killed by even a mild frost.

For the purposes of this book, therefore, borderline half-hardy annuals and borderline hardy perennials (such as pampas plume) are not included. The focus, instead, is on what I term "iron-clad hardy" plants, encompassing hardy annuals and perennials, woody plants, even herbs, fruit and vegetables that can survive severe winters, especially in areas where the ground freezes. This book represents a collection of the most important hardy plants for temperate gardens, with an emphasis on those that are relatively carefree, easy to obtain and likely to add the strongest visual interest in a garden setting.

Most of these plants are "survivors"—some prominent in home gardens, and others less familiar, but certainly worthy of garden space. The ornamentals are arranged alphabetically by botanical name, with a cross-reference common name index, and the edibles are arranged by common name because their botanical names are unfamiliar to most people. This organization of the ornamental section by Latin name is essential since common names vary from one area to another, and several plants can have the same common name, such as forget-me-not, which can include species in the family *Myosotis* and *Cynoglossum* as well as others.

Annuals

In nature there is nobody to till the soil and plant seeds to their recommended depth. Most hardy plants spill their seed abundantly on the ground in autumn, remain dormant during cold winter months and sprout when the temperature rises. Subjected to freezing temperatures and even a blanket of snow, the warmth of a spring thaw will open up cracks in the soil for seed to fall into. If the temperature rise is sustained and there is sufficient moisture to swell the embryo then germination is triggered. This is true of all hardy plants, whether they are hardy annuals, hardy perennials or hardy woody plants. With annuals, the ability for some to overwinter

TOP: Blue Siberian iris and ox-eye daisies make perfect companions in a cottage garden.

ABOVE LEFT: Mixed border combines hardy annuals like larkspur and hardy perennials like coreopsis.

ABOVE RIGHT: 'Dragon's Blood' sedum spreads a red carpet besides clumps of Irish moss.

OPPOSITE: Hardy evergreen *Leucothoe fontanesinana* (center) and deciduous Japanese maple enliven a woodland garden in autumn.

Introduction

Self-seeded pot marigold (*Calendula officinalis*) enjoys a cool coastal location.

from an autumn sowing, or even a winter or early spring sowing, even before the last spring frosts, classifies them as hardy annuals.

Annuals are the first plant group we can turn to for "instant" color. Many can be purchased locally from garden centers, ready grown in convenient transplant pots for you to plant before the last spring frosts. They are classified as tender (damaged by mild frosts), half-hardy (damaged by harsh frosts) and hardy. Generally speaking, these hardy annuals will survive even harsh frosts, and so they can be planted into flowering positions several weeks before the last expected frost date in spring. Some can even be planted in autumn to survive

winter as a dormant green mound of leaves for extra-early flowering in spring. Seed of many other hardy annuals can be sown after the first frost date in autumn to remain dormant until a prolonged warming spell in spring causes the seed to germinate.

There is a problem classifying certain hardy annuals as "hardy." For example, many seed catalogs classify sweet peas as hardy and recommend them for autumn planting. This is certainly true of virtually all parts of the U.K., Australia and New Zealand, for example. However, in North America where winters are more severe, with frozen soil possible in zone 7 and colder, sweet peas are unlikely to survive an autumn planting. Nor will sweet pea seed sown on top of frozen soil remain dormant. Too often, it will soak up too much moisture and rot. Therefore, they are included with this cautionary note.

Perennials

Since perennials live from year to year, and generally bloom the second season after seed starting, hardy perennials selected for this book must tolerate more than light frosts and even contend with frozen soil, though the dangers of frozen soil can be lessened by mulching heavily. Like trees and shrubs, hardy perennials can be deciduous or evergreen. With evergreen perennials the foliage remains visible during winter (such as Oriental poppies), while others are root hardy (such as Japanese bleeding hearts).

A large number of deciduous perennials, such as daffodils and tulips, survive harsh winters by means of fleshy storage organs collectively called bulbs. The top growth dies down but the bulb remains firm, with enough energy reserves to sprout new green growth as soon as a warming trend occurs in spring. Indeed, there are many perennials, especially those that form bulbs, that must have a prolonged cold spell in order to return. Tulips, for example, require a cold period—below 40°F (4°C)—of at least 10 weeks, and the same is true of tree peonies.

Biennials are included in this section because they generally require two seasons to bloom before dying. However, many biennials, such as foxgloves, dames rocket and honesty, set prodigious amounts of seed to self-sow and come back year after year as if they were perennials.

Shrubs and Trees

Shrubs bridge the gap between perennials and trees. Though there is no difference botanically between a shrub and a tree (they are both termed "woody plants," forming a strong cell structure called wood), a shrub tends to be multi-stemmed, while a tree grows a strong, straight trunk. Also, shrubs tend to stay under 15 ft (4.5 m) in height. Trees and shrubs carry their ornamental effect higher than annuals or perennials, which are collectively known as herbaceous plants because of their soft stems. When young they are most susceptible to winterkill through desiccation, whereby cold winds and a dry period can combine to dehydrate the life out of them. To prevent desiccation there are anti-desiccant sprays that can be applied to newly planted young trees and shrubs. This helps them through their first winters until established. Also, the practice of wrapping valuable young trees and shrubs in burlap sacking is advisable to break the force of the wind, especially those in exposed positions. Be aware also that though a plant, such as a wisteria or a forsythia, may be sufficiently root hardy to survive severe winters, the flower buds themselves can be killed, particularly during a premature thaw. This forces them to unfold, and exposes them to freezing when colder temperatures return.

TOP: Shade garden at Cedaridge Farm features mostly hardy primroses for floral color.

ABOVE: Hardy river birch (*Betula nigra* 'Heritage') contrasts decorative bark with pink redbuds and azaleas at Cedaridge Farm.

Roses and many perennials have roots that rodents will eat to survive winters. Though they may not eat the entire root, they often eat enough to deprive the plant of proper anchorage. Movement from wind will rock the roots, exposing them to the cold air that may lead to winterkill. Squirrels are a potential hazard to newly planted bulbs, especially lilies and crocus, since they regard them as food and will dig down to acquire them. Rodent-repellent mothballs or rodent-repellent flakes worked into the soil around susceptible roots will reduce rodent damage.

Edible Plants

Culinary herbs, dessert fruits and vegetables can be herbaceous or woody, and they can be classified as annual, biennial or perennial. For example, parsley is a hardy biennial that grows a healthy clump of edible leaves the first year, and persists even through harsh winters before it dies down in the second season. Vegetables are more often divided into cool-season crops (like lettuce and peas) and warm-season crops (like tomatoes and melons). Though many cool-season crops will tolerate even severe frost (like cabbage and lettuce), they will rot when the ground freezes.

A Word about Lawn Grasses

The most commonly used lawn grasses for hardiness are Kentucky bluegrass (*Poa pratensis*) and perennial ryegrass (*Lolium perenne*). In tests by the Canadian Prairie Turfgrass Research Centre, it was found that cold hardiness differs between varieties. For example, the popular perennial ryegrass variety 'Manhattan' has hardiness levels between 23ºF (−5ºC) and 5ºF (−15ºC), whereas the hardiness range for 'Fiesta 3', 'Pennfine' and 'PickPC' was 17.6ºF (−8ºC) and 1.4ºF (−17ºC). Kentucky bluegrass generally showed 3.2ºF (−15ºC) to −14.8ºF (−26ºC) cold tolerance. Though Kentucky bluegrass is the hardiest lawn grass tested, it is not as hardwearing as perennial ryegrass, and so a mixture of the two is advisable in regions with cold winters, allowing the bluegrass to fill in where the ryegrass suffers winter damage.

TOP: Raised beds feature cool season vegetables such as cabbage and peas at Cedaridge Farm.
ABOVE: The decorative bark of white birch (*Betula papyrifera*) is striking beside an azalea hedge.
OPPOSITE: Boxwood topiary at 'Green Animals' garden, Rhode Island, U.S.A.

Introduction

Spring bulb garden features tulips and blue grape hyacinth in beds surrounding a front lawn.

Conditions That Affect Cold Hardiness

Conditions other than degrees of cold can affect plant hardiness. Temperature extremes, such as alternate freezing and thawing during winter, are a major cause of casualties. A way to avoid winterkill due to alternate thawing and freezing is to mulch the soil around plants. A 3 to 6 inch (8 to 15 cm) layer of organic mulch (such as shredded leaves, wood chips, pine needles and straw) will help to maintain a stable soil temperature. In areas where the ground actually freezes, this is vital. The mulch blanket will prevent the ground from warming too early when an unseasonable warm spell thaws out the soil prematurely, heaving plant roots out of the ground and exposing them to damaging cold when the temperature drops.

In regions with severe winters, it is advisable to add the mulch *after* the ground freezes since the mulch blanket will help to keep the ground frozen. Most hardy plants, once they are dormant, can survive freezing temperatures if they stay dormant, but an early thaw can cause the plant to break dormancy and leave it susceptible to damage from re-freezing. Even hardy spring-blooming bulbs, such as tulips and hyacinths, that are not visible during winter will benefit from a mulch blanket.

Exposure to drying winds is especially harmful to many hardy evergreens. In areas susceptible to high winds, such as coastal locations, even windbreak plants like holly and boxwood may need temporary protection by a twig fence or a burlap barrier until the plants are well established. Susceptibility to salt spray can also weaken plants and cause their demise.

Many gardens have microclimates, allowing some borderline hardy plants to survive in a sheltered position, such as a courtyard, while plants considered hardy might expire in a highly frost prone position such as an exposed slope. The depth of plant roots is often a factor, causing plants with shallow roots and those in containers left outdoors during winter to be exposed to too much cold. Even hardy water lilies will survive only if their roots are below the ice line of a pond, and unless hardy foxtail lilies have exceedingly sharp drainage, their roots are likely to rot. Moreover, soil that puddles not only induces rot from water excess, but also tends to make plants more susceptible to soil diseases.

Variety selection is especially important when considering hardiness. The powdery blue English lavender 'Munstead' is a zone hardier than the violet-blue variety, 'Hidcote'; similarly American holly is a zone hardier than English holly. In my own garden, Cedaridge Farm, the most cold-hardy azalea has proven to be *Rhododendron yedoense* var. *poukhanense*. Most others struggle to survive. Provenance can also affect hardiness. A plant raised in a mild-climate nursery (azaleas in particular) may not adjust to a colder zone even though genetically it has the capability. As a rule I like to grow only local, field-grown plants.

Be aware that some of the most desirable hardy plants, though they can survive extremely cold winters, may perish during hot summers. This is especially true of the blue poppies (*Meconopsis*) and species of cotton grass (*Eriophorum*).

Hardiness Zones

The maps shown on the following page are a general guide to plant hardiness based on average winter temperatures. Within these zones, especially along rivers and close to large lakes, milder temperatures are possible. Also realize that any property can have microclimates that can be warmer or colder than the surrounding area—for example, the south side of a house, where exposure to sun and escaping heat from the house can keep soil warm enough to keep calla (arum) lilies alive in zone 6. Walk around the house after a snowfall, and you will notice areas where the snow melts first, indicating a warm microclimate. A courtyard open to the elements but sheltered on three or four sides by walls can also temper winter temperatures, allowing borderline hardy plants to survive.

Areas of the world with mountains, and especially those with maritime climates like coastal California, New Zealand and Great Britain, can have microclimates. These can be produced from sudden changes of elevation and also from invisible offshore currents, such as the Australian Current that sweeps across the Tasman Sea to warm the northwest coast of New Zealand's South Island and much of the North Island. The influence of the North Atlantic Current that sweeps up from Africa to warm Britain's

Self-seeded hardy corn poppies cover an alpine meadow, flowering in spring from an autumn seeding.

Scilly Isles and parts of coastal Cornwall, and the Gulf Stream that warms the west coast of Ireland and the Western Isles of Scotland, allow subtropical plants to overwinter in sheltered areas. This can be witnessed most notably at Tresco Abbey Gardens, in the Scilly Isles, Heligan garden in Cornwall and Inverewe garden on Scotland's rugged northwest coast.

Anchorage, Alaska, is considered zone 2, but when I visited there one summer, I was amazed to discover meadows and gardens filled with floral color from a wealth of annuals and perennials. A garden writer friend living in Anchorage confirmed that, in reality, Anchorage has three climate zones warmer than zone 2, and because of global warming, gardeners in the zone 2 area are finding it possible to grow zone 3 plants. Even the most highly respected reference books can be wrong. More than once I have seen the hardy prickly pear *Opuntia humifusa* listed as hardy only for zone 9 and warmer, whereas it is reliably hardy down to zone 6, where the ground can freeze every winter.

On a recent trip to the Shetlands, the U.K.'s most northerly outpost, I marveled at its beautiful wildflowers, such as bog orchids, blue vetch, pink ragged robin and white cottongrass. The islands have a reputation for being bleak and treeless, yet I discovered it has a garden club with plans to develop a botanical garden at Lea Gardens, Rosa Stepanova's sheltered property an hour north of Berwick. I was surprised to see she overwinters pampas plume and New Zealand flaxes outdoors, largely because of the influence of the Gulf Stream that peters out among the Shetlands.

Each year in January (spring in the sub-Antarctic), on 15 miles (24 km) wide Campbell Island, located 500 miles (805 km) south of New Zealand, occurs one of the most beautiful wildflower displays on earth. Jumbo-size hardy perennial plants called mega-herbs grow under extremely harsh weather conditions, and yet attempts to grow them in other temperate climates produce only sickly-looking plants. The two most beautiful mega-herbs are the yellow *Bulbinella rossii* (Ross lily) and blue *Pleurophyllum speciosum* (Campbell Island daisy). A theory concerning their hardiness is that in addition to high rainfall and acid soil, they demand a constant change in wind direction to thrive. This can also be true of many temperamental alpine plant species, which is why the botanical gardens' alpine house in Frankfurt, Germany, uses two fans at opposite ends of the house that blow on alternate days.

Introduction

Hardiness Zone Maps

The maps on this spread are a general guide to plant hardiness based on the average annual minimum temperature for each zone. They have been prepared to agree with a system of plant hardiness zones ranging from 1 to 12 that has been accepted as an international standard.

Zone		°F	°C
1		below −50	below −46
2		−50 to −40	−46 to −40
3		−40 to −30	−40 to −34
4		−30 to −20	−34 to −29
5		−20 to −10	−29 to −23
6		−10 to 0	−23 to −18
7		0 to 10	−18 to −12
8		10 to 20	−12 to −7
9		20 to 30	−7 to −1
10		30 to 40	−1 to 4
11		40 to 50	4 to 10
12		50 to 60	10 to 16

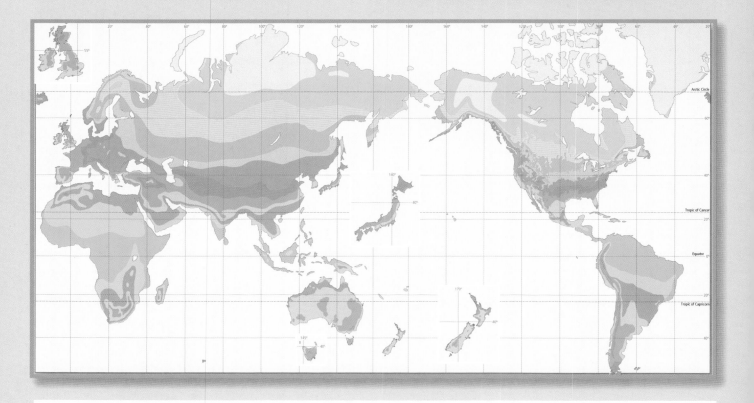

World hardiness zones

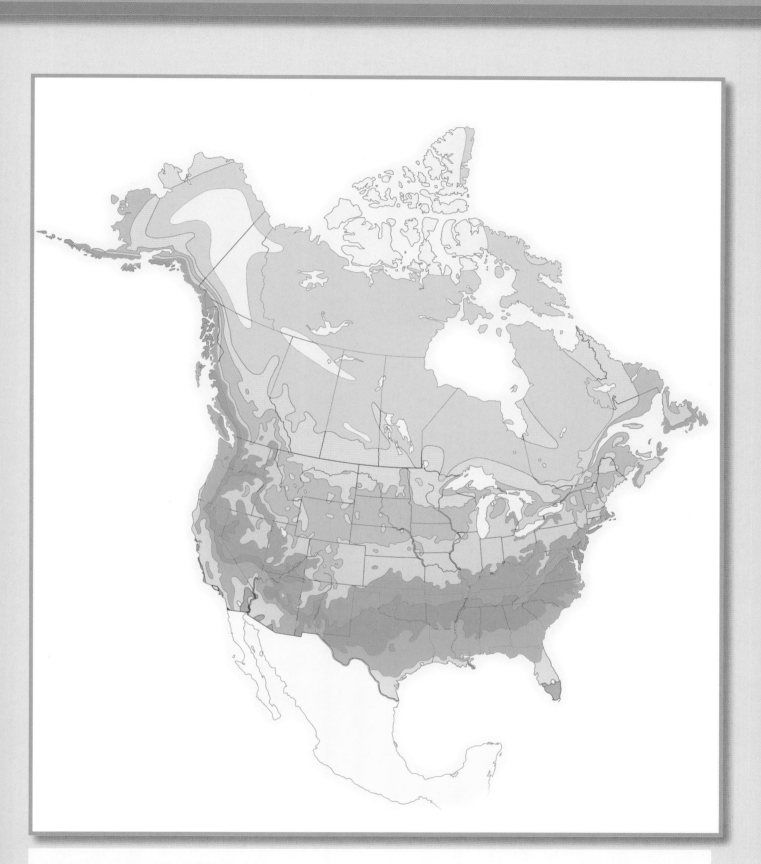

North American hardiness zones

Introduction

An assortment of hardy gooseberries and currants grown at Cedaridge Farm.

The Listings

In a sense, this is a personal selection of hardy garden-worthy plants. Perennials are the largest category, since gardeners seem to seek hardiness in perennials above all else.

Plant Names

The plant names used in this book are those accepted as accurate at the time of going to press. Unfortunately, a confusing situation exists in horticulture, with teams of taxonomists searching herbariums worldwide to determine if a generally accepted botanical name for a plant is predated by another name. At annual meetings of these taxonomists, name changes are recommended on the basis of their findings. And so, a well-established botanical name can undergo several changes over as many years if new, earlier names are discovered. Sometimes there is such a public outcry over a name change that the taxonomists bend to public pressure and restore a popular name—for example, when Chrysanthemum was changed to Dendranthemum, and then changed back to Chrysanthemum. But even when a name change becomes official, other sections of the garden industry may not follow suit. This is especially true for nursery catalogs and florists, who feel they will suffer confusion and reduced sales from an unpopular and unfamiliar name change.

Cedaridge Farm

My own garden, Cedaridge Farm, is located in zone 6 on the official zone map, but because of our high elevation compared to the surrounding area, we consider ourselves a zone 5 garden. In summer we can have cool-temperature plants like Russell lupins and nasturtiums blooming much longer than the surrounding area because we are always a few degrees cooler. At Cedaridge Farm hardiness is critical because we do not have time to coddle plants, and we are open to the public. If a plant does not provide a "big bang for the buck," it gets replaced. This is especially important in our theme gardens that rely mostly on ornamental shrubs and perennials. We can experience frozen soil to the depth of a spade for several months, and due to our north-facing location, we are susceptible to prolonged and late frost, and also to desiccating winds. I've therefore compiled this book on hardy plants as a reference for myself as well as a guide for others.

Many of the images in this book show scenes at Cedaridge Farm through all four seasons. The 24-acre (9.7 ha) farm was established in 1791 and was at one time a Mennonite dairy farm. My wife and I purchased the property in 1990 to serve as an outdoor studio, to evaluate plant hardiness and plant performance, and also to stage plant partnerships that can be photographed for the books and calendars I publish. The design philosophy is to maintain an old-fashioned appearance and to use growing techniques that can be labor saving. Our biggest problem is depredation by rabbits and deer that wander in from an adjacent nature preserve, and so we are constantly testing the effectiveness of rabbit and deer repellents. We garden organically, and therefore, any fertilizer or sprays we use must be made from organic compounds. For example, an effective rabbit and deer repellent for us is an environment-friendly product made from garlic concentrate and powdered eggs called Liquid Fence, which we apply to ornamental plantings at least once a month. And although we compost tons of garden and kitchen waste to keep our beds and borders in good heart, we do use supplemental feeding such as Spray 'n Gro (a liquid fertilizer made from seaweed concentrate) and Nitron (a balanced fertilizer made from all-natural ingredients).

Hardiness in Containers

The smaller the container, the less likely even hardy plants will survive winter, since containers expose plant roots to greater degrees of cold than if they were in the soil. This is particularly true of hanging baskets and window box planters, but even urns and whisky barrel planters on a deck or patio will be susceptible to winterkill. Where freezing can occur, move containers to a sheltered position so they can benefit from escaping house heat, or sink them up to their rims in a pit with mulch piled around the lip. Even then, there is danger of ceramic or clay pots cracking from the moist soil freezing and expanding. The ultimate solution is to remove plants from their pots, and plant them temporarily into soil. Then remove all soil from the container and up-end it so it cannot collect water and crack from freezing.

Organization

I was tempted to organize this book as a straight A–Z encyclopedia listing, but decided that it would serve gardeners better if it were arranged by category: Annuals, Perennials, Trees, Shrubs and Edibles, because it then allows a brief discussion of design principles for each category.

TOP: Oriental-style rock garden features mostly evergreens, including sweeps of English ivy and rug juniper.
LEFT: A tapestry of hardy deciduous trees with lavender in foreground, Kerdalo Garden, Britanny, France.
RIGHT: Self-seeded winter aconites (*Eranthis hymenalis*) shrug off a dusting of snow.

Annuals

There are two kinds of hardy annuals. One type can be sown in late summer or early autumn to survive winter as mature seedlings, such as poppies and cornflowers. Others have seeds that can be sown in late autumn after frost, or during winter months, to remain dormant until a warming trend in spring energizes them into bloom. These varieties are mostly used in prepackaged "Wildflower Mixtures" for sowing in autumn to germinate in early spring and flower in early summer. Reference books do not give zones of hardiness for annuals because their life cycle is completed in a single season, and so they are considered suitable for growing in all zones. Instead, annuals are usually classified as hardy (such as calendula), meaning they tolerate severe frost; half-hardy (such as marigolds), meaning they tolerate mild frost; and tender (such as impatiens), meaning they are sensitive to even mild frost.

Also, annuals can be classified as cool season (generally flowering best when night-time temperatures remain below 70°F (21°C) and warm season (generally flowering best when temperatures are above 70°F). Planting of cool-season varieties (like stocks and sweet peas) should be made so that flowering occurs in spring or autumn during relatively cool weather. High elevations and coastal locations may be especially suitable for growing cool-season annuals during summer.

Agrostemma githago
Corn cockle
Native to the Mediterranean. Slender plants with grasslike leaves grow to 4 feet (1.2 m) high and are topped by five-petalled white, pink or lavender flowers that resemble miniature hibiscus. The shimmering blooms have spotted throats and are good for cutting gardens and meadow plantings. Seed sown in winter or early spring will break dormancy in spring to flower extra early.

Alyssum maritimum aka *Lobularia maritima*
Sweet alyssum
Native to the Mediterranean, these low ground-hugging plants form a cushion of tiny white, pink, red or purple flowers borne in tight clusters. Leaves are small, narrow and pointed, but are mostly hidden by the flowers, which bloom all season. Use for edging borders and containers, allowing plants to spill over the rim. Best sown in early spring.

Ammi majus
Annual Queen Ann's lace
Native to northeast Africa and Eurasia, the white, umbrella-shaped flower clusters resemble Queen Ann's lace. The flowers sit atop 4 foot (1.2 m) long stems above fernlike, lacy foliage. Suitable for cutting gardens, mixed with perennials, and a component of meadow plantings in full sun and well-drained soil. Seed can be sown in autumn, as seedlings will tolerate severe winters.

LEFT: A wildflower meadow featuring bright orange *Eschscholzia californica* (Californian poppy) and *Linaria maroccana* (toadflax).

Annuals

Brassica oleracea var. *acephala*
Ornamental kale

Native to Europe, these relatives of the cabbage family are grown mostly for autumn and winter bedding displays and for containers such as window box planters. Seed needs starting in pots to gain transplants with frilled leaves and white, pink or red centers. Plants produce their best colors after frost and even tolerate frozen soil. Prefers full sun and good drainage.

Calendula officinalis
Pot marigold

Native to the Mediterranean, the chrysanthemum-like double flowers are mostly shades of yellow and orange, up to 4 inches (10 cm) across, usually with a dark center. Plants grow to 2 feet (61 cm) high and form a cushion shape. The lance-like leaves are sticky and have a spicy odor. The fragrant petals are edible and are often used to garnish salads. Useful for spring bedding in company with violas and pansies, and also for container plantings. Provide full sun and good drainage. 'Geisha Girl' (an orange) has unusual incurved petals. Seed sown in early spring will germinate early and tolerate frost.

Centaurea cyanus
Cornflower, Bachelor's buttons

Native to Europe, beautiful, fringed, button-shaped flowers up to 1 inch (2.5 cm) across are borne atop slender, gray-green stems with slender, grasslike leaves. Color range includes shades of blue, pink and red, plus maroon and white. Plants grow to 2 feet (61 cm) high and prefer full sun and good drainage. They combine well with poppies in meadow plantings and are valued for cutting. The variety 'Blue Diadem' has flowers up to 2 inches (5 cm) across, and 'Frosted Queen' has unusual white petal tips. Mature seedlings will tolerate freezing for sowing in early autumn. Also, seed sown in early spring will germinate at 40°F (4°C) soil temperature and tolerate frosts.

Anagallis monelli
Blue pimpernel

Native to the Mediterranean, the mound-shaped plants resemble forget-me-nots. They produce small sky-blue flowers during summer with slender, lance-like leaves. Plants grow to 12 inches (31 cm) high, and are suitable for edging borders. Prefers full sun and good drainage. Seed sown in autumn after frost can survive freezing, to germinate in early spring.

Cerinthe major 'Purpurascens'
Honeywort

Native to the Mediterranean, pendant blue, bell-shaped flowers hang from arching stems among smooth, oval, blue-green foliage. Plants grow to 2 feet (61 cm) high, bloom in summer and prefer full sun and good drainage. Useful massed in mixed borders, and a favorite for cottage gardens partnered with yellow flowers such as calendula. Sow seed in early spring, as seedlings will tolerate frost.

Chrysanthemum carinatum
Painted daisy

Native to Morocco, these colorful daisies grow bushy and erect with feathery leaves. They have strong stems topped by 3-inch (8 cm) wide flowers that are mostly tricolored—usually white or yellow petal tips, then a red zone and a yellow zone surrounding a black button center. Plants grow to 3 feet (91 cm) high and flower best during cool weather in summer and autumn. They prefer full sun and good drainage. While good for cutting, they are also suitable for massing in mixed borders and as a component of meadow plantings. Sow seed in early spring.

Chrysanthemum coronarium
Crown daisy

Native to North Africa, these cheerful daisies are mostly yellow with deeper yellow petal centers. Cushion-shaped plants grow to 2 feet (61 cm) high with finely indented leaves that are edible as chop suey greens. Plants prefer full sun and good drainage, and flower during cool weather. Suitable for massing in mixed borders and as a component of meadow planting, especially partnered with annual poppies. Sow seed in autumn or early spring as seedlings will tolerate frost.

Clarkia unguiculata
Farewell-to-spring

Native to California, plants grow slender stems up to 3 feet (91 cm) high, studded with 1-inch (2.5 cm) wide double flowers that resemble miniature roses, almost hiding the slender, lance-like leaves. Colors include all shades of pink, red, purple and apricot, plus white. Good for cutting and meadow plantings. They prefer full sun and good drainage and are summer flowering. Sow seed in autumn after frost, or early spring, since seedlings tolerate frosts.

Annuals

Consolida ajacis aka Delphinium ajacis
Larkspur
This Mediterranean native grows erect stems of finely cut, feathery foliage topped by spikes of 1-inch (2.5 cm) wide flowers resembling delphinium. Colors include all shades of red, pink, blue and purple, plus white. Provide full sun and good drainage. Though popular for massing in mixed borders, larkspur is valued highly as a cut flower. Since the best garden strains can grow to 4 feet (1.2 m) high with top-heavy flower spikes, they generally need staking. Sow seed in late summer, as mature seedlings can survive severe winters. Or sow in autumn after frost, or early spring, so seed germinates early, even before the last spring frost.

Coreopsis tinctoria
Calliopsis
Native to the prairie grasslands of North America, the 1-inch (2.5 cm) daisylike flowers are borne continuously all summer until severe autumn frosts. Though dwarf, cushion-shaped varieties are available, plants can grow to 4 feet (1.2 m) high. Flowers are mostly yellow, red and mahogany, and often are bicolored. Leaves are small and slender. Useful as a cut flower and as a component of meadow plantings, especially when partnered with Shirley poppies and cornflowers. Sow seed in autumn, after frost, or early spring, since seedlings tolerate mild frosts.

Cynoglossum amabile
Chinese forget-me-not
Native to China, masses of blue or white nodding forget-me-not flowers are borne on tall stems up to 3 feet (91 cm) high. The leaves are small, slender and sticky to touch. Plants prefer full sun and good drainage, and are mostly massed in mixed borders, meadow plantings and cutting gardens. Sow seed in early spring, as seedlings will tolerate mild frost.

Emilia coccinea
Tassel flower

Native to Africa, the small, button-shaped, flame-red flowers are clustered atop slender, bunching stems up to 2 feet (61 cm) high; small, slender leaves allow the flowers to dominate. Plants prefer full sun and good drainage. Useful massed in mixed borders, meadow plantings and cutting gardens. Sow seed in early spring, as seedlings tolerate mild frosts.

Eschscholzia californica
California poppy

Native to California, these mound-shaped plants with feathery blue-green leaves are covered with mostly cup-shaped, four-petalled or semi-double flowers all summer. The petals close on cloudy days and have a shimmering, satinlike sheen in full sun. Colors include red, pink, orange, yellow and white. Most often used as an edging, as a component of mixed meadow plantings and massed in rock gardens. In zone 7 and colder, sow seed in early spring, as seedlings will tolerate mild frosts.

Gaillardia pulchella
Indian blanket

Native to the U.S. prairie states, plants form colonies of bright red, daisylike flowers with yellow petal tips. Plants grow to 2 feet (61 cm) high and thrive in full sun or poor soil, providing it has good drainage. Sow seed in autumn, after frost or in early spring, several weeks before the last frost, for summer flowering. A good component of mixed meadow plantings.

Gilia tricolor
Bird's eyes

Native to the western U.S., plants resemble pink forget-me-not but with black eyes instead of white. Flowering in spring, plants grow to 18 inches (46 cm) high and have fine, needle-like foliage. Useful in mixed meadow plantings in full sun and soil with good drainage. Sow seed in autumn after frost, or early spring for summer flowering.

Godetia amoena aka Clarkia amoena
Satin flower

Native to California, masses of cup-shaped flowers with shimmering petals are borne in such profusion that they almost hide the small, lance-like leaves. Colors include all shades of pink, red and purple, usually with white petal tips. Plants prefer full sun and good drainage, and bloom in early summer while the nights are cool. Useful as an edging to borders, and also in containers such as window box planters. Sow seed in early spring, as seedlings will tolerate mild frosts.

Gypsophila elegans
Baby's breath

Native to the Caucasus Mountains, these mounded plants have fine, slender leaves and produce cloudlike clusters of small white or pink flowers, depending on the variety. Grows to 2 feet (61 cm) high and more. Plants prefer full sun and good drainage, are valued for cutting and are often a feature in mixed meadow plantings. A similar species, G. muralis 'Gypsy', grows mounded, cushion-shaped plants with pink flowers just 6 inches (15 cm) high, suitable for edging. Sow seed in early spring, as seedlings will tolerate mild frosts.

Helianthus annuus
Sunflower

Annual sunflowers are a diverse group of daisylike plants mostly native to North America. They range in height from the tall 'Russian Mammoth' growing to 10 feet (3 m) high, topped by yellow flowers up to 12 inches (31 cm) across, to dwarf varieties up to 15 inches (38 cm) high with 6-inch (15 cm) wide yellow flowers that are perfect miniatures of the 'Russian Mammoth'.

The most common colors are yellow and orange. The single-flowered kinds generally display a large central disk that becomes a seed head, usually black in color but sometimes brown and green, depending on variety. Other common colors include white, red and mahogany, sometimes seen as bicolors and tricolors, such as in the 'Autumn Beauty' series. This mixture has branching stems that bloom continuously from midsummer until severe autumn frost. Give them full sun and good drainage.

Double-flowered sunflowers can be tall or dwarf, notably 'Teddy Bear' [up to 2 feet (61 cm) high], capable of forming a low hedge. Sunflowers are invaluable for adding height to border plantings, and they are valued for cutting. The edible seeds attract songbirds. Seed can be sown up to 100 days before the last killing frost. For perennial sunflowers, see page 86.

Helipterum roseum aka Rhodanthe chlorocephala aka Acroclinium roseum
Everlasting, Immortelle

These daisylike plants from south-western Australia resemble strawflowers with papery petals up to 2 inches (5 cm) across, mostly in shades of pink, red and white, usually with dark button centers. Give them full sun and good drainage. Plants grow to 3 feet (91 cm) high with slender, gray-green leaves suitable for massing in mixed borders and cutting gardens. Valued especially for dried arrangements. Sow seed in early spring, since seedlings tolerate frost and flower best when night temperatures are cool.

Iberis umbellata
Globe candytuft

Native to central Europe and the Mediterranean. Small, four-petalled flowers in shades of red, pink and purple, plus white, form 1-inch (2.5 cm), dome-shaped flower clusters on cushion-shaped plants. Plants grow to 12 inches (31 cm) high, suitable for edging borders and massing in rock gardens. Give them full sun and good drainage. Sow seed in early spring, as seedlings tolerate frost.

Lathyrus odoratus
Sweet peas

Though classified as a hardy annual, if the seed is direct sown in autumn, it often rots during winter. If sown earlier to create a mound of green leaves for winter dormancy, it often does not survive severe winters. In severe winter areas, such as zones 7 and colder, sweet peas are best direct sown in early spring or four weeks before the last frost date. The seed can also be started in pots eight weeks before outdoor planting, and placed in their permanent planting positions at the onset of mild spring weather.

Before World War II, the sweet pea was the most popular flowering annual in the world with significant sales in the U.K., North America, Australia, New Zealand, South Africa and many parts of Asia. They are still as much a part of British culture as Yorkshire pudding. Such was the demand for sweet peas that thousands of acres were devoted to seed production in the Lompoc Valley of California, where cool coastal mists and sandy soil produce ideal growing conditions. Truckloads of sweet pea seeds were shipped worldwide for planting in early spring for early summer flowering. But this widespread popularity in the U.S. induced disease, and the disease that struck sweet peas a fatal blow is hard to treat, because it is a fungus disease that attacks the roots and kills the vines before they have a chance to flower. Such was the rapid demise of the sweet pea across North America that breeders turned their attention to improving other promising annuals to replace it. In fact, the disease is still widespread in the northeastern U.S., and there are no resistant varieties. However, by planting sweet peas in a different location each season, or planting in containers with sterile soil, it's possible to grow and enjoy them.

Layia platyglossa
Tidy tips
Native to California, the 2-inch (5 cm), daisylike flowers are yellow with white petal tips, held erect on stiff stems up to 12 inches (31 cm) high. Plants bloom in summer and prefer full sun, good drainage and cool nights. Useful for massing in mixed borders and as a component of meadow plantings. Sow seed in early spring, as seedlings tolerate frost.

Limnanthes douglasii
Poached-egg plant
A ground-hugging, spreading plant native to California, the half-inch (1.3 cm), star-shaped, yellow flowers have white petal tips, and are produced so freely in early summer they almost completely hide the fine, feathery foliage. Useful for edging paths and borders and massing in rock gardens. Provide full sun and good drainage. Sow seed in early spring, as seedlings tolerate frost.

Linaria maroccana
Toadflax
Resembling miniature snapdragons, these desert wildflowers from Morocco have fine grasslike foliage and small, spurred flowers arranged in a spike. The color range is astonishing, and includes many shades of red, pink, purple, orange and yellow, plus white and bicolors. Plants prefer full sun and good drainage, and are good for edging and container plantings. They are also a popular component of meadow plantings and make good companions for California poppies. Dwarf types, such as the 'Fantasy' series, grow cushionlike to 8 inches (20 cm) high, while tall types grow to 18 inches (46 cm) high and are suitable for cutting. Sow seed in autumn after frost, or early spring, since seedlings tolerate frost.

Linum grandiflorum rubrum
Scarlet flax
Native to Algeria, erect stems with slender leaves are topped by shimmering, five-petalled, blood-red flowers with black centers. Plants grow to 18 inches (46 cm) high and prefer full sun with good drainage. They are good to mass in mixed borders for early summer flowering, and also as components of meadow plantings. Sow seed in early spring, as seedlings tolerate frost.

Lychnis coeli-rosa aka *Silene coeli-rosa*
Rose of heaven
Native to Siberia, these cushion-shaped plants have delicate branching stems and narrow pointed leaves. Masses of five-petalled, 1-inch (2.5 cm) flowers bloom in early summer during cool weather. They are mostly blue but also produce pink, red and white flowers. Plants prefer full sun and good drainage. Useful for edging borders, planting as drifts in rock gardens and as components of meadow plantings. Sow seed in early spring, as seedlings tolerate frost.

Malcolmia maritima
Virginia stock
Native to the Mediterranean, dainty, four-petalled, half-inch (1.3 cm), fragrant flowers in mostly white, pink, purple and red cover cushion-shaped plants up to 12 inches (31 cm) high during cool weather. Plants prefer full sun and good drainage, but tolerate light shade. Sow seed in early spring, as seedlings tolerate frost.

Matthiola longipetala
Evening scented stock
Native to Europe, plants grow delicate upright stems to 2 feet (61 cm) high, covered with four-petalled, half-inch (1.3 cm), highly fragrant flowers during cool weather. Colors include white, pink and purple. Prefers full sun and good drainage. Their scent intensifies at night. Good for massing in mixed borders and cutting gardens. Sow seed in early spring, as seedlings tolerate frost.

Nemophila menziesii
Baby blue eyes
Native to California, cushion-shaped plants with small, oval leaves are covered in late spring and early summer with half-inch (1.3 cm), cup-shaped, blue flowers with white centers. Plants require full sun and good drainage. Suitable for edging borders, massing as drifts in rock gardens and as components of meadow plantings. The variety 'Penny Black' has black flowers with white petal tips. Sow seed in early spring, as seedlings tolerate frost.

Nigella damascena
Love-in-a-mist
Native to the Mediterranean. Slender, branching stems up to 2 feet (61 cm) high are topped by cornflowerlike flowers with black centers and a spidery arrangement of stamens. The flowers along with the fine, feathery foliage produce a misty appearance. In addition to blue, the flowers can be white, pink and red. After the flowers fade, they form a balloonlike seed capsule suitable for dried arrangements. Plants prefer full sun and good drainage. Popular component of cutting gardens, meadow plantings and cottage gardens. Sow seed in late summer, autumn or early spring. Mature seedlings will tolerate severe winters.

Papaver rhoeas
Corn poppy, Shirley poppy

Native to Europe. These upright plants produce serrated leaves and wiry stems up to 2 feet (61 cm) high, topped by cup-shaped blooms up to 3 inches (8 cm) across, in all shades of pink and red, plus white and bicolors. Semi-double forms are also available. Plants prefer full sun and good drainage. They are best used in meadow plantings and also massed in mixed borders. A similar hardy annual species is *P. commutatum*, known as the Flander's poppy. The variety 'Ladybird' has shimmering crimson blooms with black petal markings. Sow seed in late summer, autumn or early spring. Mature seedlings will tolerate severe winters.

The Iceland poppy (*P. nudicaule*) with mostly white, yellow, red and orange flowers (hardy zones 2–9) is best grown as a biennial.

Phacelia campanularia
California bluebell

Native to California and similar in appearance to baby blue eyes, plants grow to 12 inches (31 cm) high and form a cushion with small, hairy, oval leaves and five-petalled blue flowers with pale blue centers. Plants prefer full sun and good drainage, mostly used for edging borders and as a component of meadow plantings. Sow seed in early spring.

Rudbeckia hirta
Gloriosa daisy

Daisylike flowers derived from North American perennial plant species, these plants grow stiffly erect, topped by mostly yellow and orange flowers up to 5 inches (13 cm) across, usually with black button centers, but sometimes green. Double and quilled petal forms are also available. Though plants generally grow to 3 feet (91 cm) high, dwarf varieties such as 'Becky' remain compact at 12 inches (31 cm). Give them full sun and good drainage. Use massed in mixed borders and as components of meadow plantings, but are also suitable for cutting. Sow seed in autumn after frost, or early spring, since seed will remain dormant until warm spring weather and will tolerate frost.

Scabiosa atropurpurea
Pincushion flower

Native to Europe, the domed flowers up to 2 inches (5 cm) across have a central raised mound of inner petals, creating a pincushion effect. Colors include all shades of red, pink and blue, plus white and maroon. Give them full sun and good drainage. Although good for mixed borders, the plants are mostly grown for cutting. Sow seed in early spring or winter, since seed will remain dormant until a warming trend, and the seedlings will tolerate frost.

Silene armeria
Sweet William catchfly

Native to Europe, clusters of magenta-pink, star-shaped flowers are borne on cushion-shaped plants up to 18 inches (46 cm) high. Leaves are slender and lance-like. Prefers full sun and good drainage, suitable for massing in mixed borders, rock gardens and meadow plantings. Sow seed in autumn after frost, or early spring, since seedlings tolerate frost.

Ratibida columnifera
Mexican hat, Prairie coneflower

Native to the prairies of the U.S., plants grow to 3 feet (91 cm) high with erect stems topped by rusty-red flowers with swept-back petals and a tall black cone. Plants prefer full sun and good drainage, and tolerate high heat. Useful as a component of meadow mixtures. Sow seed in autumn after frost, or early spring for summer flowering, since seedlings tolerate frost.

Trifolium incarnatum
Crimson clover

Native to Europe, these fast-growing, bushy plants grow to 12 inches (31 cm) high and have 3-petalled, shamrocklike leaves and scarlet, cone-shaped flowers in early spring. Give them full sun and good drainage. Useful for massing on slopes and wherever a weed-suffocating groundcover is needed. Avoid planting with other annuals in wild gardens and meadows because of its aggressive nature. Sow seed in late summer or early autumn, since mature seedlings will tolerate severe winters.

Triticum aestivum
Bread wheat

Native to western Asia, erect stems with grasslike leaves are topped with whiskered blue-green flower spikes, composed of tightly packed grains that turn amber when ripe. Plants prefer full sun and good drainage, tolerate crowding and are valued for dried arrangements. Mostly grown as a broad row in cutting gardens. Sow seed in autumn after frost, or early spring, since seedlings tolerate frost.

Viola x wittrockiana
Pansy

Developed from perennial species native to the Alps, the Swiss seed company of Roggli, near Thun, is responsible for making the pansy a popular hardy annual by the introduction of their famous 'Roggli Giants' strain of large-flowered pansies. This inspired Japanese, German and American breeders to also develop hardy varieties, including the 'Majestic Giants' and 'Imperial' strains from Japan, the 'Whiskers' strain from Germany, and the 'Universal' and 'Accord' strains from North America. These plants are best used for edging tulip beds, for low bedding, and particularly as container plants such as for window box planters.

Pansy seed should not be direct seeded in autumn or early spring, but started under glass 10 weeks before placing into their permanent positions outdoors. This can occur four weeks before the last frost date, or even earlier with some varieties. Give them sun or light shade and good drainage.

Xeranthemum annuum
Immortelle

Native to the Mediterranean. These daisylike plants have papery petals in mostly white, pink, purple and red. The 1-inch (2.5 cm) diameter flowers are held erect on stems 2 feet (61 cm) high with slender, grasslike leaves. Useful for massing in mixed borders, as a component of meadow plantings, and excellent for cutting, especially in dried arrangements. Give them full sun and good drainage. Sow seed in early spring, since seedlings tolerate frost.

Bulbs

Throughout the world, there are gardens that owe their reputations to beautiful spring bulb displays. These include Keukenhof, an hour's drive southwest of Amsterdam, where the Holland bulb industry sponsors lavish display gardens from March to May, using mostly tulips, hyacinths and daffodils, supported by dozens of minor bulb varieties. These meticulous display gardens are surrounded by thousands of acres of tulip and daffodil production fields. Other extensive production acreage can be seen around the Skagit Valley, Washington State, U.S.; the Australian island of Tasmania; and the Fenland town of Spalding, Lincolnshire, U.K.

In Ottawa, Canada, a Dutch tulip festival in spring commemorates the time during World War II when the Queen of the Netherlands and her family lived there during the Nazi occupation of Holland. In England, Hodstock Priory near Blyth, Nottinghamshire, is open for five weeks from late January to early March to celebrate a "Snowdrop Spectacular." An astonishing 30,000 visitors attend to witness the mass flowering of thousands of snowdrops in a 5 acre (2 ha) area of woodland and gardens, in company with thousands of hellebores, early-blooming cyclamen, early-blooming narcissus, aconites and snow irises.

Acidanthera bicolor aka Gladiolus callianthus
Peacock orchid

Zones 6–11

Native to South Africa, this dry landscape plant grows to 3 feet (91 cm) tall with an erect habit. The orchidlike flowers occur in summer and are pure white with handsome purple-brown markings at the petal base. The leaves are long, slender and irislike. Best grown as an accent in mixed beds and borders; it is also excellent for cutting. Similar to gladiolus in habit and appearance, they are easy to grow in most well-drained garden soils in full sun. Plant in spring, 3 inches (8 cm) deep and 6 inches (15 cm) apart.

ALLIUM SPECIES

Ornamental onion
Zones 4–10, depending on variety

The large plant family of *Allium* is widely dispersed throughout the Northern Hemisphere, perhaps totaling 700 species. They are related to the domestic onion, usually emit an onion odor when bruised and produce tubular flowers arranged in a dome or sphere. All are easily propagated from bulbs, prefer full sun but tolerate light shade and demand good drainage. The following species will produce floral displays lasting several weeks in spring and summer.

LEFT: *Narcissus* 'Bestseller' at Cedaridge Farm.

Bulbs

Allium cernuum
Nodding onion

Zones 4–10

Native to North America, plants bloom in spring, in white or mid- to deep pink with the nodding bell-shaped flowers arranged in a loose sphere above slender, erect, arching stems. Growing to 10 inches (25 cm) high, these woodland plants are also suitable for edging and as for planting as drifts in rock gardens.

Allium cristophii
Stars of Persia

Zones 5–8

Native to Turkey and central Asia, plants bloom in spring. The dusky pink, star-shaped flowers are clustered in a large sphere up to 8 inches (20 cm) across above rosettes of slender, straplike leaves. The seed heads are valued for their suitability for dried arrangements.

Allium giganteum
Giant allium

Zones 6–10

Native to Asia, plants grow tall flower stems topped by perfectly spherical, purple-pink flower clusters up to 10 inches (25 cm) across, above rosettes of arching, straplike succulent leaves. Best grouped as a colony in mixed perennial borders in full sun. Since the top-heavy stems often break from high winds, plants may need staking. Flowers appear in late spring and are spectacular among peonies and Oriental poppies.

Allium karataviense
Ornamental onion

Zones 5–9

Native to Asia, plants grow low rosettes of broad, arching, straplike leaves and a large ball-shaped cluster of white star-shaped flowers on short stems up to 10 inches (25 cm) high in spring. Best grouped at the front of mixed borders or as drifts in rock gardens in full sun.

Allium moly
Golden garlic

Zones 3–9

Native to the Mediterranean. Few low-spreading plants look better for edging and grouping as a colony in rock gardens, for plants produce tufts of slender leaf blades and masses of cheerful, bright yellow, nodding flowers that bend to soften hard edging and paths. Plants grow to 10 inches (25 cm) high, flower in late spring and early summer and prefer full sun.

Allium schoenoprasum
Chives
See Herbs, page 46.

Allium schubertii
Schubert onion

Zones 4–10

Native to the eastern Mediterranean. A real oddity for sophisticated gardens since the flower heads bloom after the leaves have died, and produce a 10-inch (25 cm) wide seed head that has radiating spidery stalks of different lengths. Plants grow to just 10 inches (25 cm) high and are best situated where a companion plant, such as lamb's ears, will cover the dead foliage, thus allowing the strange flower head to be highlighted against a contrasting background in late spring. Especially good for containers in full sun.

Allium senescens
German garlic

Zones 5–9

Resembling chives, these drought-resistant, sun-loving plants flower in summer. Masses of ball-shaped, pink flowers on 10-inch (25 cm) stems occur above clumps of slender, grasslike leaves. These plants are excellent for edging mixed perennial borders as well as for planting as drifts in rock gardens.

Allium sphaerocephalon
Drumstick allium

Zones 4–10

Native to North Africa, these dry landscape plants grow long, slender, grasslike leaves and tall flower stems topped by a cone-shaped, purple flower cluster in early summer. The strong flower stems grow to 3 feet (91 cm) high in full sun and are excellent for cutting.

Anemone blanda
Grecian windflower

Zones 4–8

Native to the eastern Mediterranean, this woodland plant grows 4 inches (10 cm) tall with a low-spreading habit. Purple, rose and white daisylike flowers appear in early spring and close at dusk or during bad weather. With its dainty, fernlike foliage, they are mostly planted in colonies to produce a mass of bloom over several weeks. Good for naturalizing. Recommended varieties are 'Rosea' (pink) and 'White Splendor'. Suitable for rock gardens, especially planted in a crescent around a boulder. Prefers a moist, humus-rich loam soil in sun or partial shade. Plant tubers 4 inches (10 cm) deep, spaced 3 inches (8 cm) apart in autumn.

Belamcanda chinensis
Blackberry lily

Zones 5–9

Native to China, this dry landscape plant grows 3 feet (91 cm) tall with an erect, clump-forming habit. Exotic orange flowers are spotted red and cluster at the top of strong, slender stems in summer. Leaves are narrow, arching and grasslike. After flowers fade, decorative seedpods form, revealing shiny black seeds as the pods dry. Popular for massing in mixed beds and borders. Both the flowers and the dried pods with seeds are good for cutting. A hybrid between *Belamcanda* and *Pardanthopsis* called 'Candy Lily' has an extremely rich color range including yellow, orange, pink and white, as well as combinations of these colors in the same flower. Easy to grow in most well-drained loam soils in full sun. Plant rhizomes 2 inches (5 cm) deep, spaced 6 inches (15 cm) apart, in spring or autumn.

Camassia cusickii
Cammass
Zones 4–7

Native mostly to North America, this meadow plant grows to 3 feet (91 cm) tall with an upright, spire-like habit. Blue starlike flowers form a loose flower spike in spring. Grasslike leaves die down soon after flowering. Plant in groups in mixed beds and borders. Good for naturalizing, especially in moist meadows and rock gardens. *C. esculenta* (Quamash) and *C. leichtlinii* are similar in appearance. All prefer full sun in well-drained, humus-rich soil. Propagate by seeds or bulbs with flowers developing in four years from seed. Superb partnered with late-flowering tulips. Plant the bulbs 4 inches (10 cm) deep in autumn.

Chionodoxa luciliae
Glory of the snow
Zones 3–8

Native to Asia Minor, this alpine plant from the Caucasus Mountains grows to 6 inches (15 cm) with a low, mounded, fountainlike habit. Delicate blue or pink, star-shaped flowers have contrasting white centers and are attractive in masses under deciduous trees. Prefers full sun or partial shade in well-drained soil. Propagate by bulbs planted 2 inches (5 cm) deep in autumn.

Colchicum autumnale
Autumn crocus
Zones 4–9

Native to Europe and Africa, this autumn-flowering plant grows 8 inches (20 cm) tall with a low-growing, clump-forming habit. Plants resemble giant crocus with rose-pink flowers, which appear after the large, straplike leaves have died. Double-flowered forms are available. Popular for edging paths, beds and borders. Can be naturalized in rock gardens and grassy slopes. A similar species, *C. speciosum*, has flowers that resemble pink water lilies. Prefers fertile, well-drained, humus-rich soil in sun or partial shade. Plant corms 4 inches (10 cm) deep from the crown, spaced 6 inches (15 cm) apart, in spring or autumn.

Convallaria majalis
Lily-of-the-valley
Zones 3–7

Native to Europe, this drought-tolerant plant grows 6 inches (15 cm) high with a low-spreading habit. Highly fragrant spring-flowering, white or pink bell-shaped, nodding flowers are borne on arching stems, which are produced among the broad, pointed, bright green leaves. Popular as a groundcover to edge paths and borders. Commonly forced in pots to flower early indoors in winter. Good for cutting to make dainty flower arrangements. Easy to grow in most well-drained soils in sun or partial shade. Plant rhizomes 1 inch (2.5 cm) deep, 4 inches (10 cm) apart in fall.

Crocosmia x crocosmiiflora
Montbretia
Zones 6–9

Native to South Africa, this dry landscape plant grows to 4 feet (1.2 m) tall with an erect, clump-forming habit. Orange-red, freesia-like flowers are borne in summer on slender, arching stems. Bright green leaves are swordlike. Popular for massing in mixed beds and borders but can form thick clumps, which may need dividing after three years. Excellent for cutting. Prefers a fertile, well-drained, humus-rich soil in sun or partial shade. Plant corms in fall or spring, 3 inches (8 cm) deep, spaced 4 inches (10 cm) apart. Can be aggressive, especially in coastal gardens.

Crocus tommasinianus
Snow crocus

Zones 4–8

Native to Dalmatia, this diminutive plant grows to 3 inches (8 cm) tall with a low, colony-forming habit. Purple flowers are produced in small clusters in early spring. Petals with prominent orange-yellow stamens open almost flat on sunny days. Leaves are dark green with a prominent white midrib. Self-seeds to form extensive colonies. Good for rock gardens and woodland. Will grow and bloom through grass. Other varieties include *C. chrysanthus* and *C. flavus*. Prefers well-drained, humus-rich loam soil in sun or partial shade. Plant corms in autumn, 3 inches (8 cm) deep, spaced 3 inches (8 cm) apart.

Crocus vernus
Dutch crocus

Zones 4–8

Native to the Pyrenees, Alps and Carpathian Mountains, this early-spring flower grows to 4 inches (10 cm) and is capable of forming large colonies. Purple, white and bicolor striped flowers are clustered several to each corm. Dark green with white midribs, the leaves appear after flowers fade. Popular for edging paths, beds and borders. Suitable for naturalizing in lawns and good for pot culture. 'Pickwick' has purple petals streaked white. *C. flavus* (a yellow) is similar in appearance. Easy to grow in most well-drained garden soils in full sun or light shade. Plant corms in autumn, 3 inches (8 cm) deep, spaced 3 inches (8 cm) apart.

Cyclamen neapolitanum aka C. hederifolium
Hardy cyclamen

Zones 6–8

Native to Greece, these diminutive plants grow to 6 inches (15 cm) and are capable of forming colonies. Flowers in pink or white are perfect miniatures of florists' cyclamen. Leaves are ivy shaped with silver markings. Popular for naturalizing in shady wildflower gardens, woodland and in sink gardens. Prefers moist, humus-rich loam soil in partial shade. Plant corms in spring, 2 inches (5 cm) deep, spaced 3 inches (8 cm) apart, with bloom occurring in autumn. Related species: *C. purpurascens* and *C. coum* are both spring flowering.

Eranthis hyemalis
Winter aconite

Zones 4–7

Native to Europe, this buttercuplike plant grows 2 inches (5 cm) high with a low, clump-forming habit. The shimmering yellow flowers appear before the leaves, which are dark green and deeply indented. Popular for planting in woodland where it will naturalize freely from self-seeding. Often blooms during early spring thaws before the last snows of winter. Prefers a well-drained, humus-rich soil in sun or partial shade. Plant tubers in autumn, 3 inches (8 cm) deep, spaced 3 inches (8 cm) apart.

Eremurus aitchisonii aka E. elwesii
Foxtail lily

Zones 5–8

Native to the deserts of Asia, this striking plant grows to 6 feet (1.8 m) high with an erect, spire-like habit. Fringed white florets form a towering pointed flower spike in late spring, held erect by a strong, slender stem. Leaves are sword shaped, like a yucca. Popular for tall backgrounds in mixed beds and borders (especially with a tall hedge behind to provide shelter from wind). Several hybrid mixtures include orange and apricot in their color range. Prefers fertile, well-drained loam soil in full sun and thrives in pure gravel. Plant the tubers in autumn, with the roots splayed out like an octopus and the crown covered by 3 inches (8 cm) of soil.

Bulbs

Erythronium 'Pagoda'
Dog's-tooth violet

Zones 4–8

A hybrid of species native to the West Coast of North America, this alpine plant grows 10 inches (25 cm) high with an erect, colony-forming habit. Yellow flowers have swept-back petals on a slender stem and appear in spring. Leaves are broad and pointed. Popular for rock gardens and woodland wildflower gardens. Related species: *E. montanum* (white avalanche-lily), white with orange throat and *E. grandiflorum* (yellow avalanche-lily), yellow with white throat. Prefers a well-drained, humus-rich soil in sun or partial shade. Plant tubers in autumn, 4 inches (10 cm) deep, spaced 4 inches (10 cm) apart.

Fritillaria imperialis
Crown imperial

Zones 3–8

Native to Iran, this stately plant grows 2 feet (61 cm) tall with an erect habit. Orange and yellow bell-shaped flowers hang from thick, succulent stalks in spring. A tuft of green spiky leaves crown the flower head while longer pointed leaves crowd the stem. If the leaves are cut or bruised, a skunklike odor pervades the air. Popular for mixed beds and borders, and also planted at the edge of woodland. Good companions for late daffodils and early tulips. Prefers well-drained, fertile, humus-rich soil in sun or partial shade. Plant bulbs in autumn, 6 inches (15 cm) deep, spaced 12 inches (31 cm) apart. The bulbs should be planted on their sides to keep water from collecting in the hollow on top of the bulb and rotting it.

Fritillaria meleagris
Checkered lily

Zones 3–7

Native to Europe, this meadow plant grows to 8 inches (20 cm) high with an erect, clump-forming habit. Nodding, bell-shaped flowers are white or purple with a dark checkered pattern on the petals and appear in spring. Leaves are thin, inconspicuous and grasslike. Popular for rock gardens, wildflower meadows, and woodland gardens. Easy to grow in most well-drained garden soils in sun or partial shade. Plant bulbs in autumn, 4 inches (10 cm) deep, 3 inches (8 cm) apart.

Galanthus elwesii
Giant snowdrop

Zones 3–7

Native to Europe and west Asia, this harbinger of spring grows 6 inches (15 cm) high with a low-growing, clump-forming habit. Nodding, white, teardrop-shaped flowers are held above the slender green foliage on erect stems. There is a double form, 'Flore Pleno'. Good for edging paths, beds and borders, and for naturalizing in woodland. Bulbs increase readily by division and also self-seed. Prefers a well-drained, fertile, humus-rich soil, particularly one with leaf mold. Plant bulbs in autumn, 4 inches (10 cm) deep, spaced 3 inches (8 cm) apart. Beautiful partnered with yellow aconites and pink hellebores.

Hyacinthus orientalis
Dutch hyacinth

Zones 3–8

Native to Mediterranean countries, this plant grows 10 inches (25 cm) high with an erect habit. Highly fragrant, star-shaped florets are closely set around a thick, fleshy stem, producing an erect flower column above several green, straplike leaves in spring. Color range includes red, blue, pink, yellow, white and purple. Good for massing in beds and borders and popular for pot culture. Prechilled bulbs are offered by many bulb dealers for growing in special hyacinth vases, filled only with water. 'Woodstock' is an unusual maroon. Prefers fertile, humus-rich loam soil in full sun. Plant bulbs in autumn 6 inches (15 cm) deep, spaced 6 inches (15 cm) apart. Good companions for late daffodils and early tulips.

Hyacinthoides hispanica aka *Endymion hispanicus*
Spanish bluebell

Zones 6–10

Native to Europe, this woodland plant grows 12 inches (31 cm) high with an erect habit. Nodding, spring-flowering, blue, bell-shaped flowers are clustered at the top of arching stems. Leaves are green and sword shaped. Popular for shade gardens, where they will naturalize; they are excellent for cutting. Prefers fertile, moist, humus-rich soil. Plant bulbs in autumn, 3 inches (8 cm) deep, spaced 6 inches (15 cm) apart. Related species: *H. non-scripta* (English bluebell) is similar in appearance and fragrant, but generally not as showy.

Incarvillea delavayi
Hardy gloxinia

Zones 5–7

Native to China, this is not a true gloxinia, but is instead related to trumpet vines. These alpine plants grow to 12 inches (31 cm) high with a low, rosette-forming habit. Lovely gloxinia-shaped pink, rosy-red or white blooms have purple and yellow throats clustered at the top of slender stems. The flowers appear in spring. Leaves are glossy, dark green, heavily veined and indented. Popular for rock gardens. Prefers well-drained, fertile, humus-rich, acid soil in sun or partial shade. Plant tubers in autumn with tips angled down just below the soil surface, spaced 8 inches (20 cm) apart.

Bulbs

Ipheion uniflorum aka *Triteleia uniflorum*
Spring starflower
Zones 6–9

Native to Argentina, this meadow plant grows 5 inches (13 cm) high with a low, colony-forming habit. It has six-petalled, light blue, star-shaped, lightly fragrant flowers that bloom in spring. Leaves are narrow and grasslike, emitting an odor of onion when bruised. Popular for rock gardens. In warm, sunny, sheltered locations, clumps can spread rapidly from bulb division and self-seeding. Easy to grow in most well-drained garden soils in sun or partial shade. Plant bulbs in autumn, 4 inches (10 cm) deep, and spaced 3 inches (8 cm) apart.

Iris reticulata
Snow iris
Zones 3–7

Native to the Caucasus Mountains, this alpine plant grows to 6 inches (15 cm) high, forming colonies. Mostly blue, purple and white flowers appear in early spring. Sometimes sold as a mixture with *I. danfordiae* to introduce yellow into its color range. Leaves are narrow, green and spiky. Popular planted as drifts in rock gardens in company with crocus and also for forcing in containers. Prefers well-drained, fertile, humus-rich soil in full sun. Plant bulbs in autumn, 4 inches (10 cm) deep, spaced 3 inches (8 cm) apart.

Leucojum vernum
Spring snowflake
Zones 2–9

Native to Europe, this plant resembles a large snowdrop and grows 9 inches (23 cm) tall with a low-growing, clump-forming habit. Dainty, pendulous, white flowers cluster along short, arching stems with narrow, pointed leaves. Popular for naturalizing in woodland and shade gardens. Often flowers before the last snowfalls of spring. *L. aestivum* (summer snowflake) flowers a little later in spring and grows to 2 feet (61 cm) with larger flowers, especially in the variety 'Gravetye Giant'. Prefers a moist, well-drained, humus-rich soil in partial shade. Plant bulbs in autumn, 3 inches (8 cm) deep, spaced 3 inches (8 cm) apart.

LILIUM

Lilies
Zones 3–9 depending on variety

The true family of lilies has nine classifications but there are many imposters including calla lilies and lily-of-the-valley. Lilies, in general, grow in sun or shade and prefer a cool, organic-rich soil. They like good drainage and mulching around the stems to keep the soil cool. They are mostly massed in mixed borders and along woodland paths, and they are excellent for cutting. Most are propagated by division of the segmented bulbs, and some are easily raised from seed, though results from seed can be variable. Some kinds, such as the tiger lilies (*L. lancifolium*), produce black bulblets along the stem at the base of the leaves. These can be rubbed off and planted to produce exact replicas of the parent plant. The main classifications are these:

Asiatic hybrids
Asiatic lilies
Zones 3–8

These are early summer-flowering plants with mostly upward-facing flowers, but also some outward-facing and some nodding. They have been hybridized from Asian species, and they are the most popular group, ideal for massing and also for cutting. Some dwarf varieties, such as the 'Pixies', are suitable for container plantings. Color range includes all shades of red, pink, yellow, orange and purple, plus white and many bicolored.

Martagon hybrids
Zones 4–9

Also called Turk's cap lilies, these are mostly summer flowering and hybridized from *L. martagon*, which is found across Europe and Asia. Flowers are pendant with recurved petal tips, and they prefer afternoon shade. The wide color range is mostly shades of red, pink and purple, plus white.

Candidum hybrids

Zones 6–9

These are derived from the white Madonna lily, *L. candidum*, probably native to China though their precise origin is unknown. They grow tall flower spikes with mostly fragrant flowers.

American hybrids

Mostly zones 5–9, depending on variety
These are derived from American species, heavy into the yellows, orange and red. They are mostly spotted with nodding recurved petals such as the Bellingham hybrid mixture.

LONGIFLORUM AND FORMOSANUM HYBRIDS

Zones 6–11

Commonly called Easter lilies because of their ability to be easily forced into bloom at Easter. They have mostly trumpet-shaped, fragrant blooms and tall stems. Derived from crosses involving *L. longiflorum* from Japan and *L. formosanum* from Taiwan and the Philippines, valued for its late summer flowering. Certain selections, such as 'White Swan', can be flowered the first year from seed.

Trumpet hybrids
Zones 5–9
Mostly obtained from crosses involving *L. henryi* from China, these have a wide color range including all shades of red, pink, yellow and orange, plus white. 'Black Dragon', which has large white flowers and dark maroon on the petal reverse, belongs to this group.

Oriental hybrids
Zones 4–8
These are crosses involving large-flowering lilies from China and Japan, mostly *L. auratum*, *L. japonicum* and *L. speciosum*. The flower can be trumpet shaped, but most are flared with recurved petals. The popular florist varieties 'Star Gazer' (rosy-red and handsomely spotted) and the pure white, New Zealand-bred 'Casa Blanca' belong here. They are rich in red and pink shades but can also be found in yellow, and they are often exotically spotted.

Miscellaneous hybrids
Zones 3–10
This catch-all category includes all other hybrids. These include crosses between trumpet and Oriental lilies (dubbed 'Orienpets') and Asiatic and trumpet lilies (called 'LA Hybrids').

Species
Zones 2–11, depending on the species
These lilies are found in the wild, mostly from Europe, Asia and North America. *L. canadense* (Zones 2–7), from North America, is one of the hardiest. *L. pyrenaicum*, from the Pyrenees, is almost as hardy.

Bulbs

Lycoris squamigera
Naked ladies
Zones 6–10
Native to Japan, this meadow plant grows to 2 feet (61 cm) tall with an erect, colony-forming habit. Pink, trumpet-shaped flowers appear in late summer at the top of a thick, fleshy stem after the straplike leaves have died. Popular as an accent in mixed beds and borders and for naturalizing in drifts. Closely related to amaryllis. Prefers well-drained, fertile, sandy soil in full sun. Plant bulbs in spring or autumn, 4 inches (10 cm) deep, spaced 6 inches (15 cm) apart.

Muscari armeniacum
Grape hyacinth
Zones 3–8
Native to Asia Minor, this easily naturalized plant grows 5 inches (13 cm) tall with a low, clump-forming habit. Tiny, bell-shaped, blue flowers are clustered on top of slender stems above narrow, pointed leaves in spring. Readily increases by division of the bulbs and by self-seeding. Popular for edging paths, beds and borders, and also for colonizing in rock gardens. Easy to grow in most well-drained garden soil in sun or partial shade. Plant bulbs in autumn, 4 inches (10 cm) deep, spaced 3 inches (8 cm) apart. Striking when partnered with yellow daffodils.

NARCISSUS

Daffodils
Zones 4–9 depending on variety
Of all hardy perennials, the daffodil is one of the most cherished. This is mainly because it is the most eye-catching of early spring flowers, capable of creating magnificent sweeps of cheerful yellow or white trumpet blooms, which can also be tinted pink or orange. Many are delightfully fragrant, and even the miniatures have stems long enough for cutting to create beautiful, long-lasting floral arrangements.

Native to the Pyrenees Mountains bordering Spain and France, wild species also occur in other parts of Europe at high elevations, especially in the Alps, and this gives them inherent hardiness. They survive in all but the hottest subtropical and tropical areas (climate zone 10) and the coldest (climate zones 2 and 3). Plants prefer full sun but will tolerate partial shade, especially beneath deciduous trees. Drought tolerant during all seasons except spring, they flourish in most soils with good drainage. Beautiful planted alone or partnered with early-flowering perennials and shrubs such as pansies, early tulips, hellebores, forsythia, magnolia and quince.

Planting of bulbs should occur in autumn until the ground freezes, at a depth of 6 inches (15 cm) from the base of the bulb, pointed side up. To keep daffodils coming back and increasing from year to year, feed with a high phosphorus fertilizer in spring before the plants bloom, and again in autumn after the first frost. Deadheading blooms after the flower fades helps reblooming, and allowing the leaves to die down naturally also preserves the vigor. Britain's Royal Horticultural Society has established 12 classifications for daffodils. They include:

Trumpet daffodils
These grow one large flower to a stem with a trumpet as long as, or longer than the petals, for example: 'King Alfred' (canary yellow).

Large-cupped daffodils
These grow one large flower to a stem, the cup more than a third, but less than equal to the length of the petals, for example: 'Ice Follies' (white, canary-yellow cup).

Small-cupped daffodils

These grow one flower to a stem, the cup not more than one-third the length of the petals, for example: 'Barrett Browning' (white, bright orange cup).

Double daffodils

These grow one or more flowers to a stem with a doubling of the outer rim of petals, for example: 'Golden Ducat' (perianth and cup golden yellow).

Cyclamineus daffodils

These usually grow one flower to a stem, the outer rim of petals significantly reflexed, for example: 'Jack Snipe' (ivory-white, yellow trumpet).

Triandrus daffodils

These usually display two or more pendant flowers per stem with the outer rim of petals reflexed, or swept back, for example: 'Thalia' (white, highly fragrant).

Jonquilla daffodils

These have one to three flowers to a stem. The outer rim of petals are not reflexed. The flowers are fragrant and the leaves narrow and grasslike, for example: 'Suzy' (gold-yellow, cup bright orange).

Bulbs

Tazetta daffodils

These can have three to 20 fragrant flowers in a cluster, and the petals are not reflexed. They are the least hardy. For example, 'Paper white', which is usually grown indoors as a winter-flowering house plant, overwinters mostly in zones 8 and 9. The variety 'Cragford' (left) is hardy zones 5–9.

Poeticus daffodils

Also known as Poet's daffodils, these usually have one flower to a stem. The outer rim of petals is white and the cup is small, usually a contrasting color, for example: 'Actaea' (pure white perianth, gold-yellow cup with bright red edge).

Papillon daffodils

Similar to the split-coronas except the cup is usually shaped like a star or sunburst, for example: 'Dolly Mollinger'.

Species daffodils

These are wild types or hybrids found in the wild: for example, *N. bulbocodium* (Hoop petticoat daffodil), which generally is not hardy north of zone 7.

Miniature daffodils

Represent other divisions, except the flowers are small, and many grow no more than 6 inches (15 cm), for example: 'Tête-À-Tête'. Daffodils are also classified as early, midseason and late. Therefore, by choosing the right varieties, color from daffodils can extend for three months, from early spring with a miniature daffodil like 'Tête-À-Tête' to late spring with the double-flowered poet's daffodil known as 'Gardenia'.

Split-corona daffodils

These have the cup split into segments for at least a third of its length. The cup is usually wide, almost as wide as the outer rim of petals, and they tend to be the most eye-catching in mass plantings, for example: 'Chanterelle' (creamy white perianth, lemon-yellow cup).

Ornithogalum umbellatum
Star-of-Bethlehem
Zones 6–10

Native to the Mediterranean and naturalized throughout North America, this meadow plant grows 6 inches (15 cm) tall with a low, clump-forming habit. White starlike flowers are spring blooming; leaves are narrow and pointed. Usually form dense clumps by division of bulbs and self-seeding. Popular for edging paths and naturalizing in rock gardens. Easy to grow in most well-drained garden soils in sun or partial shade. Plant bulbs in autumn, 4 inches (10 cm) deep, and spaced 3 inches (8 cm) apart.

Puschkinia scilloides
Striped squill
Zones 3–9
Native of the Caucasus Mountains and southwest Asia, this alpine plant grows to 6 inches (15 cm) tall with an upright, clump-forming habit. Bluish-white flowers are star shaped and clustered at the top of a slender stem in spring. Green leaves are straplike. Popular for naturalizing in rock gardens. Increases by division of bulbs and self-seeding. Easy to grow in most well-drained garden soils in full sun. Plant bulbs in autumn, 4 inches (10 cm) deep, and spaced 3 inches (8 cm) apart. Effective when partnered with early daffodils.

Ranunculus ficaria
Celandine
Zones 5–9
Native to Europe and Asia, this is among the first bulbs to flower in spring. Plants produce masses of yellow, star-shaped flowers on low, 4-inch (10 cm) high spreading mats of glossy, heart-shaped leaves. Suitable for sun or shade, plant it where you don't mind its invasiveness. They tolerate boggy soil and summer drought. In addition to white, there is a double-flowered form.

Scilla siberica
Siberian squill
Zones 5–8
Native to the Caucasus Mountains, this alpine plant grows 5 inches (13 cm) high with a low-growing, erect, clump-forming habit. Each bulb bears several stems of nodding, bell-shaped, blue flowers above straplike leaves in early spring. Popular for forming drifts in rock gardens and naturalizing in woodland to form a dense, blue carpet. Increases by bulb division and self-seeding. Often blooms during a thaw while snow is still on the ground. Recommended variety: 'Spring Beauty', a sterile selection with extra-large flowers. Easy to grow in most well-drained garden soils in sun or partial shade. Plant bulbs in autumn, 4 inches (10 cm) deep, and spaced 3 inches (8 cm) apart. Especially beautiful partnered with early daffodils.

TULIPA
Tulip
Zones 4–8, depending on variety
Although not generally as early flowering as the earliest daffodils, tulips are cherished for the bold splash of color they can make in spring. Their color range is almost as diverse as orchids, being especially rich in shades of red, pink, orange, yellow, white, green and even black.

Indigenous mainly to Asia, particularly in the mountainous regions from Turkey to China, tulips survive cold, freezing winters and hot, dry summers. They are happiest in zones 4 to 7. A tulip's flower form, color and height vary according to variety. The most common flower shape is urn shaped, but on sunny days, the petals will often splay out flat like a water lily. There are also tulips with pointed petals, fringed petals and bizarre "feathered" petals called parrots. They make especially good companions to daffodils, hyacinths, bleeding hearts and other early-flowering perennials, along with trees and shrubs such as azaleas, cherries and crabapples.

Tulips prefer to be planted in full sun, although they will tolerate partial shade. They relish well-drained, sandy, fertile soils. Bulb size can vary, but most prefer to be planted 6 inches (15 cm) deep from the base of the bulb.

Although most of the species tulips, such as *Tulipa tarda*, will come back faithfully each year and multiply, most of the highly-bred tulips will fail to return after the first season. This is not because of lack of hardiness but because the bulb often will divide and produce only leaves.

Tulips are grouped into categories that were recently changed by the Dutch bulb growers for sake of simplicity.

Single Early tulips
Include some of the oldest garden tulips. Most are urn shaped with one flower to a stem and are commonly seen in company with daffodils.

Double Early tulips
Mainly short stemmed and early flowering. The flower form resembles a peony, for example: pink 'Peach Blossom'.

Triumph tulips
Urn-shaped, single-flowered varieties. There are more Triumph tulips than any other type, for example: 'Gavota' (a mahogany and yellow bicolor).

Darwin Hybrid tulips
Generally larger flowered than the Triumphs and shorter lived, primarily the result of parentage with the short-lived species, *T. fosteriana*. This lineage gives the petals a shimmering or satinlike sheen. Sometimes called perennial tulips, they have sufficient vigor to bloom over several seasons, for example: 'Gudoshnik', a yellow that is streaked with red.

Lily-flowered tulips
Have elegant pointed petals, one flower to a stem, mostly midseason and late flowering, such as the red and yellow bicolor 'Queen of Sheba'.

Single Late tulips
Mostly long-stemmed with urn-shaped blooms that can be cluster-flowered, several flowers to a stem. Sometimes known as cottage tulips, their late flowering allows them to be partnered with peonies, Oriental poppies and bearded irises, for example: 'Sorbet' (white with rosy-red streaks).

Fringed tulips
Have lacy or fringed petal tips, for example: 'Blue Heron', a violet-blue with frosted petal edges.

Viridiflora tulips

Also known as artist tulips, they are mostly late flowered and have streaks of green along the petal midrib. They are especially valued for floral arrangements, where their subtle beauty can be best appreciated, for example: 'Groenland'.

Kaufmanniana tulips

Reliably perennial, mostly low growing and preferred for rock garden display. On sunny days, they resemble a water lily, for example: the yellow and red bicolor 'Stresa'.

Rembrandt tulips

Urn-shaped, bicolored flowers, mostly yellow streaked with red, and white streaked with pink. Originally, the bizarre colors were caused by a virus infection, but in modern varieties, the Rembrandt streaking has been produced by mutation.

Fosteriana tulips

Similar to the Kaufmanniana, but generally they have longer stems and are larger flowered. The popular class of 'Emperor' tulips belongs to this group, coming back in subsequent years.

Parrot tulips

Can be extremely large flowered, up to 8 inches (20 cm) across with the petals frilled, or feathered like the tail feathers of a parrot, for example: 'Flaming Parrot'.

Greigii tulips

These also resemble Kaufmannianas, but they have striped, straplike leaves and are mostly maroon on green. They are popular for mass planting in rock gardens, forming long-lived colonies. 'Plaisir' is a red and white bicolor.

Double Late tulips

Resemble peonies. They are also among the largest flowered of tulips, valued in flower arrangements, for example: 'Carnaval de Nice', a red and white bicolor.

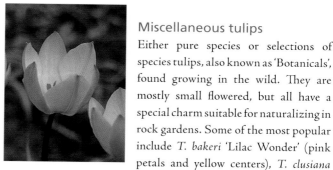

Miscellaneous tulips

Either pure species or selections of species tulips, also known as 'Botanicals', found growing in the wild. They are mostly small flowered, but all have a special charm suitable for naturalizing in rock gardens. Some of the most popular include *T. bakeri* 'Lilac Wonder' (pink petals and yellow centers), *T. clusiana* 'Cynthia' (alternating yellow and pink petals), *T. praestans* 'Fusilier' (a vivid red, cluster-flowered tulip that can repeat bloom for 20 years or more), and *T. tarda* (yellow with white petal tips).

Herbs

The following listing features useful annual, biennial and perennial herbs. Most have culinary value as a garnish, flavoring or herbal tea. Many come from areas of the Mediterranean with poor soils and are not especially ornamental (like burnet), while others have beautiful flowers (like chives) or foliage (like sage), thus allowing them to be used in perennial borders.

Using herbs to create a beautiful design takes skill because plant height and the texture of leaves often play a more important part in the overall design than flowers. Also, it is important to realize that within a herb species, there may be decorative variegated forms that will provide a better visual effect than the plain species.

When planning a herb garden, it helps to plant within a framework of low hedges or paths to create knot gardens and cartwheel designs where paths radiate from the center like the spokes of a wheel.

Agrimonia eupatoria
Agrimony

Zones 6–9

A rhizomatous perennial found in northern temperate regions, this dye plant grows to 3 feet (91 cm) tall with a wide spreading habit. Leaves and stalks are deep green and downy with slender spikes of yellow flowers. All plant parts are slightly aromatic with the flowers emitting an apricotlike spicy scent. Propagate by seed and cuttings. Prefers partial shade in sandy, well-drained soil. After drying, the stems, leaves and flowers can be used to make tea, as well as a yellow dye.

Allium cepa var. proliferum
Egyptian onion

Zones 4–9

This perennial bulb grows to 3 feet (91 cm) tall with an erect, clump-forming habit, and it forms edible onion-flavored bulblets on top of pungent, hollow, onionlike stalks. Plants also multiply by forming edible bulblets in the soil. Both the bulbs in the soil and the bulblets that form on the flowering stems are the chief means of propagation. Use as a substitute for onions as a seasoning in soups, sandwiches and salads.

Allium fistulosum
Welsh onion

Zones 4–9

This perennial bulb grows to 3 feet (91 cm) high with an upright, clump-forming habit. It bears rounded white flower clusters on hollow green stems with new leaves forming from bulblets at the base of the plant. Propagate from the seeds that follow flowering in the second season of growth and also by division of the underground bulblets. Prefers moist, fertile loam soil in full sun or partial shade. The young leaves are chopped into rings and used as a garnish like chives, while the bulbs are used as a substitute for onions in cooking.

LEFT: Herb garden at Cedaridge Farm features hardy annual herbs such as nasturtium, and hardy perennial herbs such as catmint and chives.

Herbs

Allium schoenoprasum
Chives

Zones 3–9

Native to Europe, Asia and North America, this hardy perennial bulb grows 12 inches (31 cm) tall with a clump-forming habit. It bears rounded pink or purple flowers which appear in spring on top of slender stalks above the clumps of arching, hollow, pointed leaves. Both leaves and flowers emit a mild onion flavor. Propagated by seed and by dividing established clumps, chives are easy to grow in most well-drained loam soils in full sun or partial shade. The leaves are chopped and used fresh, frozen or dried as a garnish in cooking and on salads. In flower, chives are highly ornamental and popular to use as an edging for paths and borders.

Allium tuberosum
Garlic chives

Zones 3–9

Native to Southeast Asia, this hardy perennial bulb grows 3 feet (91 cm) tall with an upright, clump-forming habit. The vigorous plants produce flat, slender leaves and masses of showy, white, rounded blossoms in summer. The flowers are sweetly scented, while the leaves and bulb have a garlic flavor and odor. Highly ornamental when in bloom. Propagate by seed and by dividing established clumps. Easy to grow in most well-drained loam soils in full sun or partial shade. Leaves are snipped into salads, soups and sauces. The dried green seed head makes an excellent garlic vinegar.

Anethum graveolens
Dill

All zones as an annual

This ornamental, annual culinary herb usually has one main upright hollow stem and blue-green foliage divided into threadlike segments. Umbels of yellow flowers are borne in summer, followed by ovoid, flattened, aromatic seeds. Plants grow to 3 feet (91 cm) high. Direct-seed three weeks before last spring frost date, since seedlings tolerate mild frost. Edible leaves ready to harvest in 60 days for use as a garnish, especially with eggs and fish. The dried seeds are used for flavoring cabbage and pickles.

Angelica archangelica
Angelica

Zones 4–9

Native to northern Europe, this aromatic biennial grows up to 6 feet (1.8 m) tall with a clump-forming habit. Clusters of large yellow-green flowers bloom in summer. Dark green leaves are up to 3 feet (91 cm) long with toothed edges, borne on hollow stems that are purplish at the base. All plant parts are fragrant. Plants prefer cool, moist, alkaline soils in sun or partial shade. The entire plant, finely chopped, is used mainly as a garnish. Oils extracted from the seeds are used as perfume fragrance and for flavoring. Propagate from seed.

Anthemis nobilis aka Chamaemelum nobile
Chamomile

Zones 4–9

Native to western Europe, this evergreen hardy perennial grows to 12 inches (31 cm) high with a bushy habit. Small, yellow, buttonlike blossoms appear in summer. Leaves are light green and segmented. All parts are highly fragrant. Propagate by seed and division of established clumps. Easy to grow in most well-drained loam soils in full sun. Flowers can be used fresh or dried to make a refreshing tea. 'Treneague' (lawn chamomile) is a variety that forms a 1-inch (2.5 cm) high mossy carpet suitable for creating a fragrant lawn. The flowers are inconspicuous and have no petals.

Anthriscus cerefolium
Chervil

All zones as an annual

This fast-growing hardy annual grows to 3 feet (91 cm) high with an erect, clump-forming habit. Dainty white flower clusters appear on thin, brittle stems in summer. Leaves are bright green and resemble parsley. Plants prefer a moist, fertile loam soil in full sun. Young leaves can be used fresh, dried or frozen as a garnish, especially on fish and fruit salads. It is an essential ingredient in bearnaise sauce. Also used on salads, in soups and marinades, and for a chicken or fish baste. Seed can be direct sown in early spring before the last frost date and in autumn to remain dormant until an early spring thaw. Edible leaves ready to harvest in 50 days for use as a garnish.

Carthamus tinctorius
Safflower

All zones as an annual

Native to western Asia, this tender annual grows 3 feet (91 cm) tall with an erect, branching habit. Bright orange, thistle-like flowers appear in summer. Indented, shiny green leaves are covered in spines. Propagated from seed, this plant tolerates a wide range of soils including impoverished, dry soil, in full sun. The white seeds are harvested commercially to make safflower oil for cooking. Seeds are frequently incorporated into wild bird foods. The dried petals are used to color food and can be substituted for saffron powder in a variety of dishes. The petals also yield a natural dye for cloth.

Artemisia dracunculus var. sativa
French tarragon

Zones 3–7

Native to central and eastern Europe, this aromatic hardy perennial grows to 3 feet (91 cm) high with an erect, clump-forming habit. Anise-flavored, shiny, green leaves are willowlike. Inconspicuous greenish white blooms are produced sporadically. The plant is propagated by division or cuttings. There is a related variety, *A. dracunculus* var. *inodora* (Russian tarragon), which can be grown from seeds, but it is inferior in quality to the true French tarragon, which is sterile. Plants prefer fertile, well-drained loam soil in full sun or partial shade. Divide every three years to maintain vigor. The chopped leaves are used to flavor vinegar and also to season spinach, mushrooms, chicken, beef and fish.

Chenopodium bonus-henricus
Good King Henry, Goosefoot

Zones 5–8

Native to Europe, this hardy perennial salad green grows to 2 feet (61 cm) high with a clump-forming habit. The upper surface of the spear-shaped leaves are dark green with a lighter, slightly downy underside. Spire-like, green flower clusters appear in spring. Plants prefer fertile loam soil in full sun but tolerate impoverished soil. Young leaves are harvested and cooked like spinach. Propagate from seed.

Herbs

Chrysanthemum coccineum
aka *Tanacetum coccineum*
Pyrethrum, Painted daisy
Zones 5–9

Native to southwest Asia, this decorative hardy perennial grows to 3 feet (91 cm) high with a bushy habit. The beautiful, daisylike flowers with yellow centers are red, pink and white, mostly single, but occasionally double flowered. The feathery leaves are silvery green. Easy to grow in most well-drained loam soils in full sun. Propagate from seed. Powdered petals are a source of an effective natural insecticide. Worth growing in mixed borders and for cutting.

Cichorium intybus
Chicory
Zones 4–8

Native to northern Europe, Africa and western Asia, this meadow plant produces charming blue cornflowerlike flowers that are especially beautiful partnered with Queen Anne's lace in wildflower gardens. Only a few wavy green leaves appear on the flower stems which grow to 3 feet (91 cm) high. Though it thrives in impoverished soil, the heaviest bloom occurs in fertile loam in full sun. Propagate by seed. Medicinally, the young leaves are edible as a salad green. Also, the root can be ground to make a substitute for coffee. A similar species, *C. endivia*, is a high-quality salad green and the source of "chicons", also known as Belgian endive.

Coriandrum sativum
Cilantro aka Coriander
All zones as an annual

This erect, ornamental annual herb has pungently aromatic, divided leaves. In summer, white flowers are followed by pale brown seed capsules with a fruity scent when ripe. Direct seed three weeks before last spring frost date, since seedlings tolerate mild frost. Edible leaves ready to harvest in 60 days for use as a garnish, especially in Mexican dishes.

Chrysanthemum balsamita aka *Tanacetum balsamita*
Costmary, Bible leaf
Zones 6–8

Native to Europe and western Asia, this shy-flowering hardy perennial grows to 3 feet (91 cm) high, forming clumps of broad, pointed, mint-scented leaves. The blossoms resemble pale yellow buttons on leggy stems in late summer. They are best removed to keep plants looking attractive. Propagate by root cuttings. Plants prefer fertile loam soil in sun or partial shade. The young leaves are used fresh or dried as a substitute for mint. Small quantities can be sprinkled on salads and also to flavor soups, poultry and bread.

Crocus sativus
Saffron
Zones 5–8

Origin uncertain but probably Spain. This hardy perennial bulb grows to 6 inches (15 cm) high with a low, clump-forming habit. Blue or purple crocus flowers, occurring in autumn, have conspicuous orange-red stigmas that hang over the petals. The long, pointed leaves are dark green and grasslike. Propagate by corms. Plant in spring into a well-drained, fertile loam or sandy soil in full sun. The orange stigmas when dried and crushed into a powder are used to flavor many ethnic foods such as Indian (saffron rice), French (bouillabaisse), Spanish (paella) and Swedish (saffron bread). Since 10,000 flowers are needed to make one pound of saffron, it is a costly herb to buy. Saffron imparts an attractive yellow color to rice and is a source of beautiful yellow dye.

Dipsacus sylvestris
Teasel
Zones 5–8

Native to Europe and Asia, this hardy biennial grows to 3 feet (91 cm) high with an upright, branching habit. Cone-shaped flower heads studded with tiny lilac flowers appear in midsummer. The seed head dries, becomes hard and is covered with curly spines. Leaves are pointed and thistle-like. Propagate from seed. Plants are easy to grow in a wide range of soils, including impoverished soil. The dried, prickly seed heads are used as combs. They are also ornamental in dried flower arrangements.

Foeniculum vulgare var. azoricum
Florence fennel aka Finocchio
All zones grown as an annual

Biennial grown as an annual with foliage divided into threadlike leaflets. Umbels of yellow flowers are produced in summer, followed by gray-brown seeds. Transplant four-week old seedlings three weeks before last spring frost date. Edible bulbous stems ready to harvest in 80 days, sliced and cooked.

Galium odoratum aka Asperula odorata
Sweet woodruff
Zones 5–8

Native to Europe, northern Africa and Russia, this hardy perennial grows up to 6 inches (15 cm) high with a low, ground-hugging habit. Small clusters of tiny, starry-white flowers appear in spring among whorls of pointed leaves. The plant spreads rapidly and maintains a uniform height, making it a decorative groundcover. Propagate primarily by dividing established clumps. Prefers a moist, humus-rich soil in partial shade. The leaves are an essential flavor enhancer for "May" wine and were once used for scattering on floors to sweeten musty rooms. Ornamentally, it is a valuable groundcover for shady areas. In autumn, when the leaves wilt and dry, they pervade the air with a sweet hay-scented aroma.

Hyssopus officinalis
Hyssop
Zones 6–9

Native to southern and eastern Europe, this decorative hardy perennial grows 2 feet (61 cm) high with a shrubby, clump-forming habit. Lavenderlike flower spikes in blue, pink or white bloom throughout the summer. Aromatic leaves are narrow with a slightly musky aroma. Propagate by seed sown directly into the garden or from cuttings. Prefers fertile, well-drained loam soil in full sun or light shade. Oil from the leaves is used primarily in scented soaps and in potpourri. The strong aroma is considered an insect repellent. It is an important ingredient in Chartreuse liqueur, and the leaves can be brewed to make an invigorating tea.

Lavandula angustifolia
English lavender

Zones 5-10 depending on variety

Native to high elevation areas of the Mediterranean, lavender is a hardy perennial that produces bushy plants of gray-green leaves and blue flower spikes. The fragrant flowers appear in early summer and the entire plant is a source of oils used in soaps and perfumes. Grows two to three feet high and prefers sandy or gravel soils that drain well. The variety 'Munstead' a light blue is the hardiest, a zone hardier than 'Hidcote' which is a darker blue. Propagate by cuttings. Trim plants of excessive growth in winter to maintain a compact habit.

Levisticum officinale
Lovage

Zones 5–8

Native to southern Europe, this celerylike hardy perennial grows up to 6 feet (1.8 m) tall with an upright, clump-forming habit. Small flower umbels, resembling dill flowers, are produced in spring. Best grown from seed sown directly into the garden in autumn, or started indoors six weeks before outdoor planting in spring. Prefers a deep, fertile, moist loam soil in full sun. All parts of the plant including leaves, stems, roots and seeds have culinary value, primarily to add a celery flavor to salads, soups, stews, meat and poultry.

Marrubium vulgare
White horehound

Zones 3–8

Native to Europe, Asia and North Africa, this nondescript hardy perennial grows 2 feet (61 cm) high with an erect, clump-forming habit. Small white flowers bloom along the stems in summer. Its common name comes from the wrinkled, hoary appearance of the gray-green leaves, which have crinkled edges and curl down. Propagated mainly from seed. Tolerates poor impoverished soils in full sun. Shear old plants in spring for a compact, bushy appearance, and divide overgrown clumps every three years. Used primarily to flavor candy, the leaves can be steeped in boiling water to make a refreshing tea. *Ballota nigra* (black horehound) is much stronger in flavor and too harsh for most tastes, except as a strong herbal tea said to relieve colds and sore throats.

Melissa officinalis
Lemon balm

Zones 3–7

Native to southern Europe, this mintlike hardy perennial grows to 3 feet (91 cm) with a mounded habit. The serrated oval leaves are bright green. Small white flowers are borne along the stems in summer. Left unchecked, it can become invasive through self-seeding. Propagate by seed, cuttings or root division. Prefers fertile, moist loam soil in full sun. The lemon-scented leaves make a delicious, refreshing tea. Rubbed on hands, they act as a deodorizer, covering unpleasant smells such as fish and garlic. Dried leaves retain their lemony aroma and are popular for adding to potpourri.

Mentha x piperita
Peppermint

Zones 3–7

Native to Europe, this hardy aromatic perennial grows up to 3 feet (91 cm) high with an upright, clump-forming habit. Stems are erect and square with oval, pointed, serrated leaves. Pale lavender flower spikes appear in summer. Propagate mainly by cuttings and division of overgrown clumps. Prefers moist loam soil in full sun or light shade. Spreads quickly by underground rhizomes. Commercially grown for its oil, which is used to flavor candy, perfume and potpourri. Inhaling the aroma clears the sinuses. Leaves steeped in boiling water make a refreshing tea.

Mentha pulegium
Pennyroyal

Zones 6–9

Native to Europe, this mintlike hardy perennial grows to 12 inches (31 cm) high and has a spreading habit. The leaves are small, oval, pointed and spaced evenly along slender stems with a dainty crown of pink flowers clustered at each leaf node. Propagate by seed and by division of overgrown clumps. Tolerates a wide range of well-drained soils in full sun. The strong mint flavor is reminiscent of peppermint. Its culinary use has diminished in recent years following reports that it can be toxic if used in excess. The leaves steeped in boiling water make a refreshing tea and can also be used to add a pleasant mint flavor to iced tea. Good to use as a natural insect repellent, dried and stuffed into sachets, or sprinkled over pet bedding.

Mentha spicata
Spearmint
Zones 4–9

Native to Europe, this aggressive hardy perennial grows to 3 feet (91 cm) high with an erect, bushy habit. Pink flower clusters are borne at the top of erect stems in long, tapering spikes, usually in early summer. Narrow, pointed, bright green, serrated leaves have conspicuous veins and are highly fragrant when bruised. Propagated by seed and root division. Any 4-inch (10 cm) section of root will produce a new plant. Prefers a moist loam soil in full sun or partial shade. Spearmint is similar to peppermint in appearance and uses, though it is milder. The oil is used as a flavoring by the cosmetics industry for everything from shampoo to toothpaste. Its culinary uses include flavoring iced tea, vinegar, fruit punch and jelly. Mint cordials are common, as is mint tea.

Monarda didyma
See Perennials, page 96.

Nepeta cataria
See Perennials, page 97.

Origanum vulgare
Oregano
Zones 5–9

Native to Europe, this aromatic hardy perennial is similar to *O. majorana* (sweet marjoram) but hardier. Oregano is similar in appearance to marjoram, except the small pink flower clusters are less conspicuous and it grows to 18 inches (46 cm) high. Propagate by seed, cuttings and root division. Easy to grow in most well-drained loam soils in full sun. Fresh or dried leaves are used in a variety of dishes especially pizza, cheese casseroles, pastas, tomato and spaghetti sauces.

Panax quinquefolius
Ginseng
Zones 3–7

Native to the Appalachian forests, this hardy perennial grows to 18 inches (46 cm) high, creating a low, groundcover habit. Five pointed leaves surround a basal stem, and small greenish flowers appear on mature plants in summer, followed by bright red berries. The plant develops a curious fleshy tap root often resembling a human form. Propagate primarily by seed. Ginseng is one of the slowest-growing herbs in cultivation, requiring four years to flower and set seed. Plants demand a moist, humus-rich soil in partial shade. The powdered or shredded roots are dried to make a refreshing tea. The Chinese attribute mythical powers to ginseng as a medicinal cure-all and as a stimulant.

Petroselinum crispum
Parsley
Zones 5–8

Native to southern Europe, this hardy biennial grows to 12 inches (31 cm) with a moundlike habit and usually remains evergreen even during freezing weather. There are two kinds: Italian plain leaf and curly parsley, which has dark green leaves that are finely divided and curly, sometimes resembling a tight cushion of moss. Tiny clusters of greenish yellow flowers are produced on tall stems in the spring of the second year, setting seed and then dying. Propagate by seed, which require warm temperatures to germinate, even though the seedlings tolerate frost. Prefers a cool, humus-rich moist soil in full sun. An extremely popular garnish for all manner of culinary dishes, especially fish and potatoes. Sometimes used as an ornamental for edging flower beds. 'Hamburg' parsley, a related species, produces an edible root shaped like a parsnip. Transplant "starts" four weeks before last spring frost date. Both plain leaf and curly parsley are ready to harvest in 60 days as a garnish for soups and salads.

Pimpinella anisum
Anise

Zones 5–8

Native to Eurasia and northern Africa, this hardy annual grows 2 feet (61 cm) high with an upright, slender habit. Feathery green leaves resemble those of wild carrot. Umbels of white flower clusters resemble Queen Anne's lace and appear in summer. The entire plant has a licorice aroma. Propagate from seed. Prefers a moist, loam soil in full sun. The seeds can be collected and chewed to sweeten the breath and as a digestive aid. The seeds also yield a licorice-flavored oil used in beverages, candies and cookies, and also to make a refreshing tea.

Ruta graveolens
Rue

Zones 5–9

Native to southeastern Europe, this hardy perennial grows to 3 feet (91 cm) high. Plants usually remain evergreen throughout winter. Beautiful, indented, blue-green leaves form attractive moundlike plants, becoming bushier as the season advances. Bright yellow flower clusters appear in midsummer. Propagate by seed, root cuttings and by division. Prefers an acidic soil in full sun or partial shade, and tolerates poor soil. Dried rue is used primarily as an insect repellent, while the roots produce a rosy red dye. Popular in herb gardens for its ornamental quality, particularly the variety 'Blue Mound'.

Salvia officinalis
Garden sage

Zones 5–8

Native to the Mediterranean, this bushy hardy perennial grows to 3 feet (91 cm) high. Slender, oval leaves are gray with a blistered texture. They are highly aromatic when rubbed. Decorative spikes of white, pink or light blue flowers appear in spring. Propagate by seed and by cuttings. Easy to grow in most well-drained garden soils. Fresh sage leaves are more pungent than the dried leaves and should be used sparingly to flavor stuffing, sausage, vegetable dishes and many other foods. Oil distilled from the leaves is used to make perfume. 'Purpurescens' has purple leaves, and 'Tricolor' features white, pink and purple leaves.

Sanguisorba minor aka Poterium sanguisorba
Salad burnet

Zones 4–8

Native to Europe and Asia, this hardy perennial grows 12 inches (31 cm) high with a low, mounded habit. Long, cascading stems splay out from the center of the plant, presenting the toothed, green leaves in matched pairs along each stem. Greenish flowers, small and inconspicuous are produced in late summer. Propagate by seed and division. Prefers well-drained sandy soil in full sun. Self-seeds easily and tolerates crowding. The cucumber-flavored leaves are used in salads and vinegars.

Herbs

Satureja montana
Winter savory
Zones 5–8

Native to southern Europe, this aromatic hardy perennial usually stays evergreen during winters and grows to 12 inches (31 cm) high with a mound-shaped habit. Narrow, pointed green leaves are crowded along wiry stems. Propagate by seed and softwood cuttings. Short spikes of white flowers appear in late summer. Prefers moist, sandy soil that is not too fertile, in full sun. The root crown is susceptible to rot in moist soils. Prune tops back in spring to keep the plant looking tidy. May be used as a dwarf hedge.

Symphytum officinale
Common comfrey
Zones 3–9

Native to Europe and western Asia, this hardy perennial grows to 4 feet (1.2 m) high, forming a vigorous clump of dark green, heavily veined leaves. Pale pink tubular flowers are borne in summer on long stems. Propagate by seed and division. Prefers moist, fertile loam soil in full sun. A great number of medicinal remedies attributed to comfrey have proven false. Therefore, its place in the herb garden today is mostly historical and ornamental, though herbalists still do not hesitate to brew a cup of comfrey tea or add a chopped leaf to a spring salad.

Santolina chamaecyparissus
Lavender cotton
Zones 6–9

Native to the Mediterranean, this bushy hardy perennial grows to 2 feet (61 cm) high with a cushion-shaped habit. Attractive, silvery foliage is finely cut. In summer, masses of yellow, buttonlike blooms appear on slender stalks. Leaves are highly aromatic when touched. Propagate by seed and cuttings. These drought-tolerant plants prefer fertile, moist, well-drained, acidic loam soil in full sun. The dried foliage repels insects, especially moths. Sensational edging plant for beds and borders. Useful as a slope cover in coastal gardens, plants require heavy pruning after flowering to maintain a tidy shape. *S. virens* (green santolina) has needle-like, dark green leaves and buttonlike, pale yellow flowers in early summer, and is hardy to Zone 5.

Tanacetum vulgare
Common tansy
Zones 4–8

Native to Europe, this aggressive hardy perennial grows to 4 feet (1.2 m) high with a dense, clump-forming habit. Dark green leaves are fernlike and pungent. Yellow buttonlike flowers appear in summer. Propagate by seed and division. Easy to grow even in poor soil and prefers full sun. Spreads rapidly by underground rhizomes. Needs division annually after third year. Fresh and dried flower heads and foliage have insect-repellent properties. Both leaves and flowers are beautiful in fresh or dried arrangements.

Teucrium chamaedrys
Germander
Zones 5–9

Native to Europe and southwest Asia, this shrublike hardy perennial stays evergreen in winter and grows to 15 inches (38 cm) high. Mature plants develop woody stems crowded with small, oval, green leaves. Dainty pink flowers resembling thyme occur in midsummer. Plants tolerate crowding and can be planted to create a dwarf hedge. Propagate by cuttings or division. Prefers fertile loam soil in full sun. In areas where winters are severe, plants benefit from mulching around roots. A tea can be brewed from its leaves, although its main value is as an edging plant for beds and borders and also in creating knot designs.

Thymus vulgaris (TOP RIGHT)
Common thyme
Zones 4–9

Native to the western Mediterranean, this aromatic hardy perennial remains evergreen in winter and grows to 12 inches (31 cm) tall with a mounded, shrubby habit. Small, rounded, green leaves are almost hidden in spring by clusters of showy pink flowers. Mature stems turn woody. Propagate by seed, cuttings and division. Prefers a well-drained, garden loam soil in full sun. The most popular culinary use for thyme is as a seasoning for vegetable, meat and fish dishes. It is an essential ingredient in "bouquet garni", a cluster of five essential herbs tied together and steeped in soup or stew. *T. praecox* (creeping thyme) good for planting between flagstones in zones 4–9; *T. citriodorus* (lemon thyme) imparts a lemonlike aroma, good for zones 5–10; and *T. serpyllum* (mother of thyme) is ideal for rock gardens, walls and containers in zones 4–9.

Valeriana officinalis (LOWER RIGHT)
Common valerian
Zones 4–9

Native to western Europe, this showy hardy perennial grows to 5 feet (1.5 m) high with an erect habit. Clusters of attractive white or pink flowers are borne on stiff stems in spring, imparting a vanilla-like fragrance. Finely divided leaves are blue-green and ornamental. Propagate by seed and division. Prefers moist, well-drained loam soil in full sun or partial shade. Self-seeds easily. In ancient times, the root was used medicinally to treat hypertension. Today, the plant is used mainly for its ornamental effect and its value as a cut flower.

Perennials

Perennials represent the largest listing in this book, because as a plant category, they are more extensive than any other for garden display. The hardy perennials in the following list have been chosen for their superlative garden display, many for their beautiful flowers and others for their appealing foliage. They are arranged by botanical name; however, to find a variety by common name, you can refer to the common name index on page 220.

When grown from seed, perennials usually develop a crown of leaves the first season, survive wintry weather through a dormant root system, and flower the following season. Most, like peonies, will live on from year to year, flowering each season, and outlive the owner. Others, like columbine, have shorter life spans – usually no more than three years. Included here are also some hardy biennials that flower the second season and die after flowering. However, they generally self-seed readily, and so give the impression of being perennial. Foxgloves, dame's rocket and lupines fit in this category.

In addition to reproducing themselves from seed (which can produce variable results), many perennials can be propagated by division of healthy clumps, and also by stem cuttings and root cuttings, depending on variety. This produces offspring identical to the mother plant. Heights given refer to the mature height when the variety starts to flower. Often, soil fertility or abundant rainfall will cause excessive growth. Moreover, heights often vary according to variety. Similarly, the spread of a plant can vary among varieties and with age; many perennials double in area each season.

Perennials that live on from year to year as bulbs (such as tulips and daffodils) and reproduce from bulblets have been given a separate section.

Acanthus spinosus aka *Acanthus spinosissimus*
Bear's breeches
Zone 5–9

Native to the Mediterranean. Acanthus are handsome, thistle-like plants with a commanding presence in the landscape because of their arching, glossy, heavily indented leaves and stiff flower spikes that can grow to 5 feet (1.5 m) high. Though *A. mollis* is the species whose broad, arching leaves are sculpted into the top of Corinthian columns of ancient Greece, it is not reliably hardy in gardens colder than zone 8. *A. spinosus* is similar in appearance, growing more sharply indented leaves with spiny leaf tips. In early summer plants grow tall, tapering, flower spikes studded with tubular white flowers hooded with purple bracts. Plants can form vigorous clumps 4 feet (1.2 m) or more across. They are prized for mixed borders, adding a stately, tropical accent; also suitable to control soil erosion, especially in coastal locations. Plants thrive in sun or light shade, grow in moisture-retentive soil but prefer good drainage. The spent flower spikes make good dried arrangements. Propagate from seed or root division.

LEFT: A welcoming entranceway with bright yellow *Rudbeckia fulgida* (black-eyed Susan), *Echinacea purpurea* (purple coneflower) and *Phlox paniculata* (phlox). **ABOVE RIGHT**: Cottage garden featuring roses and perennials around a sundial.

Perennials

Achillea filipendulina
Yarrow

Zone 3–9

Native to Europe and Asia, this is the most widely grown of several hardy species suitable for summer-long garden display, especially in mixed borders. Varieties such as 'Gold Plate' (a deep golden yellow) and the hybrid 'Moonshine' (a pale yellow) are vigorous plants that can become invasive. The hybrid 'Walter Funke' is a bright cinnamon red, which perennials expert Al Russell describes as "the never to be outdone again, compact and more silvery companion of 'Fireland.'" The yellows are all ideal companions to blue *Salvia nemorosa*. Another species, *A. millefolium*, is rich in pink and red tones, notably 'Appleblossom' (pale pink), 'Lilac Beauty' (lilac-pink) and 'Paprika' (ruby-red flowers with yellow centers). Plants have aromatic, fernlike leaves and grow from 2 feet (61 cm) in the compact varieties like 'Moonshine' and 'Walter Funke' to 4 feet (1.2 m) and more for others. They spread equally wide and wider if not controlled. They are easy to grow in most well-drained soils and tolerate drought. The fresh flowers are valued for cutting, and the spent flowers are suitable for dried arrangements. Mostly propagated by root division. Hybrid mixtures are available to grow from seed, such as 'Summer Pastels'. Colors include yellow, apricot, white, all shades of pink, and red.

Aconitum carmichaelii
Monkshood

Zones 3–7

This is the hardiest of several popular species of monkshood, all native to Europe and Asia. Discovered growing on the Kamtchatka Peninsula, plants grow tall, to 5 feet (1.5 m) and more, the tapering flower spikes studded with hooded deep blue flowers that bloom in midsummer. They are most suitable for mixed borders, though plants usually will require staking. The variety 'Arendsii' is particularly desirable for garden display because its long flower clusters resemble delphinium from a distance. A less tapering species *A. napellus* is hardy to zone 5, and though variable in habit, the hooded violet-blue flowers are generally arranged in a dome. There are also blue and white bicolored hybrids. Plants are clump forming, prefer full sun or light shade, and thrive in fertile well-drained soils. The flower stems are suitable for cutting, though the sap can cause a rash, and the roots are deadly poisonous.

Acorus calamus 'Variegatus'
Sweet flag

Zones 4–11

This grasslike plant has slender green leaves edged in white, similar in appearance to variegated irises. Tolerant of boggy soil it is especially attractive massed beside ponds. The small, pokerlike, yellow flowers occur in spring and are inconspicuous. Tuberous roots have a pleasant, sweet odor reminiscent of cinnamon when crushed. Plants grow to 3 feet (91 cm) high and will survive with their roots submerged in shallow water up to 6 inches (15 cm) deep. Propagate by dividing the fleshy rhizomes, preferably in spring. In small water gardens it is advisable to grow in sunken pots in order to confine the aggressive roots. *A. gramineus* has yellow-gold leaves and a more compact habit, growing to 10 inches (25 cm) high, while 'Minimus aureus' has fine yellow foliage only 4 inches (10 cm) high, suitable for growing between flagstones.

Adenophora confusa
Ladybells

Zone 3–8

Resembling spires of campanula, plants grow long, tapering, violet-blue flower spikes up to 4 feet (1.2 m) tall, crowded with nodding, bell-shaped flowers and toothed leaves. Native to China, plants flower in late spring in sun or light shade and may need staking to keep the flower stems erect. A similar species, *Adenophora bulleyana*, is only slightly less hardy.

Adiantum pedatum
Maidenhair fern

Zones 3–8

This deciduous, slow-growing, lace-like fern is native to North America and since many tropical species of *Adiantum* are also called maidenhair ferns, it is often referred to as North American maidenhair fern. Plants grow to 3 feet (91 cm) high and create a layered effect with their splayed, deeply indented leaf clusters. They are extremely sensitive to sun burn and wind burn, and prefer to be planted in a lightly shaded, humus-rich, moist soil, particularly in woodland where mosses grow naturally. Striking when massed in a rock garden, damp grotto or along woodland paths, in company with broad-leafed hostas for leaf contrast. Propagate by spores and root division.

Adonis amurensis
Amur Adonis

Zones 4–7

Native to Japan and China, the anemone-like yellow flowers strike through the soil in early spring, at the same time as snowdrops, before the leaves appear. They are especially beautiful massed on slopes along woodland paths in company with snowdrops. In a humus-rich, acid soil with good drainage they self-seed reliably to create sheets of shimmering yellow. The feathery, fernlike, deciduous leaves appear after the main floral display and persist until midsummer. Double-flowered forms of up to 30 petals are available. Plants grow to 6 inches (15 cm) high and are easily propagated by seed or division after the leaves die down.

Aegopodium podagraria
Bishop's weed

Zones 4–9

Although the common species can be a highly invasive plant with its dark green ivy-shaped leaves and white flowers resembling Queen Ann's lace, there is a less aggressive, variegated form called 'Variegatum' that has gray-green leaves and white margins, creating a silvery appearance from a distance. Suitable for sun or light shade, it can be used for erosion control of difficult slopes and as a weed-suffocating groundcover beneath trees and poor soils where little else will grow. Native to Europe and Asia, plants grow to 12 inches (31 cm) high and bloom in early summer.

Agastache foeniculum
Anise hyssop

Zones 6–10

Native to southern and western regions of North America into Mexico, anise hyssop has a pleasant licorice-like scent. Although often grown in herb gardens to brew a delicious tea, its prominent candle-like, lavender-blue flower spikes also make it a favorite for mixed perennial borders, particularly in company with ornamental grasses. Plants have square stems and mintlike leaves, grow to 5 feet (1.5 m) high, self-seed readily and spread aggressively. They are drought resistant, thrive even in poor soils and demand good drainage. Numerous other hardy species and hybrids are available for garden display. Of particular value in the flower garden are *A. barberi* 'Firebird', bearing erect flower stems studded with orange-red flowers and 'Tutti-Frutti', a magenta. Hybrids such as 'Acapulco Rose' (a rosy-red) are highly desirable for containers. All are attractive to hummingbirds and butterflies. In addition to seed propagation among the species, plants are easily divided.

Perennials

Ajania pacifica
Pacific chrysanthemum

Zones 5–9

Native to Japan and closely related to chrysanthemums, the pachysandra-like variegated leaves and late flowering of its buttonlike, yellow flowers endear this aggressive, spreading plant to gardeners. The leaves are a dark glossy green, margined white, and during summer remain low, cushion shaped and compact at about 6 inches (15 cm) high; but in autumn plants grow taller flower spikes up to a foot (31 cm) high in sun and 2 feet (61 cm) high in light shade. The flower stems are suitable for cutting. Plants tolerate a wide range of soils, prefer good drainage and are most often used either for edging flower beds or as a groundcover along rock ledges in rock gardens. Propagated by division.

Ajuga reptans
Bugleweed, Blue bugle

Zones 3–9

The most widely planted of several *Ajuga* species from Europe and Asia, the evergreen plants flower mostly in blue but also in pink and white, depending on variety. 'Catlin's Giant' is an especially conspicuous and free-flowering blue. The tubular flowers are tightly packed around square stems, creating a stocky column, surrounded by a rosette of dark green, glossy leaves. Plants thrive in sun or light shade, self-seed readily and can become a lawn weed, but confined to the edges of mixed perennial borders and woodland paths, it is an invaluable early spring-flowering perennial good to contrast with yellow dogbane, yellow perennial alyssum and yellow 'Bowles Golden' grass. Even though the equally hardy *A. pyramidalis* has bolder leaves with a dark metallic sheen and larger flower spikes, *A. reptans* creates a bolder splash of floral color. In addition to *A. reptans* being grown for its floral display, there are several variegated forms that are valued for groundcover effect. These include 'Multicolor' with red, pink, maroon and silvery green crinkled leaves, and 'Burgundy Glow' with red, bronze and light green variegated foliage. Flowering on the variegated forms is sparse. In addition to seed, propagate by division.

Alcea rosea
Hollyhock

Zones 3–9

Plant breeders have been very busy breeding garden varieties of hollyhock; they can be perennial, biennial or annual, depending on variety. Old-fashioned single-flowered hollyhocks grow tall, taking flower spikes up to 10 feet (3 m) high, displaying cup-shaped flowers with a satinlike sheen in a rich assortment of colors including red, pink, yellow, apricot, white and maroon. They make excellent back-of-the-border accents, especially when massed, and good companions to climbing roses. The large, coarse, deeply lobed leaves resemble fig leaves in some varieties. If the stems are cut back soon after flowering, plants have a tendency to come back as perennials. However, double-flowered hollyhocks are best treated as biennials, sowing seed directly into their permanent flowering positions in summer for flowering the following summer. A few varieties will perform as hardy annuals (see page 17), flowering the first season from seed started early indoors. Choose a sunny position and a fertile soil with good drainage.

Alchemilla mollis
Lady's mantle

Zones 4–7

An amazingly popular plant for edging perennial borders and rock gardens considering its ivy-shaped leaves and sprays of lime green flowers have an understated beauty. The domes of foliage add an appealing velvety texture and the flower sprays have a tendency to arch forward informally to soften edging. Plants look particularly good planted beside pools, ponds and streams with their flower sprays dipping into the water. Plants prefer a moist soil, thrive in sun or light shade and tolerate dry spells. Floral designers value the flower sprays as a filler. Native to mountainous regions of Russia and Turkey. Propagate by seed and division. To prevent invasive self-seeding, remove faded flower stems. Plants scorched by summer heat can be cut back to produce fresh growth for autumn display. A good companion to early summer-flowering blue flowers such as Siberian irises.

Amsonia tabernaemontana
Blue star
Zones 3–9
Native to North America. Generous clusters of spring-flowering, pale blue flower clusters cover bushy plants that grow to 3 feet (91 cm) high with each floret resembling a star. The slender, bright green, willowlike leaves are decorative all season and turn yellow in autumn. Plants prefer full sun and a well-drained soil and are good for massing in mixed borders and as drifts in rock gardens. Plants grow to 2 feet (61 cm) high, tolerate dry soils and high heat. *A. hubrectii* is similar in appearance but with even more finely cut leaves and the added appeal of beautiful orange autumn coloring. Taller growing, to 4 feet (1.2 m), it has a shrub-like quality.

Anaphalis margaritacea
Pearly everlasting
Zones 4–8
Native to North America, plants grow erect stems with lance-like, silvery-green leaves and masses of papery white, button-shaped flowers held in tight clusters. Valued for cutting and dried arrangements, plants also add interest to mixed borders, especially in the company of ornamental grasses. Also a good component of all-white and "evening" gardens. Plants are drought tolerant, prefer a sunny location and good drainage. Propagated from seed and tip cuttings. *A. triplinervis*, from the Himalayas, is similar but with slightly tighter flower heads.

Anchusa azurea
Blue bugloss, Alkanet
Zones 3–8
The conventional form of this Mediterranean species is tall, up to 5 feet (1.5 m), and suitable for back-of-the-border mixed plantings. The flowers are a deep sky blue, produced in profusion on branching stems, and resemble large forget-me-nots. Flowering in late spring and early summer, good companions are pink foxgloves and yellow lupines. 'Loddon Royalist' is an especially sturdy selection that generally does not require staking. Several low-growing dwarf varieties such as 'Little John', at less than 2 feet (61 cm), have been selected for edging paths, rock gardens and massing for front-of-the-border display. The biennial *A. capensis* is a natural low-growing species from South Africa, growing to 8 inches (20 cm) high. 'Blue Angel' and 'Blue Bird' have been selected for long-flowering displays. These varieties tolerate light shade and look effective massed along paths in woodland. Plants are easily propagated from seed and root cuttings, and demand good drainage.

Perennials

Andropogon gerardii
Big bluestem, Turkeyfoot
Zones 2–7

An aggressive North American prairie grass that's highly ornamental when planted among other ornamental grasses in grass gardens and also in mixed perennial borders where its slender, arching leaf blades soften the stiff stems of most herbaceous perennials. Plants grow clumps of slender blue-green leaves that turn amber and bronze in autumn. Plants grow to 6 feet (1.8 m) high and produce wispy three-fingered flower stems that splay out like a turkey's foot. Propagate by seed and division.

Androsace lanuginosa
Rock jasmine
Zones 5–7

Most suitable for massing along ledges in rock gardens, to edge paths and spill over rock ledges, this is a low-growing, cushion-forming, evergreen alpine plant. Tiny pink or white flowers so completely cover the plants in spring, they almost hide the gray-green, densely-packed triangular leaves. One of about 100 species from Northern Hemisphere alpine regions, *Androsace lanuginosa* is native to the Himalayas. Good companions to pink thrift, perennial yellow alyssum and blue creeping phlox, plants are propagated by seed and cuttings, and work best when planted to form drifts among rock outcroppings. Plants require full sun and sharp drainage.

Anemone hupehensis
Chinese anemone
Zones 4–8

Valued for its late summer and early autumn blooms, plants stand stiffly erect. The branching stems are massed with dusky pink or rosy pink flowers and highlighted with a crown of golden stamens. This species has also been crossed with other hardy species, notably *A. japonica* and *A. vitifolia*, which has extended the color range into white, as in the large-flowered variety 'Honorine Jobert', displaying flowers up to 3½ inches (9 cm) across. 'Whirlwind' is a white, semi-double hybrid with equally large flowers and a golden boss of stamens. The ivy-shaped leaves are decorative even when the plants are not in bloom. Propagate by seed or division.

Anemone nemorosa
Wood anemone
Zones 4–8

Though there are numerous low-growing anemones known as wood anemones, this is a favorite for lightly shaded gardens. It is especially good for edging woodland paths, for massing to create a beautiful drift on a slope or even for a vast groundcover on level ground. The white, star-shaped flowers grow on cushion-shaped plants above sharply indented leaves. Flowering in spring, they are good companions to bluebells and pink western bleeding heart. In the variety 'Robinsoniana' the flowers are pale blue. Propagate by seed and division.

Antennaria dioica
Pussy-toes
Zones 5–9

A rather dainty, low-growing, spreading plant that forms a dense colony of velvety gray evergreen foliage and buttonlike flowers borne in small, tight clusters, up to 8 inches (20 cm) high. Flowering in spring, plants form rosettes of spoon-shaped leaves that knit tightly together to make a weed-suffocating groundcover, suitable for edging borders and paths, and especially for decorating dry walls and rock ledges in rock gardens. Plants tolerate drought, require full sun and good drainage. The nodding, papery flower clusters can be white and pale pink in the variety 'Rosea' and a deeper pink in 'Nyewoods'. Propagate by seed or division. Self-seeds readily.

Anthemis sancti-johannis
Golden marguerite
Zones 4–9

Beautiful, golden-yellow, daisylike blooms with golden yellow, buttonlike centers are freely produced from early summer on bushy plants up to 2 feet (61 cm) high. Finely cut green foliage is aromatic. Good for massing in mixed borders and for cutting. A similar species, *Anthemis tinctoria* 'E. C. Buxton', has lemon-yellow flowers and yellow centers, plus eye-catching gray-green foliage. 'Kelwayi' has canary-yellow flower heads and golden centers. Good partnered with blue lavender. Propagate by seed and cuttings.

AQUILEGIA HYBRIDS & SPECIES

Columbine, Granny's bonnet
Zones 3–9

An encounter with members of this family of more than 70 species and hybrids is always an uplifting experience, especially in cottage gardens where they are often seen liberally planted among more staid perennials like peonies, bearded irises and Oriental poppies. The perky, nodding, spurred outer circle of petals and rakish, trumpetlike inner circle of petals are distinct. Moreover, the encounter can occur in unexpected places—the large flowered hybrids such as 'Origami' can be massed as drifts in sunny perennial borders either as mixtures or separate colors, with the pale tones decorating lightly shaded woodland paths in the company of ferns, and the species can also enliven sunny nooks and crannies in rock gardens. The way the flowers display a star-shaped rim of outer petals and a trumpet-shaped circle of inner petals, plus a third outer ring of "spurs" combine to give the flowers a swept-back look, as though they are a flock of small birds in flight. One season at Cedaridge Farm we even made a special columbine garden by planting together the following readily available kinds.

Aquilegia caerulea
Rocky Mountain columbine
Zones 4–8
Scenes of mountain slopes in the Rocky Mountains of North America crowded with spring wildflowers and snow still on the highest peaks often feature the conspicuous blue-and-white flowers of mountain columbine. Plants form bushy clumps up to 2 feet (61 cm) high, invaluable for decorating rock gardens.

Aquilegia canadensis
Canada columbine
Zones 3–8
Native to North America, plants grow to only 12 inches (31 cm) high. Their pendant red and yellow flowers are ideal for planting in lightly shaded woodland and in sunny rock gardens and even sprouting out of dry walls. At Cedaridge Farm visitors are thrilled to see them partnered with 'Barnhaven' primroses. A yellow selection, 'Corbett', can create a shimmering effect in lightly shaded areas when the sun shines through its translucent petals from behind, creating an effect like twinkling lights.

Aquilegia hybrids
Zones 4–8
Several strains of long-spurred hybrids have been developed from *A. caerulea* to bloom the first season from seed when started early indoors. Sow in October/ November for April/May flowering. These have been produced mostly by American plant breeders and include 'McKana Giants', 'Origami' and 'Swan', all providing a rich color range that includes light blue, pink, red, yellow and white, plus bicolors. Plants grow to 16 inches (41 cm) high, thrive in light shade or full sun, and prefer soil with good drainage. Easily raised from seed.

Aquilegia vulgaris
European columbine
Zones 3–8
Indigenous to valleys in Wales and other parts of Europe, these bushy plants grow to 3 feet (91 cm) high, holding their flowers above blue-green indented foliage. Though flowers of the original species are dark blue and somewhat compressed, the color range now extends to all shades of pink, maroon and purple, plus white. The white was a favorite of Gertrude Jekyll, who liked planting them around white foxgloves. Look for 'Magpie', a unique black and white form and also the double-flowered 'Nora Barlow', a pink and white bicolor, and 'Woodside Mixture', similar to 'Nora Barlow' but with double white, rose-pink, plum and shades of blue in its color range. *A. vulgaris* has given rise to several hybrids, including the larger flowered 'Hensol Harebell'.

Arabis caucasica aka A. alpina
Rock cress
Zones 5–8
Early flowering, evergreen, spreading, low plants have toothed, evergreen gray-green leaves, and masses of four-petalled white or pink flowers in early spring, usually seen cascading over rock ledges in rock gardens in company with pink and purple aubretia or pink and blue creeping phlox. Growing to just 4 inches (10 cm) high, plants are also suitable for edging sunny borders and to cover slopes. Indigenous to rock screes in the Caucasus Mountains, plants demand good drainage. Propagate from seed and by division. 'Flore Plena' has double white flowers. 'Variegata' has bicolored green and creamy white leaves.

Arenaria verna
Irish moss, Sandwort
Zones 5–7
Native to Europe, this low-growing, cushionlike plant has fine leaves that resemble moss, and small white starry flowers. Plants demand full sun and good drainage, and grow best in coastal locations where cool coastal mists can keep the plants healthy. Useful for planting at the edges of lawn, around stepping stones and wherever a low, soft groundcover is desired. Propagate by division.

Arisaema sikokianum
Japanese arum
Zones 5–9

Native to Japan, this is a fine shade-loving, spring-flowering plant for moist woodland and humus-rich soil. Plants have trifoliate leaves and a hooded spathe, mostly maroon striped white. A prominent, club-shaped, white spadix rises inside the hood and resembles porcelain. Useful along woodland paths, and certainly the most coveted of a large number of hardy arisaemas.

Armeria maritima
Sea pinks, Thrift
Zones 6–8

Perky, clump-forming plants up to 10 inches (25 cm) high have slender, grasslike leaves and masses of spring-flowering globular pink flowers. Salt tolerant, it is an uplifting sight to see acres of sea pinks forming soft cushions along exposed cliff-tops of the U.K. right up to the shoreline, often in the company of English bluebells. In cultivation they are best used for edging or massing in rock gardens. Propagated by seed and division. 'Bees hybrids' include the common pink, shades of red, and white.

Artemisia ludoviciana
Mugwort
Zones 4–9

This North American native is grown mostly for its decorative silvery foliage. The bushy plants have willowy, toothed leaves arranged in whorls and in summer bear slender plumes of tiny yellow flowers. The aggressive roots can become invasive. Silver foliage is most desirable in partnership with red and pink flowers, such as the 'Meidiland Red' shrub rose, red lupins and red Oriental poppies. Other artemisias that produce mounds of attractive silver foliage include *A. stelleriana* with broader, flatter clusters of silvery foliage, and the hybrid 'Powis Castle', which has feathery silver leaves and a billowing, shrublike appearance, growing up to 4 feet (1.2 m) high.

Arum italicum
Italian arum
Zones 6–10

Native to moist meadows around the Mediterranean, plants produce large, arrow-shaped, dark green, glossy leaves and lime-green flower spathes. These appear in early spring usually before the leaves, which grow on erect stems up to 3 feet (91 cm) high. The leaves generally die down in late summer, leaving a decorative orange-red berry cluster. Plant in sun or light shade, in humus-rich soil. Useful as a component of bog gardens and along woodland paths. 'Marmoratum' and 'Pictum' have white leaf veins and are more decorative than the species.

Aruncus dioicus
Goatsbeard
Zones 3–7

A bold plant with large, white, frothy flower plumes resembling a giant astilbe. The fernlike foliage creates a cloudlike bush with flower stems up to 6 feet (1.8 m) high held well above the foliage in early summer. Good for placing at the back of mixed borders and also in bog gardens since the plants tolerate moist soil. Though plants prefer full sun they will tolerate light shade, especially along streams. A smaller species, *A. aethusifolius*, is more compact, growing to 16 inches (41 cm) high and popular for the margins of small ponds. Give them a fertile, humus-rich, moisture-retentive soil. Propagate from seed or by division.

Asarum europaeum
European ginger
Zones 4–8

This handsome, low-growing plant is grown mostly for its glossy, evergreen, heart-shaped leaves and its ability to tolerate even deeply shaded locations such as dense woodland. It is especially good to use as a groundcover around azaleas, ferns and hostas in shade gardens. Plants grow to 4 inches (10 cm) high and spread 12 inches (31 cm) or more. Though the greenish-purple flowers are inconspicuous, being hidden by the leaves and pollinated by slugs, they have an interesting bell shape. American ginger (*A. canadense*) is hardy to zone 2 and also useful as a groundcover but with smaller leaves and inconspicuous bell-shaped brown flowers also pollinated by slugs.

Asclepias incarnata
Swamp milkweed
Zones 3–8

Milkweeds are a family of more than 100 species of perennials and shrubs. When the stems are cut, they exude a sticky, milky sap that can be a skin irritant. Swamp milkweed has attractive rosy-pink, star-shaped flowers arranged in clusters on branching stems up to 2 feet (61 cm) high in early summer. These are followed by fleshy horned pods that split when dry to release silky seeds for dispersal by the wind. Plants have broad, lance-like leaves, thrive in full sun and tolerate moist soil. They are suitable for wildflower meadows and mixed borders, attracting bees and butterflies. The fleshy, aggressive roots can become invasive. Propagate by seed and root division. *A. syriaca* is also known as swamp milkweed and common milkweed. Though ornamental, with erect 4-foot (1.2 m) high stems bearing nodding clusters of pink star-shaped flowers, its aggressive stoloniferous root system can be too invasive for border plantings, but it is suitable for wildflower meadows.

Asclepias tuberosa
Butterfly weed
Zones 4–9

Bushy plants with lance-like leaves grow to 3 feet (91 cm) high. They produce generous clusters of deep orange, star-shaped flowers in early summer and make good companions with blue veronica to create a blue and orange color harmony. They are popular for wildflower meadows, as drifts in rock gardens and massed in mixed borders. They require a sunny position and soil with good drainage. A mixture known as 'Gay Butterflies' includes yellow, red and orange in its color range. Propagate by seed and root division.

Asphodeline lutea
Jacob's rod
Zones 6–9

From the Mediterranean and related to lilies, plants grow strong, stiff flower stems up to 5 feet (1.5 m) high around a basal rosette of blue-green, slender leaves. The star-shaped, pale yellow flowers appear as a poker at the top of the stems in early summer. They make good companions to blue campanula and are mostly seen in mixed borders, but also make fine highlights in large rock gardens since they relish full sun and good drainage. Propagate by seed and by division.

Asplenium scolopendrium
Hart's tongue fern
Zones 6–8

Grown for its erect, straplike, evergreen, translucent green leaves extending 2 feet (61 cm) high, plants thrive in shade and cool soil, and spread by creeping rhizomes. Though attractive planted singly in rock gardens and dry walls among cushion-shaped plants like armeria, alpine columbine and androsace, they are especially beautiful massed on slopes in humus-rich soils near streams, waterfalls and pools in the company of woodland wildflowers like primroses and bluebells. Propagate by spores and division.

ASTER

Zones 3–8, depending on variety

This large genus within the daisy plant family has more than 250 species that give rise to many more hybrids. Perennial asters should not be confused with the much larger flowered and half-hardy annual China asters that are grouped under the botanical name *Callistephus*. An extremely popular hardy perennial, asters are valued for their late summer and autumn bloom, and are capable of filling the garden with a riot of color as the season winds down. So many kinds of perennial aster are useful for garden display—in borders all to their own, mixed with other late-flowering perennials and in cutting gardens—that it is difficult to pick out the best. Here is my choice based on performance at Cedaridge Farm:

Aster ericoides
Heath aster
Zones 5–9

Indigenous to North America, bushy plants grow erect, freely branching stems covered with clouds of tiny star-shaped flowers mostly in white or dusky pink with yellow centers, among slender, serrated, green leaves. When massed they look like a cloud of mist from a distance, and for this reason are good to use in meadow gardens and among ornamental grasses. Plants grow to 3 feet (91 cm) high, prefer full sun and a fertile, well-drained soil. Propagate by division and by cuttings. *A. laterifolius* 'Horizontalis' is similar in appearance but is more compact.

Aster x frikartii
Blue starwort
Zones 5–8

'Mönch' and 'Wunder von Stäfa' are two popular varieties of this long-flowering hybrid that are difficult to tell apart for they both have beautiful deep blue flowers 2 inches (5 cm) across with golden yellow centers, freely produced on strong, erect stems among slender, serrated green leaves up to 3 feet (91 cm) high. Though generally not long lived as a perennial, 'Mönch' is the earliest and longest flowering of the two, starting in July and continuing into October. "'Mönch' is not only the best perennial aster, it is among the 10 best perennial plants, and should be in every garden," notes the late Graham Stuart Thomas, in his book *Perennial Garden Plants*. Plants prefer full sun, good drainage and a fertile soil. Propagate by division. Use in mixed borders among pink Japanese anemone, rusty red 'Autumn Joy' sedum and white boltonia. Invaluable for cutting since an entire plant, when cut just above the soil line, will make an instant bouquet.

Aster novi-belgii
Michaelmas daisy aka New York aster
Zones 3–8

Similar in appearance to *A. novae-angliae*, plants will take light shade and boggy soil better than New England asters. They are suitable for mixed borders and for occupying a garden border all to themselves since the number of named varieties, colors and forms far exceeds those bred into New England asters. Some of the best named varieties include 'Wood's Pink', 'Wood's Blue' (a better selection than 'Professor Anton Kippenberg') and 'Wood's Purple'. All three stay moderately neat and compact at 2 feet (61 cm) high and are mildew resistant. They are suitable for containers, including window box planters. Propagate by division.

Astilbe x arendsii
False spiraea, Goatsbeard
Zones 4–8

One of the most thrilling sights of early summer occurs at Hodnet Hall, Shropshire, where a large bog garden features numerous species and varieties of astilbe massed in shades of pink and red, plus white. A path follows a small stream planted along its length with the astilbe on both sides in company with hostas, ferns, gunnera and aruncas. The most popular forms of astilbe are hybrids that resulted from a breeding program by the late George Arends, a German nurseryman, of which the dark red 'Fanal', dark pink 'Cattleya' and white 'Bridal Veil' are most impressive. Growing to 3 feet (91 cm) high, the flowers are formed into pyramid-shaped, frothy flower plumes held well above serrated leaflets. Plants thrive in full sun or light shade and prefer a humus-rich, moisture-retentive soil. They are good for massing in mixed borders and look especially attractive when seen against a lake, pond or stream. *A. chinensis* var. *pumila* is a dwarf dusky-pink species suitable for groundcover. Propagate astilbes by division.

Aster novae-angliae
New England aster
Zones 4–8

Though the original species is a rather coarse purple hue with yellow centers, many named selections have extended the color to include pure white, sky blue, deep blue, plus all shades of pink and red. Flowering from late summer to mid-autumn, some of the most popular varieties include 'Alma Potschka' (bright rose-pink), 'Harrington's Pink' (light pink), 'Purple Dome' [purple, growing to only 2 feet (61 cm) high], 'September Ruby' (red) and 'Wedding Lace' (white). Plants grow to 5 feet (1.5 m) high, prefer full sun and a fertile soil that drains well. The flower heads are often so heavy with flowers they may need staking. Propagate these named varieties by division. In Monet's garden in France, blue New England asters are partnered with yellow perennial sunflowers for a striking yellow-and-blue color harmony.

Astrantia major
Masterwort

Zones 4–7

Native to Europe, pincushion, papery flowers in mostly white, pink and red, are clustered atop 3-foot (91 cm) tall stems in late spring. Plants have deeply toothed, palm-shaped leaves and thrive in full sun or light shade in a fertile, humus-rich soil. They are good for mixed borders and excellent for cutting. 'Sunningdale Variegated' has creamy yellow leaf tips and pinkish-white flowers. Propagate by seed and by division.

Athyrium niponicum
Japanese painted fern
Zones 5–8

The variety 'Pictum' is a beautiful, deciduous, woodland fern that displays unusual bicolored fronds in green and silver. The elegant, finely indented, arching fronds form vigorous clumps from creeping rhizomes, suitable for massing to create a durable groundcover. They are especially attractive used as an edging to woodland paths, to cascade over boulders in shady areas of rock gardens and as a contrast to hostas. Several selections of 'Pictum' are available with predominantly pink-and-silver fronds. 'Ursula's Red' even combines maroon, pink and silver to create an especially dramatic effect. *A. filix-femina*, the lady fern, is an attractive North American species with bright green, feathery fronds growing 2½ feet (76 cm) high, and is good for massing under groves of trees, especially in partnership with the Japanese painted fern.

Aubrieta deltoidea
Rock cress
Zones 5–7

These low-growing, cushion-forming, spring-flowering plants have small, indented leaves and masses of four-petalled flowers. They are sensational for massing along dry walls, rock ledges in rock gardens and also for edging paths. All the beds and borders in Claude Monet's garden are edged in aubretia. Flowers are mostly pink but also come in white, shades of red and violet blue. Plants grow to 4 inches (10 cm) high, spread to 12 inches (31 cm) or more, and are easily propagated from seed or division.

Aurinia saxatilis aka *Alyssum saxatilis*
Basket of gold
Zones 3–8

This low-growing, cushion-forming, short-lived perennial from mountainous regions of Europe produces masses of small golden-yellow flowers. They enliven rock gardens, dry walls and dry slopes in early spring, especially in the company of rock garden tulips, such as *Tulipa greigii* and *T. fosteriana*, and minor bulbs such as blue grape hyacinths and blue squill. Plants demand full sun and well-drained soil; they grow to 10 inches (25 cm) high and spread up to 3 feet (91 cm) or more, and display gray-green, evergreen, toothed leaves. Unless pruned back to the soil line, plants tend to fall apart after the second season. Propagate by seed and division. 'Citrina' has distinctive lemon-yellow flowers.

Baptisia australis
False indigo
Zones 3–9

Native to the southeastern U.S., this lupin look-alike produces erect, spring-flowering spikes clustered with deep blue or white pea flowers. The bushy, cloverlike plants grow to 4 feet (1.2 m) high and are mostly used in mixed borders. Give them full sun and good drainage. They make good companions to pale blue amsonia and deciduous azaleas in rock gardens. Propagate by seed and by division.

Bergenia cordifolia
Pigsqueak, Heartleaf

Zones 3–8

This Siberian plant was a favorite of Gertrude Jekyll, who liked its bold, evergreen, heart-shaped ruffled leaves and spring-flowering umbels of mostly pink flowers, even massing them within boxwood parterres for permanent groundcover effect. Plants grow to 2 feet (61 cm) high, prefer full sun and a well-drained soil, but will tolerate light shade. Use as edging to mixed borders, also massed as drifts along rock ledges in rock gardens. Beautiful bronze, red and even orange coloring can infuse the leaves in autumn. Propagate by seed and division. *B. crassifolia* is a similar species with mostly rose-pink flowers. Hybridizing between these and other species has produced a large number of hybrids, including 'Silverlight', a white that makes a welcome change from the rather harsh pinks of most other species and hybrids. A good companion with blue-flowering *Brunnera macrophylla*.

Boltonia asteroides
Autumn aster

Zones 4–9

The pure white daisylike flowers with golden centers are produced in unbelievable profusion atop 5-foot (1.5 m) stems. The flower clusters are so dense and heavy with flowers that they need staking. The leaves are slender and pointed. Native to North America, plants prefer full sun and good drainage, flowering in late summer and early autumn. They make good companions to ornamental grasses and Japanese anemone in mixed borders and meadow gardens. Good for cutting. Propagate by seed and division. 'Pink Beauty' is a dwarf variety growing to 2 feet (61 cm) high with pale pink flowers.

Brunnera macrophylla
Siberian bugloss

Zones 3–8

Masses of forget-me-not blue flowers occur in early spring on thin, branching stems above heart-shaped, leathery, dark green leaves. However, the introduction of varieties with variegated foliage like 'Jack Frost' (whose leaves appear to be metallic silver) and 'Hadspen Cream' (dark green leaves bordered with cream) have all but overshadowed the plain green species. Plants grow to 2 feet (61 cm) high and thrive in sun or light shade. Give them good drainage or a moisture-retentive soil. Invaluable for shade gardens, especially edging woodland paths and in company with primulas.

Calamagrostis x *acutiflora*
Reed grass

Zones 5–9

Native to meadows of Eurasia, this popular ornamental grass is often used to soften mixed borders and is massed for groundcover. From a fountain of stiff, green, slender leaves arise amber flower plumes that persist from midsummer through autumn. 'Karl Foerster' is a particularly good selection for profuse flowering. Plants grow to 5 feet (1.5 m) high, are clump forming and make good companions to pink shades of summer phlox, yellow black-eyed Susans and purple cone flowers. Propagate by division.

Perennials

Caltha palustris
Marsh marigold
Zones 3–7

Buttercuplike flowers occur in early spring and have shimmering yellow flowers in single and double forms. Leaves are glossy dark green and heart shaped. Native to northern Europe, plants grow to 12 inches (31 cm) high and form mounded clumps in moisture-retentive, humus-rich soil. Plants will even thrive with their roots permanently covered in shallow water. Prefers full sun but tolerates light shade. Popular along woodland paths where soil remains moist, and an excellent component of boggy soils surrounding wildlife ponds and stream banks. Propagate by seed and root division.

Campanula carpatica
Bellflower
Zones 4–8

Native to the Carpathian Mountains, cushion-shaped plants grow to 8 inches (20 cm) high and are covered in blue or white cup-shaped flowers in spring. The tooth-edged foliage is dense and bushy. Valued for edging mixed borders and massing in rock gardens, the varieties 'Blue Clips' and 'Bliss' are extra free flowering. Two similar alpine species suitable for edging and massing in rock gardens are *C. portenschlagiana* (zones 4–9) and *C. poscharskyana* (zones 6–9). Both cover the ground with blue star-shaped flowers. Propagate by seed and division.

Campanula glomerata
Globe bellflower
Zones 3–8

Beautiful violet-blue, star-shaped flowers are clustered in a perfect sphere on strong stems studded with spear-shaped leaves. Native to southern parts of Europe, these early summer-flowering plants prefer a moisture-retentive soil in full sun. Popular in mixed borders in the company of yellow lysimachia, these flowers are also good for cutting. Propagate from seed and root division.

Campanula persicifolia
Peachleaf bellflower
Zones 3–8

Native to Europe, from southern Russia to Turkey, large bell-shaped blue or white flowers are crowded along slender stems. Leaves are narrow and willowlike. Popular in mixed beds and borders, also good for cutting. Easy to grow in most organic-rich, well-drained garden soils in full sun. Late spring flowering, plants grow to 3 feet (91 cm) and make good companions for pink-flowering shrub roses such as 'Betty Prior'. Propagate by seed and root division. Hardier than the similar *C. lactiflora* (milky bellflower) and *C. latifolia* (great bellflower).

Campanula punctata
Cathedral bells
Zones 6–9

Native to Siberia, masses of tubular, pendant bells in mostly white and pink hang from erect, tapering stems. Plants grow to 12 inches (31 cm) high and have spear-shaped leaves. Suitable for massing in mixed borders and for cutting. Provide full sun and good drainage. Propagate by seed and division.

Carex elata 'Bowles' Golden'
Bowles' golden sedge
Zones 5–9

Unmistakable for its golden yellow, arching leaf blades, plants seem to grab all the sunshine and reflect it right back. Tolerant of light shade and moist soil, plants grow to 2 feet (61 cm) high, are good for edging woodland paths and also for growing near water features such as streams and ponds. Indeed, plants will thrive with their roots permanently submerged in shallow water. At Cedaridge Farm we confine several to sunken containers and place them in the company of hardy water lilies. The brown, nodding flower clusters occur in spring and are mostly inconspicuous. Propagate by division.

Many other kinds of hardy carex, known as sedge grass, are worthy of garden space. *C. hachijoensis* 'Evergold' (Zones 5–9) grows to just 12 inches (31 cm) high, creating a fountain of green and gold variegated leaves. *C. flagellifera* has a similar distinctive bronze color and elegant weeping habit (zones 5–11). 'Toffee Twist' is highly recommended.

Catananche caerulea
Cupid's dart
Zones 3–8

Native to the Mediterranean, the pale blue, cornflowerlike flowers are held erect on slender stems. Growing to 3 feet (91 cm) high, leaves are gray-green and grasslike. They are popular for mixed borders, meadow gardens and for cutting. Easy to grow in most well-drained garden soils in full sun. Drought resistant and summer flowering, plants are easily propagated from seed and division.

Cerastium tomentosum
Snow in summer
Zones 3–7

Native mostly to Italy, plants have naturalized throughout Europe and North America. Small white star-shaped flowers occur in spring and almost smother the small, narrow, silvery leaves, creating a carpet of white, resembling drifts of snow. These plants are popular for rock gardens where they will cascade over rock ledges and dry walls, also good for edging mixed beds and borders. They are a popular component of all-white gardens. Plants grow to 6 inches (15 cm) high. Easy to grow in most well-drained soils in full sun. Propagate by seed and root division.

Centranthus ruber
Valerian
Zones 5–8

Native to the Mediterranean, red, pink or white flowers are clustered in a cone-shaped dome on slender stems. Flowering in early summer, leaves are gray-green, narrow and pointed. Does best in cool locations where it self-sows readily. Drought resistant, plants are suitable for dry landscapes such as rock gardens, dry walls and also for mixed borders. Excellent cut flower, plants grow to 3 feet (91 cm) high with a bushy habit. Propagate by seed and cuttings.

Chelone lyonii
Turtlehead
Zones 4–9

Native to the eastern U.S., plants grow to 2 feet (61 cm) high, forming a dense clump of dark green leaves and erect stems topped by short spikes of tubular white or pink flowers in late summer. It is the shape of the flowers that suggests the common name, turtlehead. Plants prefer full sun and good drainage but tolerate moist soil. Useful in mixed borders.

Perennials

Chrysanthemum x morifolium
Garden mum, Cushion mum

Zones 5–9, depending on variety

Hybrids of species mostly native to China; flower shape and size depend on variety. Indeed, there are at least a dozen common flower forms including daisy, spoon, quilled, pompon and spider. Height varies according to variety, from 12 inches (31 cm) high and a mounded habit in cushion mums up to 4 feet (1.2 m) in tall-stemmed varieties such as football mums, which are mostly grown for the show bench. Color range includes yellow, red, pink, bronze, purple and white. Leaves are dark green, narrow and toothed. Popular for massing in beds, edging borders and container planting; the tall kinds are good for cutting. Plants prefer full sun and good drainage. Propagate by stem cuttings and root division. Maintain a good dome shape in the cushion mums by pinching out the growing tip in spring, and again in summer, forcing basal branching. Winter hardiness is highly variable depending on the type of mum. Varieties developed by a breeding program at the University of Minnesota, U.S., tend to be the hardiest, such as the 'My Favorite' series.

Chrysanthemum nipponicum
Montauk daisy
Zones 5–7

Native to Japan, they are identical in flower form to ox-eye daisies with two basic differences: they have scalloped leaves that are succulent and a blooming period that extends from late summer into autumn. Plants like full sun and good drainage, are useful for mixed borders and grow to 2 feet (61 cm) high. Propagate by division and cuttings.

Chrysanthemum parthenium aka *Tanacetum parthenium*
Feverfew
Zones 4–9

Small white daisylike flowers have conspicuous yellow centers, except in the double-flowered forms, which form a completely white button shape. Leaves are typically chrysanthemum shaped and finely toothed. Popular in mixed borders as a cloudlike accent. Also an excellent cut flower for late spring and summer flowering. Native to the Mediterranean, plants grow to 3 feet (91 cm) high, tolerate drought and prefer full sun and good drainage. Feverfew self-seeds readily. Propagate by seed and root division.

Chrysanthemum x superbum aka *Leucanthemum x superbum*
Shasta daisy
Zones 3–8

Emanating from a hybridizing program by the late Luther Burbank, plant breeder, who used European species of the ox-eye daisy. Plants produce large daisy flowers with golden centers up to 4 inches (10 cm) across, in early summer. Some varieties are double-flowered. Dark green leaves are slender and toothed. Plants grow to 3 feet (91 cm) high, are popular for mixed borders and for cutting. Dwarf varieties such as 'Silver Princess' and 'Miss Muffet' are suitable for containers and edging, growing just 12 inches (31 cm) high. Give them a fertile, well-drained soil in full sun. Propagate by seed and cuttings. Young plants need the tip pinched back to encourage basal branching.

Chrysogonum virginianum
Golden star, Green and gold
Zones 6–8

Native to North America, this low-growing, drought tolerant, spreading plant has woolly, dark green leaves and yellow, starlike flowers. Plants grow to just 8 inches (20 cm) high and are suitable for massing in rock gardens and as an edging. Prefers full sun and good drainage but tolerates light shade. Propagate by division.

Cimicifuga racemosa aka *Actaea racemosa*
Snakeroot
Zones 3–8

Tall, towering flower spikes are crowded with tiny white or cream-colored flowers. Leaves are dark green, fernlike and finely toothed. Native to North America, plants grow in full sun or light shade and are popular for woodland gardens, and also as backgrounds in mixed beds and borders. Prefers moist, fertile, humus-rich soil. Propagate by root division. Plants grow to 5 feet (1.5 m) high, flower in early summer and may need staking. *C. simplex* is a later-flowering species that grows to 4 feet (1.2 m).

Clematis recta
Ground clematis
Zones 4–7

Mostly from central Europe, this differs from vining clematis (Shrubs, see page 121) by growing bushy with erect stems that support a cloud of starry white flowers in summer. Plants can grow to 5 feet (1.5 m) high and generally need staking. Useful in mixed borders. Propagate by division.

Coreopsis grandiflora
Tickseed
Zones 4–9

Golden-yellow, daisylike flowers are produced in profusion all summer on bushy, 2- to 3-foot (61 to 91 cm) high plants. Easy to grow in most well-drained soils in full sun. Native to North American prairies, leaves are narrow and spear shaped. Popular for mixed borders and cutting. The variety 'Sunburst' has double golden yellow flowers; 'Rising Sun' is semi-double with red flecks in the center; the semi-double dwarf variety 'Early Sunrise' will bloom the first year from seed started early indoors. Also propagated by division.

Similarly hardy are *C. lanceolata*, especially the bushy, low-growing 'Baby Sun'; *C. rosea*, a cushion-shaped, pink-flowering variety just 18 inches (46 cm) high; and *C. verticillata*, particularly the ever-blooming, lemon-yellow 'Moonbeam' of similar height. However, all of these pale in comparison to 'Sweet Dreams', a low-growing, ever-blooming hybrid colored white with raspberry red eyes.

Coronilla varia
Crown vetch
Zones 4–7

Though this cloverlike plant from Asia can be aggressive and is not recommended for small gardens, it is useful for covering difficult-to-plant dry slopes in need of erosion control. Masses of cloverlike pink flowers occur in summer on dense mounded plants up to 2 feet (61 cm) high. Mostly propagated from seed.

Corydalis cheilanthifolia
Yellow corydalis
Zones 6–9

Native to China, the delicate, fernlike, blue-green foliage is reason enough to grow this carefree spring-flowering perennial. The mound-shaped plants, up to 12 inches (31 cm) high, produce clusters of yellow tubular flowers that self-sow readily, even into cracks in dry walls. Suitable for sun or shade, this is a good companion for ferns and hostas in rock gardens and along woodland paths.

Corydalis flexuosa
Blue corydalis
Zones 5–9

Native to China, this is a connoisseur's plant on account of its bright blue tubular flowers and finely cut, fernlike foliage. Plants grow to 2 feet (61 cm) high, form a cushion shape and die down after flowering in spring. Prefers light shade and a well-drained, but moisture-retentive soil. Suitable for edging woodland paths, stream banks and shady rock gardens. Propagate by seed and division.

Crambe cordifolia
Colewort
Zones 6–9

Native to the Caucasus Mountains, plants first produce a large rosette of glossy, dark green, heart-shaped leaves up to 4 feet (1.2 m) wide, and a tall flower stalk up to 6 feet (1.8 m) high. The stalk is topped by a cloud of white, star-shaped flowers resembling baby's breath. Useful as a highlight in mixed borders. Prefers full sun and well-drained soil. Propagate by seed.

Deschampsia caespitosa
Tufted hair grass
Zones 4–9

Plants form a mass of tufted green leaves in spring, followed by wispy, pale green flower spikes that look like a cloud of mist. These turn amber along with the leaves in autumn. Indigenous to open meadows throughout the Northern Hemisphere on all continents, plants grow to 3 feet (91 cm) high, tolerate light shade, grow in dry soils and can be massed on slopes to control soil erosion. Propagate by seed and division.

Dianthus barbatus
Sweet William
Zones 4–9

Without question, this biennial is the showiest of the 300 dianthus species. Of Mediterranean origin, many forms are available from dwarf, cushion-shaped plants 8 inches (20 cm) high to tall varieties, up to 2 feet (61 cm) high. Flowering in late spring and early summer, plants produce domed flower clusters up to 4 inches (10 cm) across with individual flowers in shades of red, pink and white, usually zoned with a contrasting color. Give them full sun and good drainage. Useful massed in mixed borders, the dwarf kinds are suitable for edging. Start seed in late summer prior to flowering in spring.

Dianthus caryophyllus
Carnation
Zones 6–9

Famous for their sweet fragrance in wedding bouquets, the domed flowers have ruffled or laced petals in a wide color range, including all shades of pink and red, purple, yellow, white and maroon, plus bicolors. 'Chabaud Giants' grow to 3 feet (91 cm) high and have blue-green, slender leaves. Native to the Mediterranean, use them in mixed borders and containers, even window box plants, where the flower stems are allowed to bend forward and cascade over the edge.

Dianthus plumarius
Cottage pinks
Zones 4–9

Fragrant, single and double carnationlike flowers, mostly with fringed petals, form a cushion of blooms up to 12 inches (31 cm) high. Native to Europe, plants are easy to grow in sunny locations with good drainage. Popular for cascading over rock ledges in rock gardens and also for edging borders. Leaves are grasslike, evergreen and blue-green. Flower colors include all shades of pink, red and purple, plus white. Many beautiful hybrids, such as *D. allwoodii*, have been created from crossing with other species of dianthus. Similar in appearance are *D. deltoides* (maiden pinks), of which the variety 'Brilliant' is an outstanding red and *D. gratianopolitanus* (Cheddar pinks), notably the variety 'Spotty', a red with white spots. Propagate all these by seed and root division.

Dicentra spectabilis
Japanese bleeding heart
Zones 3–9

Heart-shaped pink or white flowers are borne on graceful arching stems in early spring. The finely cut, mid-green leaves die down during hot weather, but the roots remain viable and will survive freezing winters to come back reliably year after year. Plants prefer a slightly acidic, humus-rich, well-drained soil in sun or light shade. Native to Japan, plants grow to 3 feet (91 cm) high and make good companions to bluebells and forget-me-nots. Propagate by root division. Good to use in mixed borders, rock gardens and along woodland paths.

The *D. eximia*, eastern bleeding heart (zones 4–8), and *D. formosa*, western bleeding heart (zones 4–8), are native to the eastern and western coastal forests of the United States. Pink flowering, they are more compact in habit and are good massed with bluebells in woodland.

Dictamnus albus
Gas plant
Zones 3–10
Native to southwest Europe and Asia, plants form erect clumps up to 3 feet (91 cm) high and bear conspicuous flower spikes in white or pink. Prefers full sun and good drainage. Useful massed in mixed borders. Propagate by division. On warm nights, it is possible to light a match close to the large, fleshy, cloverlike leaves and ignite a gas exuded by the plant, hence its common name.

Digitalis purpurea
Foxglove
Zones 4–9
Native to Europe, this tall, spirelike biennial produces flower stems up to 5 feet (1.5 m) high, studded with tubular flowers with spotted throats. Colors include white and shades of pink, red, purple and yellow. Plants grow in sun or light shade and prefer soil with good drainage. Heart-shaped, blistered leaves form a rosette until the flower stalk emerges. Use massed in woodland and meadow gardens, and as highlights in mixed borders. *D. grandiflora* (zones 6–9) is similar with pale yellow flowers.

Dodecatheon meadia
Shooting star
Zones 3–9

Native to the Pacific Northwest, these unusual woodland plants have flowers resembling cyclamen with nodding, swept-back petals that are most shades of red and pink, plus white. Growing to 2 feet (61 cm) high, the erect flower stems appear in spring, arising from a rosette of oblong leaves. Give them full sun or light shade. Useful massed in rock gardens, especially close to water, and along woodland paths. Propagate by seeds and division.

Doronicum caucasicum aka Doronicum orientale
Leopard's bane
Zones 5–8

Gold-yellow daisylike flowers appear in spring on long stems among spear-shaped, serrated leaves. Growing to 2 feet (61 cm) high, plants form a spreading mass of roots. Though they flower prolifically in full sun, leopard's bane tolerates light shade and looks sensational along woodland paths in company with blue flowers such as bluebells, or pink flowers such as bleeding heart. Also popular for mixed borders and rock gardens. Excellent for cutting. Native to China, leopard's bane is naturalized throughout Europe. Propagate by seed or root division.

Echinacea purpurea
Purple coneflower
Zones 3–9

Native to North America, these daisylike flowers have swept-back, pinkish-purple petals surrounding a prominent maroon-colored dome. Summer flowering, the 4-foot (1.2 m) high plants have spear-shaped, toothed leaves and stout stems; they are suitable for mixed borders and as drifts in meadow gardens, especially in company with the yellow black-eyed Susan (*Rudbeckia hirta*). Prefers full sun but tolerates poor soil. 'Magnus' is extra-large flowered, up to 5 inches (13 cm) across. 'White Swan' is pure white with a copper-colored cone. The coneflower species *E. paradoxa* has yellow and orange in its color range, while *E. tennesseensis* displays flowers with up-curved rose-pink petals that look especially beautiful when backlit. Propagate by seed and division.

Echinops ritro
Globe thistle
Zones 3–9

Native to the Mediterranean and tolerant of poor soil, the metallic-blue globular flower heads are borne in summer atop silvery stems on billowing, thistle-like plants with prickly leaves. Popular for mixed borders and cutting gardens. Plants prefer full sun and good drainage. Propagate by seed and division.

Other species offer similar steel-blue flowers, including *E. bannaticus* 'Blue Globe', displaying navy blue flowers. All combine well with yellow perennial sunflowers such as *Helianthus* x *multiflorus*.

EPIMEDIUM HYBRIDS

Barrenwort
Zones 5–9

These airy plants will grow in the shade and very dry soil of surface-rooted trees; they are good when used as a groundcover in these locations. They are low growing, not more than 20 inches (50 cm) high, with thin wiry stems holding leathery, heart-shaped leaves. In spring, loose spikes of small waxy flowers are produced in pink, red, red-orange, creamy yellow or white, according to species. Its delicate appearance is belied by its tough constitution once established, although it is necessary to mulch for the first few years to prevent weed incursion.

Perennials

Epimedium x versicolor 'Sulphureum'
Barrenwort
Zones 5–9

This is undoubtedly the best of a large number of epimediums from Europe used for low groundcover effect, especially along lightly shaded woodland paths. That is because the yellow nodding flowers in spring are more conspicuous than other epimediums, and also because the heart-shaped leaves are more decorative, displaying chocolate edging and bright green leaf veins. Plants grow to 12 inches (31 cm) high, prefer humus-rich, well-drained soil and look especially good planted at the base of azaleas and rhododendrons. Propagate by division.

Eragrostis elliotti
Love grass
Zones 6–9

This native to North American meadows starts the season with an explosion of blue-green, narrow arching leaves. By midsummer, masses of airy, silvery flower plumes rise like a mist above the foliage to 4 feet (1.2 m) high, turning amber as the season advances. Plants demand full sun, tolerate dry soil and are not invasive. 'Wind Dancer' is an especially fine selection. Propagate by division.

Erianthus ravennae
Plume grass
Zones 5–9

This giant among grasses will quickly grow to 14 feet (4.3 m) high. Consequently, it should be used sparingly at the back of mixed borders and for a tall background hedge effect in ornamental grass gardens. Plants produce stiff, erect stems and ribbonlike, blue-green leaves that turn amber in autumn. The flower plumes are silvery-white, changing to amber and are valued for cutting. Prefers fertile, well-drained soil in full sun. Propagate by division.

Erigeron glaucus
Beach aster
Zones 4–8

Native to coastal California and Oregon, this plant grows 18 to 24 inches (46 to 61 cm) tall with a bushy, rounded habit. Clusters of daisylike purple or pink flowers have yellow centers. Popular in rock gardens, mixed borders and especially in coastal gardens, it is also attractive as a cut flower. 'Adria' is an especially good free-flowering variety bearing masses of deep rosy pink flowers with bright yellow centers; 'Azure Beauty' has beautiful blue flowers. Combines well with ornamental grasses. Prefers full sun in well-drained, sandy or loamy soil. Tolerates salt spray and high winds. Propagate by cuttings and division. Midsummer flowering.

Erigeron karvinskianus
Fleabane
Zones 3–8

The profusion of daisylike flowers and its low-spreading, cloudlike habit have many admirers though its propensity for self-seeding in mild winter areas can make it a nuisance. Plants grow to 9 inches (23 cm) high and spread 3 feet (91 cm) or more. They like full sun and tolerate poor soil, even drought-prone gravel soil. The daisylike flowers bloom all summer, opening white and changing to pink with red centers. Leaves are small, narrow and toothed. The variety 'Wayne Roderick' has lavender-blue flowers. Use in rock gardens and as an edging to paths and mixed borders. Propagate by seed and division.

Eriophorum angustifolium
Cotton grass
Zones 4–7

Native to boggy soils of Europe, such as the Scottish Highlands, plants have slender sedge-like leaves and unusual flowers that resemble balls of cotton. Mostly growing as drifts in peaty soil, cotton grass looks sensational grown beside water features such as ponds and streams, and also in containers. A similar species *E. latifolium* has broader leaves and nodding flowers, and therefore is not quite as appealing. Propagate by seed and division. Plants are generally unsuitable where summers are hot.

Erysimum x *allionii* aka *Cheiranthus* x *allionii*
Siberian wallflower
Zones 3–7

Hybridized from species mostly native to North Africa, this eye-catching biennial has orange or yellow flowers that resemble English wallflowers but are easier to grow and less demanding of cool conditions. Plants grow to 18 inches (46 cm) high, flower in spring, and prefer full sun and good drainage, though they are tolerant of light shade. Useful massed as an edging to mixed borders and as a component of meadow gardens. Propagate from seed started in late summer of the season prior to flowering.

Eryngium giganteum
Sea holly, Miss Willmott's ghost
Zones 5–8

Silvery, spiny flower heads are composed of a prickly, silvery collar tinted blue or purple and a blue-green domed column of small, prickly, white flowers. These occur in summer and can measure up to 5 inches (13 cm) across, on silvery stems above blue-green, thistle-like foliage. Plants grow to 3 feet (91 cm) high, look good in mixed borders, are valuable for cutting fresh or dried. Give them full sun and good drainage. Propagate by seed and division. *E. giganteum* is native to Mexico and gets the name Miss Willmott's ghost from a wealthy Victorian who visited gardens and scattered its seed as she went. There are many other species popular for mixed borders including the hardiest of all, *E. amethystinum* (zones 3–8), a European species with smaller blue flowers and the largest, *E. alpinum* (zones 6–9), from the European Alps.

Eupatorium coelestinum
Perennial ageratum, Mistflower
Zones 3–7

Fluffy flower clusters are mostly in shades of blue and white, and appear in midsummer. Leaves are dark green and spear shaped, forming a bushy plant up to 2 feet (61 cm) high. Native to the eastern U.S., give them full sun and good drainage. Useful for mixed borders, meadow gardens and cutting. Propagate by seed and division. The variety 'Cory' has powder-blue flowers, a more compact habit and produces more lustrous leaves than the species.

Perennials

Eupatorium maculatum
Joe Pye weed
Zones 3–8

The variety 'Gateway' produces enormous dusky pink flower heads up to 10 inches (25 cm) across on tall, wine-red stems. The plants grow up to 6 feet (1.8 m) high. Leaves are whorled, serrated and spear shaped. Native to damp meadows of the eastern U.S., plants flower in mid- to late summer, demand full sun and thrive in a variety of soils. Attractive to butterflies, use 'Gateway' in meadow gardens and at the back of mixed borders. Propagate by seed and division. Combine with other tall-flowering plants, such as perennial sunflowers, and among ornamental grasses.

Euphorbia epithymoides aka E. polychroma
Cushion spurge
Zones 4–9

Low-growing, drought-resistant plants that grow up to 12 inches (31 cm) high create a cushion of smooth, oval leaves completely covered in spring with dazzling yellow flower clusters. Popular for massing in the front of mixed borders, edging paths in rock gardens and for slope cover. Native to Europe, give them full sun and good drainage. Propagate by seed, tip cuttings and division. A similar species, *E. myrsinites* (myrtle spurge) is hardy from zones 5–8. Growing sprawling, succulent stems and yellow flowers in early spring, it is invaluable for slope cover.

Euphorbia griffithii
Fireglow
Zones 5–10

If you have a space for only one hardy euphorbia, make it this one, since its fiery-red flower clusters up to 4 inches (10 cm) across are outstanding. Plants grow to 3 feet (91 cm) high, displaying red stems and slender, willowlike leaves that bleed a milky sap when cut, which is an irritant. Useful in mixed borders in full sun and soil that drains well. Propagate by tip cuttings and division.

Festuca glauca
Blue fescue
Zones 4–8

Native to coastal meadows of Europe; a Dutch nurseryman once advised: "Do not water until it looks dead." A compact, clump-forming grass with blue-green leaves that resemble a porcupine, its silvery, featherlike flowers occur in early summer and change to amber as the season advances. The variety 'Elijah Blue' has the deepest blue coloring. Growing to just 8 inches (20 cm) high, plants are useful for edging sunny borders and massing as a groundcover on dry slopes. Excellent drainage is the key to longevity. Propagate by division.

Filipendula rubra
Queen of the prairie
Zones 4–8

Native to the eastern United States, this plant grows up to 6 feet (1.8 m) tall, is clump-forming and aggressive in habit. Fluffy pink flowers cluster up to 12 inches (31 cm) across on strong, wiry stems. Good tall background accent to mixed perennial borders. Prefers full sun or light shade and moist, fertile, loam soil. Tolerates boggy soil. Propagate by division. Early summer blooming.

Gaillardia x grandiflora
Blanket flower
Zones 3–8

Mostly red, daisylike flowers with yellow petal tips are produced on erect, bushy plants up to 3 feet (91 cm) high. Other colors include yellow and burgundy. The gray-green leaves are slender and deeply indented. Native to meadows of North America, plants prefer full sun and good drainage. Popular for wildflower meadows, planting as drifts in mixed borders and also for cutting gardens. An especially eye-catching tall variety is 'Dazzler', displaying golden-yellow flowers with rich wine-red centers. Dwarf varieties like 'Goblin', a yellow and red bicolor, are everblooming, ideal for edging borders and for rock gardens. Propagate from seed and root division.

Galega officinalis
Goat's rue
Zones 4–9

Native to the Mediterranean, these lupinlike plants grow bushy, up to 5 feet (1.5 m) high. The erect flower spikes borne in early summer are mostly white and light blue but not as tall as a lupin. Plants prefer full sun and good drainage. Useful in mixed borders. Propagate by seed and division.

Gaura lindheimeri
Gaura
Zones 6–10

This native of Texas looks like nothing special when grown individually, but when massed in a colony, it is one of the finest "see-through" plants you can use for decorating mixed borders. The compact, basal-branching, erect stems produce four-petalled white or pink flowers that resemble a mass of butterflies in flight. Plants grow to 18 inches (46 cm) high and produce smooth, narrow, willowlike leaves. They tolerate poor soil if it drains well and full sun. Flowering continuously from early summer until fall frost, the best selections include 'Siskiyou Pink' (a bright reddish-pink) and 'Whirling Butterflies' (pure white flowers with red stems). Propagate from seed and division.

Geranium himalayense
Blue cranesbill
Zones 4–7

Perennial geraniums are a large plant family and should not be confused with the common bedding geranium, botanically known as *Pelargonium* and widely used as a tender annual for summer display in beds and borders. Indigenous to the Himalayan Mountains of Northern India, the blue cranesbill features masses of gorgeous, lilac-blue, cup-shaped flowers in late spring and early summer. The flowers are the largest in hardy perennial geraniums, up to 2 inches (5 cm) wide, held above bushy plants on airy stems. The ivy-shaped leaves are deeply serrated. Use as drifts in mixed borders and rock gardens. Propagate by seed and root division. 'Johnson's Blue' is a profuse-blooming hybrid growing to 18 inches (46 cm) high. They are especially appealing when mixed with ornamental grasses.

Geranium psilostemon
Armenian cranesbill
Zones 4–9

This is a large geranium, growing to 4 feet (1.2 m) tall with magenta flowers with dark centers. The leaves turn a brilliant color in the fall.

Geranium sanguineum
Bloody cranesbill
Zones 3–9

Grows 9 to 18 inches (23 to 46 cm) tall, with long-blooming flowers ranging from white to deep pink, depending on the cultivar. The leaves are deeply cut and turn crimson in the fall. It stays compact and makes a good border plant.

GEUM HYBRIDS

Avens
Zones 5–9

Mostly derived from crosses with G. *chiloense* and native to Chile, some popular varieties include 'Lady Stratheden' (yellow) and 'Mrs. J. Bradshaw' (orange-red). Other colors include red and orange. Plants grow to 3 feet (91 cm) high and equally wide, with branching stems covered in spring with double and semi-double flowers that resemble roses, up to 2 inches (5 cm) across. The slender leaves are divided and toothed. Good accents for mixed borders.

Goniolimon tartaricum aka Limonium tartaricum
Perennial statice
Zones 4–10

Native to the Russian steppes, plants form a rosette of lance-shaped green leaves and tall flower stems up to 3 feet (91 cm) high, topped by clouds of papery white or pink flowers in early summer. Give them full sun and good drainage. Useful massed in mixed beds and also for cutting to make long-lasting dried arrangements. Propagate by seed and division.

Hakonechloa macra
Japanese woodland grass,
Hakone grass

Zones 6–9

Though generally slow growing, this native of Japan's mountainous regions has a special variegated form, 'Aureola'. It is highly rated among ornamental grasses because of its dome of mostly yellow leaves that arch out in perfect symmetry all around the plant to create a fleecy appearance. The slender, bamboolike leaves are thickly layered and soft, and valued for edging lightly shaded paths and as a woodland groundcover since the leaves tend to bleach in full sun. Also good for containers. Small, inconspicuous weeping flowers are produced in spring. Plants grow to 18 inches (46 cm) high, turn pink in autumn and prefer a humus-rich, moisture-retentive soil with good drainage. Sensational combined with hostas, ferns and blue forget-me-nots. Propagate by seed and division.

Gypsophila paniculata
Baby's breath

Zones 4–9

Summer-flowering, dainty white or pink, star-shaped flowers are borne in such profusion on brittle, slender stems that the whole plant can look like a cloud of mist from a distance. Native to Europe, plants grow to 3 feet (91 cm) high with a billowing habit and like moisture-retentive, fertile soil in full sun. Good for mixed borders and valued for cutting. 'Bristol Fairy' has white, double flowers while 'Festival Pink' has pink, double flowers. G. *repens* (zones 4–7) is a low, mat-forming, creeping species suitable for rock gardens and available in white and pink.

Helenium autumnale
Sneezeweed
Zones 4–8

Native to North America, plants grow 5 feet (1.5 m) high to create a dense bush of lance-like leaves and masses of daisylike flowers in mostly yellow, orange and rusty-red. Requires full sun and tolerates moist soil, even surviving long periods with their roots covered with shallow water. Popular for mixed beds and also cutting since a complete flower head forms an instant bouquet. Tall kinds such as 'Bruno' (a ruby red) may need staking since the summer-flowering canopy can become top-heavy. Good companions for ornamental grasses and goldenrod. Dwarf hybrids that grow up to 3 feet (91 cm) high include 'Moerheim Beauty' (a dark copper-red) and 'Wyndley' (a yellow and orange bicolor).

Helianthemum nummularium
Rock rose
Zones 4–8

Spreading, evergreen plants up to 12 inches (31 cm) high are smothered in cheerful, drought-tolerant, cup-shaped flowers. Native to Europe, the petals have the feel and texture of crepe paper in yellow, orange, red, pink and white. Popular for rock gardens, edging mixed borders, covering dry slopes and planting between flagstone to form cushions. Tolerant of a wide range of soil types providing drainage is good and plants receive full sun. Propagate from seed and division. Blooms in spring.

Helianthus atrorubens aka H. salicifolius
Yellow sunflower
Zones 5–9

This is the showy perennial sunflower that blooms in late summer and early autumn every year in Monet's garden, usually in partnership with blue New England asters to create a spectacular yellow and blue color harmony, especially along Monet's Grand Allée. The canary yellow, daisylike, 3-inch (8 cm) flowers have dark brown centers and are held erect on tall, branching stems up to 6 feet (1.8 m) high among toothed, lance-like, velvety leaves. Propagate by division.

Helianthus x multiflorus
Perennial sunflower
Zones 5–9

Native to North America, plants grow to 5 feet (1.5 m) high with an upright, bushy habit. Golden-yellow daisylike flowers can be single or double, held high on stiff, slender stems. Leaves are dark green and spear shaped. Popular as an accent in mixed beds and borders. Prefers moist, fertile, loam soil in full sun. Propagate from seed and root division. The summer-flowering plants may need staking. 'Flore Pleno' has fully double flowers and is good for cutting. *H. angustifolius*, the swamp sunflower, is a related species that tolerates boggy conditions.

Helianthus tuberosus
Jerusalem artichoke
See Vegetables, page 210.

Helleborus orientalis
Lenten rose
Zones 4–9

Native to Europe, plants grow to 12 inches (31 cm) high with a spreading habit. Color range includes purple, pink, white and cream, and some blooms have freckles. Leaves are leathery, toothed and sometimes appear after the flowers die. Good to use in rock gardens, woodland gardens and for edging mixed beds and borders. Prefers moist loam or humus-rich soil in partial shade. Propagated by seed (must be fresh) and root division. Deer resistant; blooms in late winter and early spring. Related species include *H. niger*, Christmas rose (zones 4–8), which has white flowers and *Helleborus foetidus* (zones 6–9), which has green flowers.

Helictotrichon sempervirens
Blue oat grass
Zones 3–8

Its dramatic metallic-blue arching leaves make this vigorous, clump-forming, ornamental grass one of the best to soften borders, especially in company with pink or yellow flowers. Spectacular when surrounded with clumps of pink evening primrose, *Oenothera speciosa*. Native to Eurasia, it is often confused with *Elymus arenarius* var. *glaucus*, blue dune grass (zones 4–10). These plants grow to 3 feet (91 cm) high and spread equally wide, producing silver-blue flower plumes in summer that change to amber in autumn. Provide them with full sun and good drainage. Propagate by seed or division.

Heliopsis helianthoides
False sunflower
Zones 4–9

Native to North America, plants grow to 4 feet (1.2 m) with an erect, bushy habit. Golden-yellow daisylike flowers are mostly single and semi-double, and shine brightly against dark green, spear-shaped leaves. Highly popular as an accent for mixed beds and borders, and excellent for cutting. Easy to grow in most well-drained soils in full sun. Propagated by seed and root division. 'Incomparabilis' bears both single and semi-double flowers. Late summer flowering.

Perennials

HEMEROCALLIS HYBRIDS

Daylilies

Zones 4–10, depending on variety

Mostly native to China, daylilies are valued for their rich color range and drought tolerance. Although the majority produce a two to three-week flush of lilylike flowers in midsummer, plant breeders have developed "everblooming" varieties such as 'Stella de Oro' (gold) and 'Happy Returns' (yellow) that will bloom continuously from spring to autumn frosts. These are especially suitable for growing in containers and massing to cover slopes.

Daylilies, in general, like full sun but tolerate light shade. They tolerate most well-drained soils, except boggy soil. Few sights in the plant kingdom are more glorious than a border of mixed colors, since the color range is astonishing. Although richest in yellow, orange and red shades, there are white, cream, apricot, peach, green, mahogany and violet-blue, in both solid colors and bicolors. Some of the bicolors are startling in their composition. A whole range of picotee types have a thin line around the petal edges in a contrasting color, as though applied with a paintbrush. Another range of "eyed" daylilies has a contrasting zone that rings the petal center, as though the flower has been given a black eye.

Daylilies are good companions for most summer-flowering border perennials and ornamental grass. Their long, narrow, arching, straplike leaves form a fountain up to 2 feet (61 cm) high. The flower stems extend to 3 and 4 feet (91 cm to 1.2 m), topped by a flower cluster of open flowers and buds. Each open flower lasts only a day; hence, the name "daylily." However, on the everblooming kinds, there can be 100 flower buds, giving 100 days of bloom. Propagation is mostly by division of the fleshy, potatolike tubers.

In addition to the flamboyant hybrids, there are several species with good ornamental value. These include the following:

Hemerocallis fulva
Orange daylily

Zones 4–9

This Japanese species has large, orange-red, sterile flowers that bloom for two to three weeks in late spring. It spreads aggressively by underground stolons and has populated large expanses of waysides in North America and Europe. Few hardy perennials are more successful at covering-difficult-to-plant slopes for erosion control. The fountains of slender leaves grow to 2 feet (61 cm) high with the flower stems, up to 4 feet (1.2 m).

Hemerocallis lilioasphodelus aka *H. flava*
Lemon lily

Zones 4–9

This charming Chinese species is often confused with *H. citrina* because of its similar lemon-yellow flowers and pleasant fragrance, but it is earlier flowering and is a good companion to Siberian irises. Plants bloom in spring with a leaf height of up to 2 feet (61 cm), and flower stem height of up to 3 feet (91 cm).

Hemerocallis middendorffii
Amur daylily

Zones 5–9

Native to parts of Siberia south to Japan, the orange-yellow flowers are borne in late spring above vigorous clumps of slender, straplike leaves, up to 2 feet (61 cm) high.

Heuchera sanguinea
Coral bells
Zones 3–8
Native to North America, plants grow to 2 feet (61 cm) high with a rosette-forming habit. Tiny red or pink bell-shaped flowers cluster at the top of slender, wiry stems held well above the ivy-shaped leaves. Popular for rock gardens and also as accents in mixed beds and borders. Good for cutting; deer resistant. Prefers fertile, well-drained, humus-rich soil in sun or partial shade. Propagated by seed and root division. Heuchera has been crossed with *Tiarella* (foamflower), a North American woodland wildflower, to produce a more spirelike hybrid called *Heucherella*. Early summer flowering. Related species include *H. Americana* with white flowers (zones 4–10) and *H. villosa* with late-blooming white flowers (zones 5–9).

Hibiscus moscheutos
Rose mallow
Zones 5–10
Native to North America, plants grow to 5 feet (1.5 m) high with an erect habit. Flowers of hybrid varieties are unusually large—the size of dinner plates—in white, crimson and pink, many with a contrasting center. Flowers last only a day, but plants flower continuously from midsummer to fall frost. The large green leaves are attractively heart shaped. Popular for mixed borders and edging stream banks. Prefers moist, fertile, loam soil in full sun but tolerates boggy conditions. Propagated mostly by seeds. May need staking. Recommended varieties include 'Southern Belle' (blooms first year from seed sown in January or February) and 'Super Giants' (largest flowers).

HOSTAS

Plantain lily

Zones 3–10, depending on variety

Although most hostas produce attractive tubular flowers, some the size of foxgloves, normally in white and shades of lavender-blue, they are more highly valued for their attractive leaves, which vary from heart shaped to slender and lance-like. The leaves of the large-flowered kinds are often blistered, savoyed and heavily veined, adding distinctive textures to their visual interest, in addition to color. The permutations of leaf color are amazing, not only in solid shades of green, yellow and blue, but also with white, cream or yellow variegation.

Native to Japan and China, hostas have been hybridized to produce hundreds of varieties, most of which prefer a lightly shaded location and a moisture-retentive, humus-rich soil. The larger varieties, such as 'Blue Angel' and 'Sum and Substance', can be used alone as dramatic accents in shady borders or in roomy containers. They can also be grouped to create a weed-suffocating groundcover, especially in company with ferns, astilbe and primroses. They are especially attractive planted beside streams, pools and ponds so that the leaves arch over the water, and along woodland paths to create a quilt design with their leaves. Plants die down after frost, the leaves of many varieties changing to gold in autumn. Propagate by division. Miniature hostas are suitable for creating colonies in shade parts of a rock garden.

Hosta sieboldiana (left)
Zones 6–9

A Japanese species with large, blue leaves that are heart shaped, deeply veined and puckered. The flowers appear in early summer and are usually pale mauve, but can be pure white in some varieties, such as 'Blue Angel'. 'Frances Williams', a blue-green with gold-edged leaves, is another popular variety.

Hosta plantaginea
Zones 6–10

From China, a late summer-flowering species. The varieties 'Honeybells' and 'Royal Standard' have large, glossy, pale green leaves and large, fragrant tubular flowers.

Hosta fortunei
Zones 6–10

Not known in the wild, although it is probably from Japan. Its varieties include many of the best variegated forms, including 'Albomarginata' (white-edged leaves) and 'Aureomarginata' (gold-edged leaves).

Iberis sempervirens
Perennial candytuft
Zones 5–9

Native to the Mediterranean, this plant grows to about 12 inches (31 cm) tall with a mounded, spreading habit. Dense white flower clusters cover the low, ground-hugging plants. Dark green leaves are evergreen, narrow and pointed. Popular for rock gardens, dry walls and for edging mixed beds and borders. Tolerates a wide range of soils, as long as drainage is good. Propagated by seed and root division. Spring flowering.

Inula ensifolia
Swordleaf
Zones 5–10

Native to the Caucasus Mountains, the bushy plants grow to 2 feet (61 cm) high with lance-like leaves and masses of daisylike flowers in midsummer. This species is suitable for small gardens, in full sun and soil with good drainage. Useful for massing in mixed borders. Propagate by division.

Iris cristata
Crested iris
Zones 4–8

Native to North America, this woodland and meadow plant grows to 6 inches (15 cm) high, forming low colonies. Blue or white flowers carpet the ground among broad, spear-shaped, green leaves in spring. Popular for rock gardens and edging woodland paths. Naturalizes freely. Prefers well-drained, humus-rich loam soil in sun or shade. Plant rhizomes in fall with tips just below soil surface, spaced 6 inches (15 cm) apart.

Perennials

Iris sibirica
Siberian iris
Zones 4–9

Native to north-central Europe, this plant grows to 4 feet (1.2 m) tall with an upright, clump-forming habit. Long, slender leaves emerge in spring and remain decorative all summer. Flowers are numerous on tall, slender stems. Color range is mostly shades of blue and white. They are good for mixed beds and borders, and are especially attractive massed along stream banks and pond margins. Excellent for cutting. A number of good hybrids have expanded the color range to include yellow. Prefers acidic, moist soil in full sun. Propagated by root division in spring or autumn. Blooms in late spring. Related species include *I. pseudacorus*, flag iris (zones 3–9), *I. ensata*, Japanese water iris (zones 3–9), *I. tectorum*, Japanese roof iris (zones 6–9) and *I. cristata*, crested iris (zones 4–10).

Kniphofia uvaria
Red-hot poker
Zones 6–9

Native to South Africa, this plant grows to 4 feet (1.2 m) high with an erect, clump-forming habit. Tubular flowers in red and yellow are clustered at the top of a poker-straight, thick, succulent stem held high above the leaves, which are spiky, arching up and out in a clump. Popular for mixed beds and borders, and rock gardens. Also excellent for cutting. Prefers fertile, well-drained loam or sandy soil in full sun. Drought resistant. Propagated by seed, root division and offsets. Summer flowering.

Iris germanica
Bearded iris
Zones 3–9

Native to Europe, plants grow 2 to 4 feet (61 cm to 1.2 m) high with a clump-forming habit. Slender, sword-shaped leaves emerge in spring from fleshy roots called rhizomes. Flowers are large and showy with a spicy fragrance, usually featuring a prominent arching petal called a "fall" and an eye-catching yellow arrangement of stamens known as the "beard". Color range includes white, yellow, orange, pink, red, blue, purple and black, plus bicolors. Good for mixed beds and borders, creating a temporary hedge effect, also good for large floral arrangements. Numerous hybrids have been created, including dwarfs suitable for rock gardens. Easy to grow in most well-drained garden soils in full sun. Propagated by division of rhizomes any time of year. Blooms spring and early summer.

Lamiastrum galeobdolon
Yellow archangel
Zones 3–9

Mostly grown for its mintlike, silvery leaves and propensity to create a quick weed-suffocating groundcover, particularly in light shade. Native to Europe, the 12-inch (31 cm) high plants flower prolifically in spring with yellow hooded flowers. An especially decorative variety, 'Herman's Pride', has a mosaic pattern of silver and dark green to its serrated leaves, though it is not as free flowering as the species. Propagate by division or stem cuttings, which readily root in plain water.

Lamium maculatum
Deadnettle
Zones 3–9

These low-growing, rapidly spreading plants from Europe make excellent weed-suffocating groundcovers for sun or light shade, especially variegated varieties, such as 'White Nancy' with white, hooded, tubular flowers and silver, heart-shaped, mintlike leaves edged in green. Spring-flowering plants grow to 12 inches (31 cm) high, spread by stolons and require good drainage. Propagate by division and stem cuttings, which readily root in plain water.

Lathyrus latifolius
Perennial sweet pea
Zones 5–9

Native to Europe, this vining plant grows to 9 feet (2.7 m) tall. Easy to grow, the stems and flowers are similar to sweet peas but with a more limited color range—mostly pink, white and rose red. Popular for covering unsightly slopes as a groundcover and for training up posts or walls as a tall, decorative vine. Tolerates a wide range of soils as long as drainage is good in full sun. Propagated mostly by seeds. Needs staking to climb. Summer flowering.

Liatris spicata
Gayfeather
Zones 4–9

Native to North America, this prairie plant grows to 5 feet (1.5 m) tall with an erect, clump-forming habit. Purple or white flower spikes resembling bottle brushes stand erect like pokers held well above the spear-shaped foliage. Popular as an accent in mixed beds and borders. Excellent for both fresh and dried arrangements. Easy to grow in most well-drained garden soils in full sun. Propagate by seed and root division. 'Kobold' displays deep purple flowers in a dome shape. Summer flowering.

Ligularia stenocephala
Rocket ligularia
Zones 4–8

Native to Asia, this plant grows to 6 feet (1.8 m) tall with an erect, spire-like habit. Towering flower spikes are crowded with bright golden-yellow flowers on slender black stems that contrast spectacularly with large, sharply indented, highly decorative leaves. Popular as a background for mixed beds and borders, and also stream banks and pond margins. Good for cutting. Demands a moist, humus-rich, fertile soil in partial shade. Leaves wilt during direct afternoon sunlight. Propagate by root division. 'The Rocket' has a slight bronze cast to the leaves. A related species is *L. dentata* 'Othello' with yellow, daisylike flowers and large bronze leaves.

Lilium
See Bulbs, page 36.

Linum perenne
Blue flax
Zones 5–8

Native to Europe, this Mediterranean plant grows to 2 feet (61 cm) tall and has a billowing habit. Dainty blue flowers are borne in abundance on light, airy stems with narrow leaves. Popular in mixed beds, borders and wildflower meadows. Not a long-lasting perennial but it does self-seed. Easy to grow in a wide range of soils with good drainage in full sun. Propagated by seed and cuttings, but it is difficult to divide. Spring flowering.

Liriope muscari
Lilyturf
Zones 6–10

Native to Asia, this grasslike plant grows to 18 inches (46 cm) and has a compact, clump-forming habit. Mostly grown for its slender, arching evergreen leaves, which can be dark green or variegated green and cream. Lavender-blue or white flower spikes appear among the foliage. Frequently used for edging walkways, beds and borders, also popular as a groundcover. Prefers fertile, humus-rich loam soil in sun or partial shade. Propagated by root division. Summer flowering.

Perennials

Lobelia cardinalis
Cardinal flower

Zones 3–9

Native to North America, this bog-loving plant grows to 5 feet (1.5 m) with an erect, clump-forming habit. Striking spires of cardinal-red flowers contrast well with dark green, serrated, spear-shaped leaves. Plants are usually short-lived, but readily seed themselves. Popular in mixed beds and borders, woodland gardens and along stream banks. Good for cutting. Prefers moisture-retentive, humus-rich, acidic soil in partial shade. Propagated by seed and root division. Summer flowering.

Lunaria annua
Money plant

Zones 4–7

This member of the phlox family resembles dame's rocket. Native to southern Europe, plants grow a rosette of spear-shaped, serrated leaves and 3-foot (91 cm) tall erect stems of purple or white four-petalled flowers in spring. These are followed by silvery white circular or oval seedpods that can be cut and dried for long-lasting arrangements. Plant in sun or light shade in soil with good drainage. Useful massed along woodland paths, in mixed borders and cutting gardens. Though a hardy biennial, money plant readily self-seeds into bare soil to maintain a colorful display year after year.

Lupinus hybrids
Russell lupines

Zones 4–8

Developed in England from native North American species, the Russell strain grows to 3 feet (91 cm) tall with an erect, clump-forming habit. Spires of fragrant, pealike flowers are white, yellow, red, pink, blue and purple, many bicolored. Leaves are dark green, like splayed fingers. Lupines flower best in cool conditions. Popular for mixed beds and borders, also for meadow gardens. Prefers moist, sandy soil or well-drained loam. Propagated mostly from seeds and best treated as a biennial. Self-sows easily into moisture-retentive soil. Spring flowering.

Lychnis chalcedonica
Maltese cross

Zones 4–8

Native to Siberia, this summer-flowering plant grows to 3 feet (91 cm) tall with an erect habit. Clusters of scarlet flowers are borne on slender stems, each floret in the shape of a Maltese cross. Leaves are dark green and spear shaped. Popular as an accent in beds and borders. Excellent for cutting. Easy to grow in any well-drained soil in sun or partial shade. Propagated by seed or root division. *L. coronaria* (rose campion) is a related species.

Lysimachia clethroides
Gooseneck loosestrife

Zones 4–9

Plants grow to 4 feet (1.2 m) high and bloom in early summer. Small white flowers are clustered in the shape of a goose neck. Tolerates moist soil and is disease resistant.

Lysimachia nummularia
Creeping Jenny

Zones 4–10

A ground-hugging plant with small oval leaves and yellow cup-shaped flowers. Tolerates moist soil. 'Aurea' has gold leaves, is less than 1 inch (2.5 cm) high and is good for trailing.

Lysimachia punctata
Yellow loosestrife

Zones 4–8

Native to Europe, this eye-catching plant grows to 3 feet (91 cm) tall with a spire-like habit. Erect spikes of yellow flowers grow in clumps among spear-shaped, ruffled green leaves. Popular as an accent in mixed beds and borders, pond margins and stream banks. Prefers moisture-retentive loam soil in sun or partial shade. Propagate by root division. Tolerates boggy conditions. 'Alexander' is a variegated cultivar, which grows more slowly than the species.

Lythrum salicaria
Purple loosestrife

Zones 3–10

Bushy plants grow to 4 feet (1.2 m), the erect stems topped with rosy-pink flower spikes up to 10 inches (25 cm) long. Though a beautiful summer-flowering perennial, it is banned in many parts of the U.S. for its invasiveness, especially in wetlands.

Macleaya cordata
Plume poppy

Zones 3–10

Give these tall, spreading plants plenty of room for their stoloniferous roots can be invasive. Native to China, the deeply lobed, gray-green leaves surround a 10 foot (3 m) tall stem topped by airy clusters of pink or cream-colored flowers in summer. Give them full sun and good drainage. Useful massed as a tall background to mixed borders. Propagate by division, though the plants self-seed readily.

Matteuccia struthiopteris
Ostrich fern

Zones 3–8

This North American fern is one of the most attractive for boggy and moisture-retentive soils in lightly shaded woodland because of its symmetrical, tall, feathery fronds that splay out to form the shape of a shuttlecock. Plants grow to 3 feet (91 cm) and in summer, clusters of chestnut-brown, tightly curled, fertile, spore-bearing fronds emerge from the center. Best planted in generous drifts along stream banks and pond margins in company with hosta, primula and rhododendron. Plants spread by underground rhizomes that can double the planting area each year. The young shoots called fiddleheads are edible when cooked and are sold in organic markets. Propagate by division.

Meconopsis grandis
Blue poppy
Zones 5–8

From the Himalaya Mountains, this is the hardiest of blue poppies grown in gardens. A hybrid, M. x *sheldonii* (zones 6–8), is only slightly less hardy but a deeper blue coloring. Blue poppies are the most desirable and most challenging of perennials for two reasons: the plants demand cool temperatures during summer, so their roots are kept cool; and unless the plants are deadheaded to prevent them blooming the first year, they will act like biennials and die down after setting seed. Plants prefer light shade but will grow in sun if the roots can be kept cool. They prefer a humus-rich soil and like to grow close to running water. Use them massed in woodland and bog gardens, especially in company with Japanese candelabra primulas.

Mertensia virginica
Virginia bluebells
Zones 3–9

Native to the northeastern United States, this woodland plant grows up to 2 feet (61 cm) tall with an upright, clump-forming habit. Nodding, blue, bell-shaped flowers are held in clusters like English cowslips. There is a rare white form. Pretty in shady beds and borders, and naturalized in woodland, especially when combined with late-flowering daffodils. Prefers light shade under deciduous trees in moist but well-drained, humus-rich, acid soil. Propagate by seeds or division in autumn. Since the foliage dies down by early summer, Virginia bluebells should be grown next to plants that will spread over them such as hostas. Spring blooming.

Miscanthus sinensis
Eulalia grass, Maiden grass
Zones 3–9, depending on variety

The grass family *Miscanthus* contains a large number of species and varieties, each with a distinctive characteristic. In autumn, when the flower plumes and leaf blades turn russet colors, it's worth giving them a special area to form a collection. They are best paired with some berry bushes such as hardy winterberry (*Ilex verticillata*), whose brilliant red berries provide a good contrast of color and form. 'Variegatus' (zones 5–9) has graceful green and white striped leaves that appear to be silver from a distance. 'Morning Light' (zones 5–9) has slender leaf blades tapering to white at the tips and presenting a misty, shimmering appearance, especially when backlit. 'Zebrinus' (zones 5–9) has dark green foliage with horizontal flecks of gold so that from a distance it resembles a shower of sparks. The conspicuous flower plumes occur in late summer and can be white or pink depending on variety, standing above the arching clumps of foliage to a height of 5 feet (1.5 m) and more. Plants should be used to soften mixed borders; they look good massed along stream banks and pond margins in company with astilbe and New England asters. Propagate by division.

Monarda didyma
Bee balm
Zones 4–8

Native to North America, this prairie plant grows 36 to 48 inches (91 to 121 cm) tall with an upright, bushy, clump-forming habit. Aromatic tubular flowers create a dense floral cluster resembling a crown and are held erect on stiff, square stems. Colors include scarlet, mahogany, pink and white. Use in meadow or herb gardens and as a bold accent in mixed beds and borders. Mildew is a problem, although there are a few resistant varieties such as 'Jacob Kline,' a bright red. Prefers full sun in moisture-retentive loam soil. Propagate by seed, softwood cuttings or division in spring. Can be aggressive. Summer blooming.

Myosotis scorpioides
Forget-me-not

Zones 5–9

Native to Europe, this charming plant grows to 12 inches (31 cm) tall with a low, mounded habit. Myriad, small blue flowers with yellow centers are borne in airy clusters creating a misty appearance. Leaves are paddle shaped. Popular for massing in a bed, especially among tulips. Good for edging walkways and woodland paths, also suitable for pond margins and stream banks. Prefers moist, fertile, humus-rich loam soil in sun or partial shade. Propagate by seed and root division. Early spring flowering.

Nepeta x faassenii
Ornamental catmint

Zones 4–8

This aromatic hybrid grows to 3 feet (91 cm) tall with a bushy habit. Mintlike plants produce dense clusters of mauve blue flowers. Leaves are dark green and heart shaped. Creates a hedge effect and therefore is popular for lining walkways, but can also be used in mixed beds and borders. Prefers moist, fertile, loam soil in full sun. Propagate by seed and root division. Related species *N. cataria* (catnip) has white flowers and is attractive to cats. Early summer to fall blooming.

Oenothera speciosa
Showy evening primrose

Zones 5–10

Native to the western U.S., few plants produce such a shimmering flower carpet in late spring. Spreading plants with small pointed leaves cover the ground like a carpet up to 4 inches (10 cm) high. The 3-inch (8 cm) wide, cup-shaped, pink or white flowers almost completely hide the foliage. Provide full sun and good drainage. Useful for edging mixed borders as a component of wildflower meadows and planted as drifts in rock gardens.

Oenothera tetragona
Sundrop

Zones 4–8

Native to North America, this prairie plant grows to 2 feet (61 cm) tall with an upright, clump-forming habit. Cup-shaped, yellow flowers shimmer like satin. Leaves are green and spear shaped. Popular for mixed beds and borders. Forms a dense, spreading mass of brilliant yellow in early summer. Prefers sandy or well-drained loam soil in full sun. Propagate by root division.

Omphalodes verna
Creeping forget-me-not, Navelwort

Zones 5–7

Though the beauty of its heart-shaped, blistered leaves is reason enough to grow this shade-loving, mound-shaped plant, its spring-flowering, forget-me-not blue flower sprays are a bonus. Useful in mixed borders and along woodland paths, in humus-rich soil with good drainage. Native to Europe, plants grow to 12 inches (31 cm) high. Propagate by division.

Opuntia humifusa
Hardy prickly pear
Zones 6–8

Native to North America, this excellent dry landscape plant grows 6 inches (15 cm) tall with a prostrate, ground-hugging habit. A true cactus, it features oblong pads bristling with sharp spines and produces shimmering yellow flowers up to 3 inches (8 cm) across in early summer. When the flowers die, edible red fruits develop and ripen in autumn. Popular for rock gardens and dry walls. Easy to grow in most well-drained garden soils in full sun. Propagate by rooting the leaves (pads) in moist sand. Drought resistant.

Paeonia lactiflora
Chinese peony
Zones 2–8, depending on variety

Although there are 60 species of peonies worldwide, mainly indigenous to mountains surrounding the Mediterranean and Asia, the Chinese peony (*P. lactiflora*) is the one we usually see in perennial gardens. Similar in appearance to the European peony (*P. officinalis*), it is quite distinct from the larger flowered, woody-stemmed tree peony (*P. suffruticosa*)—Shrubs, see page 140. The Chinese peony has many features gardeners appreciate in a flower—large, conspicuous, fragrant blooms up to 6 inches (15 cm) across; a robust constitution that allows them to outlive their owners; popularity as a cut flower; tolerance of a wide range of soils and climate conditions; and resistance to browsing animals such as rabbits and deer. The only complaint is the brevity of bloom. Although choosing among early, midseason and late varieties can ensure a month of color, individual plants can be devoid of bloom within a week if rain deluges the heavy flower heads and shatters the delicate petals.

The Impressionist painter Claude Monet loved peonies so much, especially in floral arrangements around the house, that he not only had dozens of varieties in his perennial borders, but he also made hedges of them around plots in his vegetable garden.

Herbaceous peonies grow multiple flowering stems that crowd together to form a bushy plant up to 4 feet (1.2 m) high. The maple-shaped green leaves emerge in early spring as red shoots, bloom in mid to late spring about the same time as bearded irises and Oriental poppies, and die down after autumn frost or excessive summer heat, remaining dormant though the winter months.

The color range is rich in shades of pink and red, plus white.

Some have globe-shaped double flowers that look like enormous scoops of ice cream. Others have a single row of petals forming a bowl shape with a crown of powdery yellow stamens in the middle. Propagation is mostly by division to ensure an exact replica of the parent. Seed propagation is possible, but produces variable results. The fully double lactiflora peonies are usually sterile, but it is possible to raise seedlings from the single types and also from the tree peonies and the species peonies.

Many older varieties developed in France are still popular, including 'Edulis Superba' (double pale pink), 'Félix Crousse' (double red) and 'Monsieur Jules Elie' (double deep pink). More recent improved varieties include the rose-pink single 'Bowl of Beauty' and the dark red 'Barrington Belle' with a dome of red and yellow stamens, and the potential for 100 blooms all open at the same time.

P. mlokosewitschii (zones 5–9), commonly called Molly the Witch, is possibly the most highly valued among peony connoisseurs. Indigenous to the Caucasus Mountains of Europe, the bushy plants produce cup-shaped yellow flowers. Plants grow to just 3 feet (91 cm) high and are eminently suitable for rock gardens.

P. tenuifolia 'Rubra' (zones 3–6) is another wonderful dwarf peony treasured by peony connoisseurs and suitable for rock gardens. Called the fernleaf peony for its feathery foliage, plants grow to just 2 feet (61 cm) high and are covered in crimson-red globular flowers.

Peonies are habit forming, and it's generally a good idea to set aside a special area for a peony garden, incorporating both species and hybrids, herbaceous and tree peonies, with a rocky area for new low-growing, cushion-shaped "rock garden peonies" that are hardy in zones 3–7.

Paeonia officinalis
Herbaceous peony
Zones 3–9

Native to Europe and Asia, this bushy plant grows to 4 feet (1.2 m) tall. The fragrant flowers are single or double, up to 6 inches (15 cm) across in white, pink and red. Leaves are dark green and deeply indented. Good accent in mixed beds or borders and also planted en masse as a spring-flowering hedge. Spectacular in arrangements. Prefers cool, moisture-retentive, fertile, humus-rich loam soil that drains well. Best in full sun. Propagate by root division. Specialist peony breeders offer hundreds of varieties, such as 'Alba Plena' (double white), 'Carmin' (semi-double pink), and 'Rubin' (a double red).

Panicum virgatum
Switch grass
Zones 4–9

Though the erect, clumping stems of this North American prairie grass feature blue stems and stiff, slender, upward-facing leaves in summer, by autumn they change to amber and all through winter will glow vibrant orange against a wintry sky. The 5-foot (1.5 m) tall flower plumes are variable, mostly pink and silver. Use in mixed borders, especially in company with yellow flowers like black-eyed Susans and coreopsis.

Papaver orientale
Oriental poppy
Zones 4–9

This exotic-looking plant grows to 4 feet (1.2 m) tall with an upright habit. Satinlike flowers shimmer atop stiff stems up to 10 inches (25 cm) across with a mass of powdery black stamens at the center. Colors include red, orange, pink, purple and white, mostly with attractive black blotches at the petal base. Leaves are green, fernlike and hairy. Popular for mixed beds and borders or massed alone. Striking cut flower if ends are quickly scorched to seal the stem and prevent wilting. Easy to grow in most well-drained garden soils in full sun. Propagate by seed and root division. Blooms in spring.

Pennisetum alopecuroides
Fountain grass
Zones 5–9

Though considered an invasive plant in warmer climes like coastal California, Australian fountain grass is better behaved in gardens with cold winters. Popular for massing around water features such as streams and even swimming pools, it is also useful for edging broad paths such as driveways. The arching leaves start off green and change to amber as the season advances and produce masses of pinkish-white flower plumes that persist well into winter months. Plants prefer full sun and good drainage. The selection known as 'Moudry' is often preferred for its broader, darker green leaf blades in summer and for its smoky black flower plumes. The black flowers make a wonderful contrast to white New England asters in autumn. Propagate by seed and division.

Perennials

Penstemon digitalis
Foxglove penstemon
Zones 3–9

Native to eastern North America, this plant grows to 3 feet (91 cm) tall in full sun to part shade but is more widely grown as the cultivar 'Husker's Red', which has pale pink flowers and deep purple foliage. This is a very adaptable *Penstemon*, even tolerating some moisture in the soil as long as it is well drained. Penstemons are usually short-lived as a group. There are many new cultivars in recent years, but most are not fully hardy except in zone 7 and milder.

Perovskia atriplicifolia
Russian sage
Zones 6–9

Native to Asia and Siberia, this dry landscape shrub grows to 4 feet (1.2 m) tall with an upright, shrubby habit. Small lavender-blue aromatic flowers form showy spikes. Twiggy stems have small, narrow, gray leaves which, when bruised, produce a sage-like aroma. A good background plant in mixed beds and borders, and an excellent cut flower, both fresh and dried. Easy to grow in most well-drained garden soils in full sun. Propagate by cuttings. Summer flowering and a good companion to tall phlox.

Phalaris arundinacea
Canary grass, Ribbon grass
Zones 3–9

The variety 'Picta' is a spreading plant with bicolored, arching, green and white leaves that are often flushed pink, especially in the selection 'Strawberries and Cream'. It is a useful plant for massing in moisture-retentive soil beside streams and ponds. Plants grow to 3 feet (91 cm) high, prefer full sun and can spread rapidly if not controlled. Small, inconspicuous pale flower clusters occur in summer. Propagate by division.

Persicaria bistorta aka Polygonum bistorta
Knotweed
Zones 4–8

Native to Europe, this bog-loving plant grows to 3 feet (91 cm) tall with an erect, clump-forming habit. Pokerlike pink flowers are held well above the green straplike foliage. Popular for mixed beds and borders, particularly as an edging. Good for cutting. Prefers moisture-retentive, fertile, loam soil in partial shade. Propagate by seed, cuttings and root division. 'Superba' has extra large flowers. Summer flowering and especially beautiful when partnered with Japanese iris.

Phlomis russeliana
Jerusalem sage
Zones 5–9

Mostly native to the Mediterranean, these erect, bushy, drought-resistant plants have feltlike, wrinkled, heart-shaped leaves and flower stems topped with yellow flowers arranged in a crown, several to a stem. Plants grow to 3 feet (91 cm) high and prefer full sun and good drainage. Useful in mixed borders. Propagate by seed, cuttings, division and tubers.

Phlox divaricata
Woodland phlox
Zones 4–9

Native to the eastern U.S. and valued for its deep blue five-petalled flowers, plants form dense colonies of low-growing rosettes that produce erect flower clusters up to 6 inches (15 cm) high in spring. Plants prefer light shade and tolerate moist soil. They make good companions for white foamflowers and yellow primroses that bloom at the same time. Invaluable for massing along woodland paths. A similar species, *P. stolonifera* (creeping phlox), has an upright, dense and mounding habit, growing to about a foot (31 cm) high and bearing fragrant flowers, usually in shades of blue.

Phlox paniculata
Summer phlox
Zones 4–8

Native to North America, this aggressive, summer-flowering plant stands up to 4 feet (1.2 m) tall with a stiff, upright habit. Bold flower clusters grow to 9 inches (23 cm) long in white and shades of red, pink, salmon, lavender and blue. Good for tall backgrounds in mixed borders and popular for cutting. 'Pinafore' is an excellent dwarf variety with clear pink flowers. 'David' and the 'Volcano' series of mixed colors have good mildew resistance. Prefers deeply cultivated, fertile loam soil in full sun. Propagate by seed and root division. May need staking. *P. maculata*, Carolina phlox (zones 5–10), is similar to *P. paniculata*, but flowers two weeks earlier in early summer.

Phlox subulata
Moss pinks
Zones 3–8

Native to North America, this dry landscape plant grows 6 inches (15 cm) tall with a low, ground-hugging habit. Small, star-shaped flowers are crowded closely together in spring to form a cushion of color in pink, red, blue and white. Narrow, gray-green leaves are evergreen. Good for rock gardens and dry walls. Creates an attractive groundcover when massed. Useful for edging beds and borders. Requires excellent drainage and full sun. Propagate by seed and root division. 'Candystripe' is an unusual pink and white bicolor.

Phragmites communis
Giant reed
Zones 4–9

Considered to be the most prolific plant on the planet, this giant reed can be found on all continents in the Northern Hemisphere. Prevalent in swamps and wetland meadows, plants grow stiff, erect, straw-colored stems up to 15 feet (4.5 m) high. The stems have arching, straplike, green leaves ending in feathery, smoky flower plumes that turn amber in autumn. Widely used for thatching, plants prefer full sun and moist soil, and spread aggressively from underground rhizomes that will tolerate being submerged permanently in shallow water. Useful as a background to bog gardens and for planting along ditches as windbreaks. Propagate by division of the rhizomes.

Physalis alkekengi
Chinese lantern
All zones

Widespread throughout eastern Europe and Asia, this aggressive spreading plant is grown primarily for its decorative orange-red, lanternlike seed cases that ripen in autumn. These are not only decorative in the garden but also make long-lasting arrangements when dried, especially mixed with the silvery dried seedpods of money plant (*Lunaria annua*). Plants grow to 2 feet (61 cm) high, resemble pepper plants (to which they are related) and require full sun and good drainage. Propagate by seed and division. Best grown either in a corner of the garden or in cutting gardens, where their invasiveness will not cause a problem.

Physostegia virginiana
Obedient plant

Zones 4–8

Native to North America, this prairie plant grows to 5 feet (1.5 m) tall with an upright, clump-forming habit. Pink or white flowers resemble snapdragons and form spikes at the top of long, slender stems. A member of the mint family, its stems are square, and the leaves are narrow, serrated and pointed. Good for late-summer display in mixed beds and borders. Spreading roots may need thinning each year to prevent them from becoming too aggressive. Called "obedient plant" because flower heads can be twisted into different positions and remain in place. Prefers moist soil and full sun. Propagate by seed and root division.

Platycodon grandiflorus
Balloon flower

Zones 4–9

Native to China, this loveable plant grows to 2 feet (61 cm) tall and has an upright habit. Beautiful, clear blue, bell-shaped flowers up to 3 inches (8 cm) across face up on erect stems in summer. White and pink forms, double and semi-double are also available. Leaves are narrow and pointed. It gets its common name from the appearance of the swollen flower buds. Excellent for mixed beds and borders, for rock gardens and also good for cutting. Prefers fertile, acidic loam soil in full sun or partial shade. Propagate by seeds. 'Miss Tilley's Blue' has the largest flower size.

Polemonium reptans
Jacob's ladder

Zones 4–8

Native to North America, this plant grows to be 12 inches (31 cm) tall with a low, spreading habit. Small, light blue, bell-shaped flowers are crowded in loose clusters in spring. Leaves are made up of oval leaflets symmetrically arranged like a ladder. Useful for edging walkways and as a groundcover in woodland gardens. Prefers moist, humus-rich, loam soil in sun or partial shade. Propagate by root division in spring. The related species *P. caeruleum* grows taller, up to 3 feet (91 cm), and is useful as a border accent.

Primrose

Zones 4–8, depending on variety

This large, spring-flowering, perennial plant family consists of species native primarily to Europe and Asia. Over the centuries, these have been crossed to create a spectacular range of hybrids split into two main groups: Polyantha, or bunch-flowered, primroses have mostly *P. veris* (the English cowslip) and *P. vulgaris* (the English primrose) in their parentage, while the Candelabra kinds have mostly *P. japonica* and other Asian species in their parentage. Propagation is by seed started indoors in spring of the season before flowering and also by dividing established clumps.

Polyantha primroses came into prominence after the Victorian plantswoman, Gertrude Jekyll, began hybridizing them. Her work was carried on by Florence Bellis, an Oregon housewife, who spent 40 years developing the finest hardy primroses the world has ever seen. Called the 'Barnhavens', these are not only hardy, they are also tolerant of hot, dry summers, which most primroses are not. The 'Barnhaven' range of colors is astonishing, for it includes the full color spectrum, including white and all shades of yellow, red, green, brown, orange, blue/violet and pink, plus bicolors. Some have their flowers arranged in a clump above crinkled, oval leaves no more than 4 inches (10 cm) high; others are clustered atop a long stem like cowslip or candelabra primroses about 8 inches (20 cm) high.

Be aware that the popular strain of hybrid primroses known as 'Pacific Giants' are not hardy. These plants have been bred for spring bedding, only to be planted in the garden after the threat of severe frost passes, or as gift plants for indoor display. They only reliably overwinter in zone 8.

Candelabra primroses are bog-loving plants and bloom a month or two after the 'Barnhavens'. They demand a moisture-retentive soil with high humus content and are mostly used along streams and beside other water features, such as pools and ponds. The leaves are usually oval and ruffled, in a rosette with a flower stem rising above the leaves to 3 feet (91 cm) high. The species *P. japonica* is mostly shades of red, pink and white, but hybrids such as 'Inshriach' and 'North Hill' have added yellow, orange and apricot to the color range. The flowers are arranged in whorls spaced equidistant along the flowering stem with three whorls that usually open at one time. Plants are best used massed in lightly shaded locations, and the soil should remain moist through summer. They are good companions to ferns, hostas, azaleas and rhododendrons.

In addition to these hybrids, the following hardy primrose species are popular in gardens:

Perennials

Primula auricula
Alpine primrose
Zones 3–9

Native to the Alps, these spring-flowering perennials are used to full exposure to sun with good drainage, but also prefer cool, misty summer temperatures. Where summers are hot and humid, they prefer a location with light shade and humus-rich, cool soil, such as close to a stone wall. A mulch of gravel also will help. Both the species and their hybrids have astonishing colors—most have a white or yellow eye surrounded by a dark zone then another color tint around the petal rim. So striking and varied are the flower forms that they are grown indoors under glass for competitions at flower shows, hence their other common name, show auriculas. Plants form a rosette of smooth oval leaves and flower stems that rarely exceed 6 inches (15 cm).

Primula denticulata
Drumstick primrose
Zones 5–9

Native to the mountains of Afghanistan, plants produce globular flower clusters in mostly shades of pink and white above rosettes of oval, toothed leaves. Plants bloom extra-early in spring, at the same time as daffodils, on flower stems up to 10 inches (25 cm) high. Use them to colonize moisture-retentive soil in sun or light shade in bog gardens and along streams.

Primula florindae
Himalayan primrose
Zones 6–9

A Tibetan species, this is a giant among bog-loving primroses, growing flower stalks up to 3 feet (91 cm) high topped by nodding, fragrant, yellow flower clusters. The leaves are heart shaped and arranged in a rosette. Spectacular partnered with hostas and ferns.

Primula veris
Cowslip
Zones 5–9

Native to open meadows in Europe, plants form a rosette of oval, ribbed leaves and erect flower stems up to 10 inches (25 cm) high topped by nodding yellow flowers. They are suitable for colonizing rock gardens or lightly shaded woodland paths in humus-rich soil and good drainage.

Primula vulgaris
English primrose
Zones 6–9

Native to woodlands and hedgerows of Europe, plants form a rosette of rounded, straplike, ribbed leaves and a dome of cheerful pale yellow flowers up to 1 1/4 inches (3 cm) across. Especially beautiful partnered with English bluebells along lightly shaded woodland paths.

Prunella grandiflora
Selfheal

Zones 5–9

A member of the mint family native to Eurasia, flowers are mostly rose-pink and form a spike. Leaves are smooth and oval. Plants grow to 12 inches (31 cm) and thrive in full sun in a well-drained soil. Suitable for planting as drifts in mixed borders and rock gardens. Propagate by division.

Rudbeckia fulgida
Black-eyed Susan

Zones 4–9

Native to North America, this wayside and prairie plant grows to 3 feet (91 cm) tall with an upright habit. Yellow, daisylike flowers have dark brown centers up to 3 inches (8 cm) wide and are produced in profusion during summer. Leaves are gray-green, pointed and narrow. Good for meadow gardens, mixed beds and borders. Easy to grow even in impoverished soils, although it flowers best in moist loam soil in full sun. Propagate by seed and root division. 'Goldsturm' is a compact sterile form that produces an especially brilliant floral display.

Rodgersia pinnata
Featherleaf rodgersia

Zones 4–9

This rodgersia forms a very large, shrublike plant upon maturity and grows up to 4 feet (1.2 m) tall with bold textured leaves and red flower blooms in early to midsummer. The cultivar 'Superba' has attractive bronze leaves. They prefer humus-rich moist to wet soil in full sun to partial shade. *R. aesculifolia* (fingerleaf rodgersia) is the largest of the rodgersias, growing to 6 feet (1.8 m) tall with creamy white flowers. *R. sambucifolia* (elderberry rodgersia) is the hardiest, smallest and earliest to bloom, reaching 4 feet (1.2 m) tall with white or pink flowers.

Sagina subulata
Pearlwort, Scotch moss

Zones 4–8

This low-growing groundcover from the coast of Scotland is a favorite for planting between flagstones and to edge mixed borders. The mat of slender, grassy leaves is soft to touch with a galaxy of small, white, daisylike flowers occurring in late spring. Plants grow to 4 inches (10 cm) high and spread 12 inches (31 cm) or more. They prefer sandy, well-drained soil, except in coastal locations, where morning mist can keep the leaves moist. Full sun can be too harsh unless some shade is provided. The variety 'Aurea' has yellow-green leaves, which allows the dark green and light green to form checkerboard squares. Propagate by seed and division.

Salvia x sylvestris
Blue sage

Zones 5–9

A hybrid of species native to Europe, this stunning border plant grows to 2 feet (61 cm) tall with an upright, spreading habit. Violet-blue flowers are borne in summer on long spikes, densely crowded together, making a strong display in mixed borders or massed alone in beds. Slender stems have narrow pointed leaves. Prefers sandy, fertile soil in full sun or light shade. Propagate by root division. Several other hardy kinds of salvia resemble *S. x sylvestris*, including *S. pratensis*, meadow clary (zones 3–9), with lavender blue flowers; *S. sylvestris* 'May Night', May night salvia (zones 5–9), with dark blue/purple flowers. Both consistently earn high praise for density of color and flawless bloom.

Perennials

Saponaria ocymoides
Soapwort
Zones 4–8

Native to Europe, this drought-resistant alpine plant grows to 6 inches (15 cm) tall with a low, ground-hugging habit. Dainty, bright pink, star-shaped flowers are produced profusely in spring on trailing stems. Dark green, lance-shaped leaves are small and pointed. Excellent choice for rock gardens and dry walls. Easy to grow in most well-drained soils in sun or partial shade. Propagated by seed and root division. Spring flowering.

Scabiosa caucasica
Pincushion flower
Zones 4–9

Native to Europe, this plant grows to 3 feet (91 cm) tall with an upright, spreading habit. The flat, ruffled, blue flowers have a pale crest in the center and are held erect on long, slender stems in summer. Leaves are narrow and indented. Popular as an accent in mixed beds and borders; it is also superb for cutting. Easy to grow in most well-drained garden soils in full sun but may need staking. Propagate by seed or root division.

Sedum spectabile
Stonecrop
Zones 4–9

Native to China and Japan, this drought-resistant plant grows 2 feet (61 cm) tall with an upright, clump-forming habit. Bright pink flower clusters are flattened and circular. Flowering in late summer, the individual star-shaped flowers are small but are crowded together in a tight mass up to 6 inches (15 cm) wide. Leaves are blue-gray, succulent, smooth and pointed. Plants are excellent for garden display in mixed borders and rock gardens, or massed alone in beds. 'Brilliant' is an extremely bold pink selection; 'Autumn Joy', a hybrid of *S. spectabile*, has deep rosy-red flowers that turn bronze and persist all winter. The dried flower heads are valued for flower arrangements. Plants tolerate poor soil but prefer fertile loam in full sun. Propagated by cuttings and root division.

Scabiosa columbaria
Pincushion flower
Zones 5–9

Though smaller flowered than its hardy cousin, *S. caucasica*, the ever-blooming character of two varieties in particular— 'Butterfly Blue' and 'Pink Mist'—have made them superior for long-lasting display. Plants grow to 18 inches (46 cm) with green indented leaves and long, wiry flower stems topped by pincushion flowers that remain in bloom from spring until autumn frost. Use them for edging mixed borders and massing in rock gardens. Give them full sun and good drainage. Propagate by cutting and division.

SOLIDAGO HYBRIDS

Goldenrod

Zones 4–9

Mostly native to North America, there are at least 130 species. The tall varieties are suitable for meadow gardens in company with New England asters and ornamental grasses, but the dwarf varieties, such as 'Peter Pan' and 'Golden Fleece', are suitable for mixed borders, grow to 3 feet (91 cm) and flower in mid- to late summer. The small, yellow, daisylike flowers are tightly clustered in a plume. Leaves are narrow and toothed. Easy to grow in full sun and moisture-retentive or well-drained soils. Useful in mixed borders and beside water features such as streams and ponds. They spread by underground stolons and can become invasive. Propagate the hybrids by division. (See photograph previous page—*Solidago* is the yellow-flowered plant behind the pink *Sedum spectabile*.)

Stachys byzantina

Lambs' ears

Zones 3–9

Native to Turkey and southwest Asia, this plant produces dense, ground-hugging rosettes of silvery-gray, silky leaves and grows to 18 inches (46 cm) tall spreading by surface runners. The plants tend to die out in the center after several years. In this case, the dead sections should be cut out, and the young plants from the outer rim of the clump can be replanted. This plant is grown mainly for its foliage effect, and the flower spikes are often cut off. Hot, humid air and continuous rain can damage the leaves, but the plant usually recovers. Several varieties are in cultivation, such as 'Silver Carpet' and 'Countess Helene von Stein', which produce few flowering stems and are therefore less of a seeding problem. Grows best in full sun but will tolerate some shade.

Silene schafta
Catchfly, Campion

Zones 5–8

Up to 500 species are widely distributed throughout the world and many are suitable for garden displays. This species comes from the Caucasus Mountains and grows to 6 inches (15 cm).

The smooth, spear-shaped leaves form a rosette, and the flowers are mostly rose-pink. Plants are suitable for edging mixed borders and rock gardens. Propagate by seed and division.

Stokesia laevis
Stokes' aster

Zones 5–9

Native to North America, this plant grows 2 feet (61 cm) tall with a bushy, spreading habit. Powder-blue flowers resembling giant cornflowers appear in spring up to 4 inches (10 cm) across. Leaves are narrow and serrated like China asters. Good for mixed beds and borders, also suitable for cutting. Easy to grow in most well-drained garden soils in sun or partial shade. Propagate by seed or root division.

Thalictrum aquilegifolium
Meadow rue

Zones 3–9

Native to Europe and Asia, this is the showiest of about 100 species. Plants grow to 3 feet (91 cm) high with clover-shaped, blue-green leaves forming a mounded bush. Out of the center rise erect flower stems up to 5 feet (1.5 m) high topped with frothy pink, white and purple flower clusters. Plants prefer full sun or light shade and good drainage. Useful as a background for mixed borders.

Perennials

Tiarella cordifolia
Foamflower
Zones 3–9

Native to the eastern U.S., plants have attractive ivy-shaped leaves and spread by stolons to form a dense groundcover. Erect flower stems up to 18 inches (46 cm) high are topped by white flower spikes. A similar species, *T. wherryi* (zones 5–9), is clump forming rather than spreading. Both are suitable for massing along woodland paths. Tiarellas have been crossed with heuchera to produce many hybrids, some with bicolored or tricolored leaves.

Trillium chloropetalum
Toad trillium
Zones 6–9

These plants are highly desirable for woodland. Mottled green leaves form a collar of threes with three-petalled flowers held erect like a candle. Colors include maroon, pink, white and creamy yellow.

Trillium grandiflorum
White wakerobin
Zones 5–9

One of a large number of shade-loving plants native to North America. Smooth, oval leaves up to 18 inches (46 cm) high form a collar for the three-petalled, 3-inch (8 cm) wide flowers. Plants prefer humus-rich soil and are suitable for massing along woodland paths. There is a double-flowered form that resembles a gardenia.

Trollius europaeus
Globeflower
Zones 5–8

Native to Europe, this bog-loving plant grows to 2 feet (61 cm) with an upright, clump-forming habit. Spring-flowering, buttercup yellow, globular flowers are borne erect on slender stems. Leaves are serrated. Popular for stream banks and pond margins; suitable for cutting. Prefers moist, fertile, humus-rich soil in sun or partial shade. Propagate by seed or root division.

VERONICA

Speedwell
Zones 4–8

Native to Europe, this is a large, highly varied, perennial plant family noted for its blue flowers. *V. longifolia* grows to 3 feet (91 cm) tall, generally with an erect habit and elegant spires of blue, white and pink flowers. Leaves are often lance-like and dark green. They are a popular accent for mixed beds and borders. Easy to grow in any well-drained garden soil in full sun. May need staking. Propagate by seed and root division. Since there is much confusion in nurseries as to the species of a cultivar, veronicas should be purchased by cultivar name. Recommended varieties include 'Sunny Border Blue', with crinkled, glossy, bright green leaves with short spikes of violet blue flowers. It is long blooming and grows to a height of 2 feet (61 cm). 'Goodness Grows' is a low-growing edging plant that also makes an excellent groundcover. It grows up to 1 foot (31 cm) tall and produces upright spikes of long-blooming, rich blue flowers. *V. spicata* (spike speedwell) has green foliage and *V. spicata* subsp. *incana* (wooly speedwell) has silvery furry foliage. Hybrids of these two species now contain the genes of both and come in all sizes, leaf textures and colors. They grow to 2 feet (61 cm) and have narrow, upright spikes of blue, pink, purple, red or white flowers. 'Red Fox' is a cultivar of this species and has deep rose pink blooms. *V. peduncularis* 'Georgia Blue' is a vigorous, low-growing, matt-forming plant that grows up to 4 inches (10 cm) tall with spring-flowering, brilliant blue, free-blooming flowers.

Veronicastrum virginicum
Culver's root

Zones 3–9

A North American native, the 'Rosea' variety produces tall, erect flower stems up to 6 feet (1.8 m) topped by a tapering spike of white or pale pink flowers. Valued for massing in mixed borders, not only for its decorative flowers, but also for its dried seed heads when planted among ornamental grasses. Leaves are spear shaped and finely toothed. Propagate by seed and division.

VIOLAS

Violets and Pansies

Zones 4–9, depending on variety

Most people think of pansies and violas only as "supporting players" in flower gardens—for interspersing among spring bulbs, as an edging to flower beds and for brightening up containers such as window box planters. However, they can be the main feature of a lightly shaded "viola garden" in front of a Victorian-style gazebo, and they stay colorful from early spring to early summer, when the heat tends to exhaust them.

The great Victorian plantswoman Gertrude Jekyll also had a pansy garden, which was immortalized in a watercolor painting by Thomas Hunn. Yellow, orange and blue varieties were planted as a mixture in front of a gardener's cottage, and a few clumps of tulips strike through to provide some contrasting height and red highlights.

Pansies are hybrids of species found in the French and Swiss Alps, notably *V. tricolor*, and bloom mostly in open, sunlit meadows. They are best treated as annuals for early spring bedding, or as biennials planted into flowering positions in autumn for extra-early spring bloom. Indeed, the oldest pansy breeder in the world is the Swiss company Roggli Seeds, which continues an aggressive hybridizing program in an Alpine village overlooking Lake Thun. Their varieties tend to honor Swiss place names, such as 'Thunersee' (a gorgeous sky blue), 'Eiger' (a bold yellow) and 'Alpenglow' (a red), all with handsome blotched faces that give them near human characteristics. They are known botanically as *V. x wittrockiana* varieties and like *V. tricolor* are hardy from zones 4–8.

Following the lead set by the Roggli family, both Japanese and American plant breeders have developed similar large-flowered hybrids, including 'Majestic Giants' from Sakata (Japan), the 'Imperial' strain from Takii (Japan), and the 'Universal' series from Goldsmith Seeds (U.S.). The 'Universal' family does not have the size of the 'Majestic Giants' and is not as long flowering as the 'Imperials', but it produces an amazing number of flowers right into the summer months. Most have black petal markings, which tend to add distinction to the flowers.

Pansies are one of the few flowers that include all the primary colors in their color range—red, yellow and blue. Even tulips are missing a true blue, and sweet peas are missing a true yellow. The 'Universal' series has 19 colors, and it is hard to beat for a mixed display.

Although the wild species of pansies are perennial, hybridized varieties are capable of blooming within 10 weeks from seed sowing. The same is true of many violas, a cross between pansies and wild violets, which are smaller flowered than pansies. Violas have never had much popularity, because they tend to be susceptible to heat stress. Two new everblooming varieties are now worth consideration: the 'Sorbet' and 'Penny' series. Similar in appearance, they create compact mounds of cheerful "whiskered" faces in mostly blue, purple, white and yellow. They are especially good for edging and for displaying in containers. Provided they are watered and fed with a diluted liquid fertilizer throughout the summer, these new violas often will bloom continuously from spring through summer and into the autumn months.

Violets, including the blue, white and yellow types, are usually native to moist woodland, shale slopes and moist meadows. They are spring flowering and are worth cultivating as a garden flower, particularly as an edging to flower beds and as drifts in rock gardens. At one time, violets were so popular as a cut flower that the town of Rhinebeck, New York, supported 138 growers with greenhouses, but now only one survives. These are the special, sweetly scented, double-flowered 'Parma' violets, grown for fashionable women to wear as a corsage with fine gowns. 'Parma' violets are sterile and can only be grown from division. They are derived from the sweetly scented violet, *V. odorata*, the English violet (zones 8–9), and prefer a frost-free Mediterranean climate, or cultivation under glass.

An especially good perennial family of violets is botanically known as *Viola tricolor*, but more commonly called 'Johnny Jump-ups'. They have the advantage of growing dense clumps of heart-shaped green leaves and masses of cheerful bicolored and tricolored faces, mostly blue and yellow with black whiskers. They are invaluable for edging. I like to see them partnered with primroses and pink, fern-leaf bleeding hearts. Although their flowering performance lasts no more than three weeks, they are perennial and self-seeding, so that it is possible to have a self-perpetuating colony.

ABOVE: *Viola odorata* (sweet violet).

Yucca filamentosa
Adam's needle

Zones 5–10

Native to Mexico and the U.S., this drought-tolerant plant grows to 6 feet (1.8 m) tall with a spiky, clump-forming habit. From the center of each clump emerges a flower spike resembling a huge asparagus spear, which opens out in early summer into a fountain of creamy white flowers. The leaves have nasty points as sharp as nails. Plants are best used as accents at the back of beds and borders, but are also suitable for massing on dry slopes for erosion control and in rock gardens. The flowers are edible in salads and taste like Belgian endive. Variegated forms with golden stripes are available such as 'Golden Sword'. Related species: *Y. glauca* (soapweed) has narrower leaves and is more ornamental when used in containers. Easy to grow in most well-drained soils in full sun. Propagated by division of offsets.

Shrubs

Although the planting of shrubs has much in common with trees, they perform different functions in the landscape; therefore, there is a good reason to list them individually. Both belong to a distinct group within the plant kingdom known as woody plants, because they form a durable cell structure called wood. Forming roots and branches, wood builds the framework that permits shrubs to grow larger, and generally live longer, than herbaceous plants such as annuals, perennials and bulbs.

The accepted definition of a tree is a woody plant that tends to form a single trunk capable of growing 15 feet (4.5 m) or higher. Shrubs are generally defined as woody plants under 15 feet (4.5 m) high that form multiple stems and a thicket of twiggy branches.

However, these definitions are arbitrary, because there are too many anomalies to make any hard and fast rules. For example, in its juvenile stage Euonymus alatus—known as burning bush for its red autumn foliage coloration—grows shrubby with a cluster of main stems and a thicket of branches. But in time it produces a thick main trunk and spreading canopy to become a handsome tree up to 20 feet (6.1 m) tall.

Conversely, many trees can be kept shrublike by heavy pruning to control size and encourage multiple stems.

From a design standpoint, shrubs are usually used as low, decorative highlights, for example, along the house foundation and as lawn accents and hedges. Some have pliable or flexible branches that can be used to climb, and many of the spreading types, such as rug junipers, are suitable for groundcover.

Abelia x grandiflora
Glossy abelia
Zones 5–9

This spreading, multi-stemmed, bushy shrub grows to 5 feet (1.5 m) high and equally as wide. Prefers moist, well-drained, acidic soil in full sun to partial shade. Generally evergreen, plants are grown primarily for the lustrous, dark green, shiny foliage that is paler green beneath. Leaves are small, slender and look bronze from a distance. The funnel-shaped flowers bloom from July in white or pink. The dense, arching branches make a good hedge or bank cover. These are readily pruned to a desirable height. 'Edward Goucher' (zones 6–9) has slightly larger flowers and a deeper pink color.

Actinidia arguta
Hardy kiwi
See Fruit & Nuts, page 215.

Aesculus parviflora
Bottlebrush buckeye
Zones 5–9

Native to North America, this suckering shrub grows to 10 feet (3 m) tall. Its leaves are typical of chestnuts, dark green, divided into oval leaflets 9 inches (23 cm) or more long and bronze when young but yellow in autumn. In midsummer, plants bear spidery white flowers with protruding stamens in conical spires up to 12 inches (31 cm) long. Tolerant of all but very poorly drained sites, it needs room to spread 10 feet (3 m) and more. Suitable for slope cover and as a lawn accent in parkland.

Aesculus pavia
Red buckeye
Zones 5–8

Native to the eastern U.S., this conical shrub or small tree grows to 15 feet (4.5 m) high, producing palmate, dark green leaves 5 inches (13 cm) or more long, and conical spires of 6-inch (15 cm) tall red flowers in early summer. This is followed by spiny nut cases containing smooth-skinned, brown, nutlike seeds. Plants tolerate a wide range of soil conditions in full sun.

LEFT: Camperdown elm at Parkside Garden, Oamaru, New Zealand, with branches trained to cover a columned shelter.

Encyclopedia of Hardy Plants | 115

Shrubs

Amorpha canescens
Lead plant
Zones 2–6

Native to central North America, this rounded shrub produces hairy, gray-white shoots and smooth, narrow leaves. Small, pea-like, dark violet-purple flowers are borne in spikes up to 6 inches (15 cm) long in late summer and early autumn. Plants grow to 4 feet (1.2 m) tall and are suitable for mixed shrub borders. *A. fruticosa*, false indigo (zones 2–8), is a related species, growing to 20 feet (6.1 m) high. Native to the eastern U.S., this fast-growing, spreading shrub has legume-like leaves up to 12 inches (31 cm) long. Orange or yellow-anthered purple-blue flowers are produced in narrow spikes to 6 inches (15 cm) long in summer. It is often a component of herb gardens.

Aronia arbutifolia
Red chokeberry
Zones 5–9

Native to the eastern U.S., this compact, erect shrub grows to 10 feet (3 m) tall, tends to sucker and forms a colony. Easily propagated by seed, it has narrow, oval, dark green leaves that turn red in autumn. Brilliant red, hawthornlike berries persist into winter months if not eaten by songbirds. Grows in most moisture-retentive but well-drained soils in sun or partial shade. 'Brilliantissima' has especially heavy berry production and strong autumn foliage color. *A. melanocarpa*, black chokeberry (zones 3–8), bears black berries 1 inch (2.5 cm) across.

Aucuba japonica 'Variegata'
Japanese laurel
Zones 6–10

Native to Japan, this eye-catching, compact, evergreen shrub grows to 10 feet (3 m) tall with a dense, bushy habit and is usually multi-stemmed with dark, lustrous, showy leaves and gold flecking. Small, purple, inconspicuous flowers are followed by red berries, which will persist until the following spring on female plants. Prefers well-drained, moist, high organic soil in dappled shade. Can be grown as a houseplant. Unless sheltered, the leaves can suffer browning from cold winds and sunburn.

Berberis thunbergii 'Crimson Pygmy'
Japanese barberry
Zones 5–8

Native to Japan, this bronze leaf variety grows to 3 feet (91 cm) high with a dense, rounded habit. Small, inconspicuous, white flowers in spring are followed by decorative, oval, red berries in autumn. Popular clustered as a colony to create a ground or slope cover. Also, it may be used as a low hedge, as a specimen in a rock garden or to create a parterre. Requires full sun to maintain the dark leaf color. Thrives in most soils and tolerates drought. Taller types, growing to 5 feet (1.5 m) high include 'Rose Glow' with leaves that appear to be pink on mature specimens. 'Aurea', of similar height, has bright yellow juvenile foliage.

Buddleia davidii
Butterfly bush
Zones 5–9

In cold winter climates, the top often freezes to the ground but roots remain hardy to sprout and flower again in spring. Native to China, this fast-growing shrub grows to 10 feet (3 m) tall with a bushy habit. Lance-shaped leaves are dark green above and downy white below. In midsummer, dense, arching, spikelike flowers resembling lilacs appear at the branch tips and attract butterflies. Prefers well-drained, fertile soil in full sun and is suitable for containers. *Buddleia alternifolia* (Fountain butterfly bush) grows 12 feet (3.6 m) high and wide. Trained as a standard tree form, it makes an excellent weeping small tree.

Buxus sempervirens
Common boxwood
Zones 5–9

Native to southern Europe, northern Africa and western Asia, this dense, slow-growing, evergreen shrub will grow to 20 feet (6.1 m) tall, but usually is kept low and bushy by pruning in winter. Lustrous, dark green, oval leaves make it a preferred choice for creating topiary figures and mazes. The true dwarf variety 'Suffruticosa' (edging box) grows to just 3 feet (91 cm) high and is suitable for edging paths and borders. Boxwood thrives in either full sun or light shade. In harsh winter climates, it is best to set the plants where they will be sheltered from cold winds, which can brown the foliage. Also, any snow that settles on the leaves should be brushed away before it has a chance to freeze, as this may also cause the leaves to turn brown.

Callicarpa dichotoma
Purple beautyberry
Zones 5–8

Native to eastern and central China, this beautiful berry-bearing shrub is the most graceful and refined of the species with a bushy arching habit. The plants grow to 4 feet (1.2 m) high and bear beautiful violet-purple berries in late summer that attract songbirds. The berries can last up to three weeks after the golden leaves fall in autumn. Tolerates most well-drained soils in full sun, but is also suitable for light shade. Plants are often pruned in the spring to within 6 inches (15 cm) of the ground in order to force juvenile growth and a bountiful crop of berries. In colder climates, the plants will freeze to the ground and reappear in the spring from dormant roots. Effective planted in groups in a shrub border.

Shrubs

Calluna vulgaris
Scotch heather
Zones 4–7

Native to Europe and Asia Minor, this cushion-shaped shrub grows to 2 feet (61 cm) high and 3 feet (91 cm) wide. There are hundreds of varieties, some selected for profuse flowering and others for colorful foliage. Dense leaves and a tight mesh of woody stems form thick mounds, making heather suitable for slope cover. The fragrant tubular flowers bloom in summer and autumn, depending on variety. Flower color includes white, pink, rose and purple. Prefers sandy, organic, moisture-retentive, well-drained, acidic soil in full sun or partial shade. Mulch to retain soil moisture. Heather is attractive to bees, and heather honey is a gourmet treat. It makes an excellent groundcover but may come under stress where summers are hot and humid.

Calycanthus floridus
Carolina allspice, Sweet shrub
Zones 5–9

Native to North America, this drought-resistant, multi-stemmed shrub grows 8 feet (2.4 m) tall by 10 feet (3 m) wide. The form varies from dense, to open and loosely branched depending on the soil and sun exposure. In clay soils and light shade, the shrub tends to grow more open. The twigs and leaves are fragrant when crushed, and the rusty-red flowers produce a strawberrylike aroma, especially at dusk. The spear-shaped leaves turn golden yellow in autumn. Grow in fertile, moist, humus-rich soil in sun or partial shade. Useful near sitting areas where the pleasant fragrance can be enjoyed in spring. 'Athens' has deeply fragrant, yellow flowers.

Camellia oleifera hybrids
Cold hardy camellia
Zones 6–9

Though *C. japonica* and *C. sasanqua*, the most widely grown camellias, are not recommended for gardens colder than zone 7, a series of interspecific crosses between these and the hardier Chinese species, *C. oleifera*, has resulted in a number of cold-hardy, evergreen camellias with good flower quality. Most are autumn flowering and have shown little or no winter injury at −12°F (−24°C).

Plants prefer a well-drained, acid soil with high humus content. Mulch should be applied at time of planting and maintained year round. These also benefit from light shade and shelter from wind. Fertilize minimally to prevent leggy, unattractive growth. They are recommended for home landscapes, especially as foundation plantings. Highly recommended are the varieties introduced by Dr. William L. Ackerman at the U.S. National Arboretum including 'Winter's Rose' (shell pink double), 'Winter's Beauty' (lavender pink double), 'Winter's Waterlily' (white double) and 'Winter Interlude' (deep pink double).

In severe winter areas, it is recommended that these plants be given a sheltered location. They should also be wrapped in burlap for their first two winters.

Caragana arborescens
Pea shrub

Zones 2–7

Native to Siberia and Mongolia, this very hardy deciduous shrub grows to 20 feet (6.1 m) tall in most soils (even almost pure sand) with an erect, oval habit. Plants are inclined to be straggly in growth unless heavily pruned at the end of each season. Can be cut to the ground to force dense juvenile growth. The flowers, which open in spring, are pealike in shape and vivid yellow in color. It creates an excellent windbreak or tall hedge.

Campsis radicans
Trumpet vine, Hummingbird vine

Zones 4–9

Native to the eastern U.S., this fast-growing vining plant grows to 40 feet (12.2 m) high. The lustrous, dark green leaves resemble wisteria. The vine clings to supports by means of aerial roots, which require a rough surface to grasp. Orange, yellow or scarlet trumpet-shaped flowers bloom non-stop all summer. Prefers full sun to bloom heavily. Prune back heavily in spring, since plants can grow 6 feet (1.8 m) or more in a season. Easily propagated by seed and can be used on strong trellises and arbors. The hybrid 'Madame Galen' has larger flowers than the species.

Caryopteris x *clandonensis*
Blue mist shrub
Zones 6–9

This bushy hybrid plant was developed from species native to Asia and grows to 3 feet (91 cm) high and wide. Generally grown with perennials, it is valued for its powder blue, mistlike flowers which occur midsummer to frost. Leaves are silvery green and narrow. Prefers light, loamy, well-drained soil in full sun. Cut back nearly to the ground in spring to encourage new growth since the flowers grow only on new shoots.

Ceanothus americanus
New Jersey tea

Zones 4–8

Native from Canada to Texas, this summer-flowering shrub grows from 4 feet (1.2 m) to 5 feet (1.5 m) wide with a broad, low-growing, compact habit. Tiny white flowers are borne in dense clusters at the tips of the branches. Tolerant of poor soil and light shade, it is a popular component of perennial borders.

Celastrus scandens
American bittersweet

Zones 3–8

Native to North America, including Canada, this vigorous vine grows 20 feet (6.1 m) or higher. It climbs by twining around tree trunks and can suffocate shrubs. The plant is grown for its generous clusters of orange fruit, which split open to reveal brilliant red-coated seeds inside. Flowers are small, white and bloom in early summer. Deep glossy green leaves turn yellowish green in winter. Grows well in most soils in full sun. Needs both a male and female plant for fruit set. Branches loaded with fruit are popular for indoor winter arrangements. *C. orbiculatus*, Chinese bittersweet (zones 4–8), is similar to American bittersweet but tends to be more rampant. While it is handsome in fruit, it has become a rather noxious weed in the northeastern U.S.

Cephalotaxus harringtonia
Plum yew

Zones 6–9

Native to southeast Asia, this evergreen coniferous shrub grows to 30 feet (9.1 m) tall and has dark, yewlike foliage, the undersurfaces of which have silver bands. It is reputed to be deer resistant. Prefers fertile, moisture-retentive, well-drained soil in partial shade and sheltered from wind. Can be severely sheared and is similar to a yew. The variety 'Prostrata' grows to 5 feet (1.5 m) high and is suitable for groundcover.

Chaenomeles speciosa
Flowering quince

Zones 5–9

Native to China, this early-flowering, dense shrub grows to 10 feet (3 m) tall and 12 feet (3.6 m) wide with a mounded, bushy habit. Grown primarily for the cup-shaped, 2-inch (5 cm) flowers with a color range from white to pink to scarlet red. Branches can be forced indoors during winter. Fragrant, yellowish, lemon-sized fruit appears in autumn. Shiny green leaves grow on thorny stems. Tolerant of poor soil, provided drainage is good. Prune to control shape and profuse bloom since flowers appear on new growth. A popular flowering shrub for Japanese gardens since the thorny branches and plumlike blossoms are a recurring motif of Japanese silk-screen art.

CLEMATIS SPECIES AND HYBRIDS

Virgin's bower

Zones 3–10, depending on variety

As a plant family, clematis offers such a wonderful assortment of colors, shapes and forms, especially the vining kinds, and in such generous flowering displays that they can be addictive. The shame is that too many of them are used alone to scramble up a trellis against a bare wall. They are best used in pairs of complementary colors and trained up into flowering trees, such as laburnum, or entwined with roses and azaleas so they mingle their blossoms with other profuse-flowering plants.

Although 300 species are known worldwide, relatively few are used for garden display with the majority of these being native mainly to China. The sight of these profuse-flowering vines climbing 20 feet (6.1 m) and higher, draped from top to toe in star-shaped flowers up to 6 inches (15 cm) across in shades of red, pink, blue and white, can be breathtaking. A particularly enchanting clematis display occurs each spring at Cross Hills Garden, New Zealand, where three varieties of *Clematis montana* (white, pale pink and deep pink) are draped like a curtain, down a cliff, in an avalanche of blossoms, mingling their colors above a stream and pond.

Clematis are classified into three groups according to their floral arrangement, and whether they bloom on old wood or new wood. The hybrids are further classified into nine groups according to their parentage. Suffice it to say that if a clematis variety blooms on old wood, it should not be pruned to the ground but thinned of weak or dead stems after flowering; and if it blooms on new wood, it can be cut to the ground to encourage as many new sprouts as possible. *C. montana*, from the Himalayas,

Shrubs

is an example of a species that blooms on old wood and is capable of covering a small cottage if desired. 'Nelly Moser' is an example of a hybrid that blooms on old wood but may benefit from thinning each season. The popular purple-flowered 'Jackmanii' is an example of a hybrid that blooms on new wood. Some clematis have a sweet scent like the late summer-flowering *C. terniflora* (sweet autumn clematis).

In nature, clematis vines scramble up into trees with their roots in cool shade, and their heads searching for the sun. This is a good way to grow them, for they demand a moisture-retentive, organic-rich soil and prefer shade or mulching to keep the soil cool. They are eminently suitable for decorating gazebos, arches and arbors. They climb by twining their stems around branches, wire or wooden slats. If trained to a wall, black invisible netting makes a good support. Described here are some popular species and varieties:

Clematis florida 'Sieboldii'
Zones 6–9

Native to China, this species has six-petalled, pointed, white flowers with a central crown of purple stamens around a green center. Individual flowers grow to 4 inches (10 cm) across and draw admiration for their similarity in appearance to hardy passion vines.

Clematis 'Duchess of Edinburgh'
Zones 4–9

There are many gorgeous white-flowered clematis, such as the single-flowered 'Henryi' [up to 8 inches (20 cm) across]. The slightly fragrant 'Duchess of Edinburgh' is a semi-double with several layers of pure white petals up to 5 inches (13 cm) wide. Both are early summer flowering and sensational as a cut flower.

Clematis 'Ernest Markham'
Zones 3–9

Although not large flowered, it makes up for lack of size by its dark red petals and free-flowering performance in summer at the same time as 'Jackmanii'. The two entwined make a stunning color combination. Flowers are up to 5 inches (13 cm) wide and are borne on new wood.

Clematis 'Jackmanii'
Zones 3–9

A popular old-fashioned variety developed by an English nursery at the turn of the century. Deep purple petals are freely produced on new wood. Flowers measure up to 4 inches (10 cm) wide and contrast well with pink roses. Many improved varieties have been introduced including 'Jackmanii Superba' with flowers up to 5 inches (13 cm) across, and often sold simply as 'Jackmanii'.

Clematis 'Nelly Moser'
Zones 4–9

An old-fashioned bicolored, pale pink with a darker pink stripe down the middle of each petal, named for the wife of a French nurseryman. Flowers are eight-petalled and up to 7 inches (18 cm) wide. 'Nelly Moser' is a very popular hybrid, although 'Dr. Ruppel' is similar but more intensely colored. Plants are good for cutting and benefit from the thinning of crowded stems after flowering in spring. Thread through rose bushes and Exbury azaleas for a stunning plant partnership.

Clematis montana
Mountain clematis

Zones 6–9

Few gardeners appreciated the full flowering potential of this Himalayan species better than Claude Monet. He erected a high, horizontal metal trellis in his garden so the vines of white and pink flowers could extend 30 feet (9.1 m) and drape their blossoms like a lace curtain or galaxy of stars above his tulip beds. The individual flowers are four-petalled, up to 3 inches (8 cm) in diameter and are produced on old wood.

Clematis tangutica
Yellow virgin's bower

Zones 4–9

Native to Mongolia, masses of pendant, golden-yellow, bell-shaped flowers bloom in midsummer and are followed by fluffy, white, decorative seed heads. Although not large, at less than 2 inches (5 cm) across, the cheerful flowers have a charm quite distinct from other flowering vines. They bloom on new wood.

Clematis terniflora
Sweet autumn clematis

Zones 5–9

This aggressive, late summer-flowering climber is native to Japan, but naturalized throughout the eastern United States, where it is known incorrectly as *C. paniculata* or *C. maximowicziana!* Small, star-shaped, white flowers cluster so densely on new wood that they create a fleece-like appearance, completely hiding the small, rounded leaves. However, it must have long, hot summers to flower well. Most vining clematis can be grown as a groundcover, but they look unnatural sprawling across the ground. Sweet autumn clematis, however, creates a splendid, tightly-knit, weed-suffocating groundcover, especially on slopes.

Clethra alnifolia
Summersweet

Zones 3–9

Native to the eastern U.S., this summer-flowering, deciduous shrub grows to 8 feet (2.4 m) high with a rounded, suckering habit. It does well in full sun or part shade, but the autumn foliage color is better in full sun. White, sweet-scented flowers in erect clusters known as "candles" appear at the branch tips when few other shrubs are blooming. Tolerant of most soils, plants grow best in acid, humus-rich situations. Use it in a perennial border, beside a pool or stream, and in wild gardens. 'Rosea' has flowers ranging in color from almost white to deeper shades of pink.

Shrubs

Comptonia peregrina
Sweet fern
Zones 4–7

Native to the northeastern U.S., this bushy, deciduous shrub is not a true fern, and though its summer flowers are inconspicuous, it merits space on account of its pleasantly aromatic, slender, serrated leaves. These plants prefer a sandy or humus-rich, acidic soil in full sun or partial shade. Sweet fern is good to use in wild gardens and as a slope cover.

Cornus sericea aka *Cornus stolonifera*
Red osier dogwood
Zones 3–9

Native to North America, this shrubby dogwood grows to 8 feet (2.4 m) high, but it is generally kept below 6 feet (1.8 m) by pruning in summer after flowering, allowing new growth to emerge by autumn frosts. Whiplike stems grow skyward; in the juvenile state, these are a brilliant red color and stand out as a beautiful ornamental accent in winter when the leaves have fallen. White flowers are borne in flat clusters and appear soon after the leaves in spring. The bright green leaves are oval, pointed and serrated with prominent leaf veins typical of dogwoods. Tolerates a wide range of soil conditions, including wet soil, in full sun. Popular for massing on berms, beside ponds and streams, it is also a good accent in mixed shrub borders and foundation plantings, especially planted against white stucco walls or white picket fences where the red winter bark color stands out dramatically. 'Flaviramea' (yellow-twig dogwood) has bright yellow stems that contrast well with the red.

C. *alba* (tatarian dogwood) and C. *sanguinea* (bloodtwig dogwood) are similar species with red stems. C. *sanguinea* 'Winter Beauty' is an unusual orange-stemmed variety, and when the red, yellow and orange-twigged kinds are clustered, the combined effect can be sensational. C. *alba* 'Elegantissima' (variegated tatarian dogwood) has red stems and attractive green and white variegated foliage.

Corylopsis glabrescens
Fragrant winter hazel
Zones 5–9

Native to China, this early spring-flowering, deciduous shrub grows to 5 feet (1.5 m) high and wide with a branching habit. It is valued for the soft yellow, fragrant flowers that bloom on bare stems. Dark green, oval-shaped leaves turn golden in the autumn. Plants prefer a well-drained, moisture-retentive, acidic soil in partial shade or in a sheltered sunny location. Branches can be cut and taken indoors in the spring to use in floral arrangements. Popular as a foundation shrub and as a winter accent underplanted with snowdrops, aconites, snow crocus and hellebores.

Corylus avellana 'Contorta'
Harry Lauder's walking stick
Zones 4–9

Native to Europe, western Asia and northern Africa, this large, multi-stemmed shrub grows to 20 feet (6.1 m) high, forming a rounded top with a leggy or open base. The stems and leaves are curled and twisted, which makes it excellent to use as cutting material for flower arrangements. Generous quantities of yellow catkins appear in early spring before the leaves unfurl. Prefers well-drained loam soil in full sun or light shade.

Cotinus coggygria
Smoke bush
Zones 5–8

Native to southern Europe and central China, this large, brittle shrub grows to 15 feet (4.5 m) high and wide with an upright, billowing habit. The regular form has brown or purplish bark with blue-green leaves. In summer, clusters of smoke-like, pale-pink flowers produce a spectacular show creating a cloudlike effect above the foliage. Small, kidney-shaped fruit develops after the flowers fade. Some varieties have purple leaves and purple flower stems. Plants are adaptable to a wide range of soil types in full sun. They can be pruned in winter to get a more compact, bushy effect. Use as a lawn accent, a foundation plant and at the edge of woodland.

Cotoneaster horizontalis
Rockspray cotoneaster
Zones 5–7

Native to China, this tightly-branched, low-growing, deciduous shrub grows to 4 feet (1.2 m) tall by 10 feet (3 m) wide. Plants prefer well-drained soil in full sun with good air circulation. Round, half-inch (1.3 cm) long leaves turn a lovely bronze color in the autumn. Branches spread by side shoots and give the overall appearance of a fish-bone pattern. The early summer pink flowers are inconspicuous, but are followed by bright red berries that last through the autumn and into the winter months. Excellent groundcover that is often used in rock gardens to spill over boulders and retaining walls.

Shrubs

Cytisus scoparius
Scotch broom

Zones 5–8

Native to central and southern Europe, this short-lived shrub grows to 6 feet (1.8 m) high and wide with a bushy, mounded habit. The outstretched, slender, medium green stems and twigs keep their color throughout the winter. Leaves are a light to medium green with no autumn color. Bright yellow, pea-like flowers bloom profusely on old wood in early summer. Plants are drought tolerant and prefer well-drained, sandy soil in full sun. Suitable for mixed perennial borders and as a hedge plant, especially in coastal gardens.

Daphne x burkwoodii
Burkwood daphne

Zones 4–8

A hybrid of wild species native to China, this compact shrub grows to 4 feet (1.2 m) high with a mounded habit. The semi-evergreen leaves are lustrous dark green above and lighter green beneath. The fragrant, pinkish-white flower clusters occur in spring, followed by bright clusters of red berries. Plants prefer well-drained, moisture-retentive and slightly acidic soil in light shade. Use in mixed perennial borders, foundation plantings and beside walkways. 'Carol Mackie' is a popular variety with blue-green foliage and a pronounced creamy leaf margin.

Deutzia gracilis
Slender deutzia

Zones 4–8

Native to Japan, this graceful weeping shrub grows to 4 feet (1.2 m) high with a compact, mounded habit. Wide-spreading and arching branches carry slender green leaves that turn slightly bronze in the autumn. Flowers profusely in spring in a mass of fragrant, white, star-shaped blooms. Prefers moist garden soils in full sun or very light shade. Prune after flowering to maintain a tidy shape and is suitable for making an informal hedge. 'Nikko' is especially compact and free flowering, growing to just 2 feet (61 cm) high and 5 feet (1.5 m) wide.

Eleutherococcus sieboldianus
'Variegatus' aka *Acanthopanax sieboldianus*
Five-leaf aralia

Zones 5–8

Native to eastern China, this eye-catching, tropical-looking, deciduous shrub has decorative greenish-white flowers in small clusters that are borne in spring. Plants grow arching stems that have short thorns situated below each bright green leaf. The leaves are attractively edged in white and are comprised of up to seven leaflets arranged like the fingers on a hand. This tough plant's virtues include a high tolerance for difficult conditions such as shade, too much or too little water, poor soil and urban air pollution.

Enkianthus campanulatus
Redvein enkianthus

Zones 4–7

Native to Japan, this large, deciduous shrub grows to 15 feet (4.5 m) tall with an upright, bushy habit. Beautiful, creamy yellow flowers resembling lily of the valley are tinged pink and appear in spring. The small, pointed, dark green leaves resembling azaleas turn orange and red in autumn. Prefers acidic soil in sun or partial shade. Good for foundation plantings, containers, bonsai and hedges. The twiggy silhouette looks beautiful in the winter landscape, especially when coated with frost or snow.

Erica carnea
Winter heath

Zones 5–7

These mounded, low-growing evergreen plants are related to *Calluna* and require the same general conditions of growth. They differ from *Calluna* in being less cold hardy and having linear, spreading leaves rather than closely packed ones. Plants flower mainly in winter or spring [although *E. cinerea*, the Scottish bell heather (zones 6–8), flowers in late summer and autumn]. The genus *Erica* also has many more species than *Calluna*. Winter heaths are plants of compact, cushionlike habit and slow growth [under 10 inches (25 cm) tall], and are often massed in rock gardens. Flowers are little bells of white, rose, purple, yellow or green, depending on variety. This plant requires acidic soils of peat and sand in open sunny sites.

Euonymus alatus
Burning bush
Zones 4–7
Native to northeastern Asia and central China, this tough, deciduous shrub grows to 10 feet (3 m) high by 15 feet (4.5 m) wide with a mounded, bushy habit in its juvenile form. The dense thicket of branches have corklike protrusions called "wings." The main interest comes in the autumn when the deep green, oval leaves turn a brilliant crimson so intense the plant seems to be on fire, especially in full sun. Inconspicuous, tiny, greenish flower clusters bloom in spring and are followed by a sparse crop of orange-red berries. Plants grow well in most well-drained soils in sun or light shade. They will eventually grow into small trees. Stunning planted against dark evergreens so the autumn color is accentuated; it is also useful as a hedge to line a driveway. The related species E. *fortunei*, wintercreeper (zones 5–8), grows to just 3 feet (91 cm) high and 5 feet (1.5 m) wide. Though lacking good autumn color, it is useful as a groundcover or climbing evergreen to cover walls.

Shrubs

Exochorda racemosa
Pearlbush
Zones 5–9
Native to China, this spring-flowering shrub grows 15 feet (4.5 m) high and just as wide with a mounded, bushy habit. Although the flowers only last for a week in midspring, they are worth planting for the spectacular show of white, pearl-shaped buds that open into gorgeous flower clusters. The leaves are pointed, oval and attractive. Grows well in most well-drained soils in full sun. Shear branch tips to a dome shape to maintain a compact, dense-flowering habit.

Forsythia x *intermedia*
Forsythia
Zones 5–9
A hybrid cross, this early-flowering, deciduous shrub grows to 10 feet (3 m) high with an equal spread and a billowing habit. Grown for its prolific, deep yellow, 1-inch (2.5 cm) flowers that bloom with daffodils. The oval-shaped green leaves turn yellowish-green in autumn. Plants grow in most well-drained soils in full sun or light shade. Effective planted as an informal hedge, although forsythia can be sheared to create a formal design. It is also useful as a slope cover to control erosion. 'Lynwood Gold' is an especially generous-flowering, canary-yellow selection. 'Golden Times' has variegated green and gold leaves.

Fothergilla gardenii
Dwarf fothergilla
Zones 5–8
Native to the eastern U.S., this spring-flowering, deciduous shrub grows to 3 feet (91 cm) high with a similar or greater spread and an upright twiggy habit. White, fragrant flower spikes resemble pussy willows, bursting into bloom on leafless branches when tulips bloom. Attractive dark green leaves are leathery and turn a brilliant yellow to orange-scarlet in the autumn. Prefers well-drained, peaty or sandy acidic soil in full sun or partial shade. Effective planted beside water in combination with early-flowering azaleas. The flowering stems make attractive indoor floral arrangements. *F. major*, large fothergilla (zones 4–8), is hardier and grows up to 10 feet (3 m) high.

Gaultheria procumbens
Wintergreen

Zones 3–8

Native to the northeastern U.S. and Canada, this low-growing, creeping, evergreen shrub makes an interesting groundcover. The leaves emit a wintergreen odor when crushed and turn red in the autumn. Round scarlet berries occur in summer and persist into the winter months. Wintergreen oil is extracted from both the leaves and berries. Plants prefer light shade and an acid, moisture-retentive, humus-rich soil in company with mosses, ferns and hostas.

Hamamelis x intermedia
Witch hazel

Zones 5–8

These large, spreading, deciduous shrubs are hybrids between *H. japonica* and *H. mollis*, and may grow to 20 feet (6.1 m) tall if left unpruned. Witch hazels flower in late winter and early spring depending on the variety. Flower colors range from bright yellow to rusty red. 'Arnold Promise' has clear yellow flowers and generous flowering potential. 'Diane' has red flowers and 'Jelena' has copper-colored flowers. A grove containing all the colors can be a sensational sight to announce the end of winter. Give them full sun or light shade in a humus-rich, moisture-retentive soil.

Hedera helix
English ivy

Zones 5–10

Native to Europe and western Asia, this evergreen vining plant grows to 20 feet (6.1 m) high, climbing by means of aerial roots with which it grips rough or porous surfaces. Thick, leathery, dark green leaves are sharply lobed in the juvenile stage and smooth in the adult phase. However, there are hundreds of varieties with distinctive variegation, as well as vastly different leaf shapes and sizes. Some leaves may turn purplish in the autumn in exposed areas. Small greenish-white flowers are borne in clusters, followed by small black fruit. Thrives in most garden soils in full sun and even deep shade. English ivy makes a very good groundcover as well as a climber. Ivy holds soil, which discourages erosion and slippage on slopes. The small leaf varieties, such as 'Duckfoot' and 'Needlepoint', are used to create topiary designs by being grown over a wire framework filled with sphagnum moss.

Hibiscus syriacus
Rose of Sharon

Zones 5–9

Native to China and India, this large, billowing, deciduous shrub grows to 20 feet (6.1 m) tall by 10 feet (3 m) wide with a bushy, mounded habit. Bears 3-inch (8 cm) wide, hibiscuslike, single or double flowers in summer. Its flowering potential is amazing, in a color range that includes red, white and blue, plus bicolors. Plants prefer moist, fertile soils in full sun. Prune to maintain compact shape by shearing the multiple trunks to make a windbreak or hedge, or prune to a single trunk to make a small-flowering tree. 'Diana' has large white flowers up to 6 inches (15 cm) wide; 'Blue Bird' has light violet-blue flowers with red centers; and 'Red Heart' has white flowers with red centers. Some nurseries sell plants with all three colors grafted onto a common rootstock.

Hippophae rhamnoides
Sea buckthorn

Zones 3–8

This potentially large, deciduous shrub grows to 20 feet (6.1 m) tall with a bushy, thorny habit. Gray-green leaves resemble a willow. On female plants, flowers are followed by masses of spherical, bright orange, edible berries. These ripen in summer and persist into the autumn and winter months. Grow in full sun in well-drained, neutral to alkaline sandy soil. Useful as a hedge and accent in mixed shrub borders.

HYDRANGEA

Hortensis

Zones 4–9, depending on variety

The large plant family known as hydrangea consists of many species and hybrids with garden-worthy qualities. The most popular are commonly called "mopheads" because of their large, globular flowers in almost all shades of red and blue, plus white.

Hydrangeas generally require a moisture-retentive soil with good drainage, because they will wilt at the slightest sign of dry conditions. For most profuse flowering, the soil should be moderately fertile and humus-rich in sun or partial shade and sheltered from cold, drying winds. Yellowing of leaves usually is a sign of poor soil fertility. *H. macrophylla*, *H. serrata*, *H. quercifolia* and *H. anomala* subsp. *petiolaris* should be pruned after blooming to force branching, as they bloom on old wood. *H. arborescens* and *H. paniculata* bloom on new wood, so they may be pruned in the spring.

Hydrangea anomala subsp. *petiolaris*
Climbing hydrangea

Zones 4–9

Native to Russia, Korea, Taiwan and Japan, this vigorous, woody, deciduous vine climbs to 50 feet (15.2 m), clinging by aerial roots. Heart-shaped leaves are dark green, sometimes turning yellow in autumn. White flower clusters up to 10 inches (25 cm) across drape down the plant in early summer.

Hydrangea arborescens 'Annabelle'
Hills of Snow

Zones 4–9

Native to the eastern U.S., this bushy variety is heavier flowering and grows more compact than the species. Plants grow to 5 feet (1.5 m) tall with a rounded habit. 'Annabelle' bears spherical white flowerheads up to 12 inches (31 cm) across, starting green and changing to white when fully mature.

Hydrangea paniculata 'Grandiflora'
Pee Gee hydrangea

Zones 4–8

Native to Russia, China and Japan, plants grow to 20 feet (6.1 m) tall and bear large flower heads up to 12 inches (31 cm) across. As the flowers mature, they turn pink and then parchment brown, remaining decorative into winter months. Though generally multi-stemmed with a bushy habit, 'Grandiflora' can be trained to grow as a small tree with a single main trunk.

Hydrangea quercifolia
Oakleaf hydrangea

Zones 5–9

Native to the southern U.S., this bold, deciduous shrub grows to 6 feet (1.8 m) tall by 8 feet (2.4 m) wide with a mounded habit. Deeply lobed, mid-green leaves grow to 8 inches (20 cm) long, are shaped like a large oak leaf and turn bronze-purple in autumn. Bears 10-inch (25 cm) conical panicles of white flowers in early summer.

Hypericum calycinum
St. John's wort

Zones 4–8

Native to southeastern Europe and Asia Minor, this small, deciduous shrub grows to 3 feet (91 cm) tall with a dense, compact habit. Plants may remain evergreen in mild winter climates. Popular for its prolific, cup-shaped, glistening yellow flowers throughout summer. Slender, oval green leaves have conspicuous veins. Prefers well-drained, moisture-retentive garden soil in full sun or partial shade but is also tolerant of sandy soil. In cold winter climates, plants are killed back to the roots, which produce new flowering stems in early spring. It makes an excellent groundcover, as well as a foundation plant, and is also used as an accent in mixed perennial borders. 'Hidcote' is an everblooming variety.

Hydrangea macrophylla
Mophead hydrangea

Zones 6–9

Native to Japan, this rounded shrub can grow to 6 feet (1.8 m) high, depending on variety. Succeeds in most well-drained soils in full sun or light shade. The blue to pink flower color is controlled by soil pH with neutral or alkaline soil producing pink or red flowers in most varieties; acidic soil produces blue flowers. In neutral or alkaline soils, the addition of aluminum sulfate will change the soil's chemistry to produce blue flowers. Plants grow especially well in coastal locations. Freezing winters often kill the top growth, but plants produce new growth from the roots, which results in a lack of blooms among varieties that bloom on old wood. The unscented, large, globular clusters of blue, pink, red or white flowers occur in summer. Bright green leaves are oval shaped and serrated, and grow up to 8 inches (20 cm) long with poor autumn color. 'Endless Summer' is a variety that produces flowers on new wood and blooms when other varieties fail.

Shrubs

ILEX

Holly

Zones 3–9, depending on variety

Although hollies can be beautiful evergreen trees, a large number are bushy and many are deciduous. Their berry-filled branches and glossy, prickly leaves are used for Christmas decorations. The hardy tree hollies are described under Trees, pages 187–188. In this section, both deciduous and evergreen hardy shrub hollies are described. Evergreen hollies should always be purchased with earth balls around their roots, since the mortality rate is high with bare-root stock. Deciduous hollies, however, can be planted in spring or autumn using bare-root stock. Plants prefer a moisture-retentive loam soil in full sun. Good drainage is important, although the winterberry holly will tolerate boggy soil. With few exceptions, male and female flowers are borne on separate plants. The female plants bear the berries, but a male plant is needed within about 40 feet (12.2 m) to pollinate the flowers of the female plant.

Ilex crenata
Japanese holly

Zones 6–9

Native to Japan and Korea, this non-prickly species can create a dense weave of leaves and branches when pruned, and so it is a favorite choice for making an evergreen hedge and topiary. Also common pruned into a low dome shape and grouped shoulder-to-shoulder to create undulating mounds.

Ilex opaca
American holly

See Trees, page 188.

Ilex glabra
Inkberry holly

Zones 4–9

Native to the eastern U.S. and Canada, this non-prickly holly is usually evergreen depending on the severity of the winter. Growing to 6 feet (1.8 m) high, it is useful as a hedge. The slender leaves are usually dark green and glossy, containing black berries in the leaf axils. Flowers are small, white and inconspicuous. Indigenous to low, damp places, inkberry also succeeds in dry soils, spreading by means of stolons and forming a dense clump.

Ilex verticillata
Winterberry
Zones 3–9

Native to the northeastern U.S. and Canada, this smooth-leafed, deciduous holly grows to 15 feet (4.5 m) high with a wide spreading habit. Indigenous to swamps, winterberry will tolerate both wet and dry soil, producing inconspicuous white flowers in summer followed by masses of scarlet berries that are relished by songbirds. After the leaves drop, the berries remain on the plants well into winter, and often are cut for Christmas decorations by commercial florists. However, since only female plants bear fruit, it is essential to have a male nearby for maximum berry production. Regular English or American male hollies can also provide pollination. In addition to red, there are orange-berried varieties.

Ilex x meserveae
Blue holly
Zones 5–9

This handsome, blue-green hybrid holly, the result of crossing *I. rugosa* (prostrate holly) and *I. aquifolium* (English holly), was first produced by a New York gardening enthusiast, Mrs. F. Leighton Meserve. Plants grow to 10 feet (3 m) tall with equal width and an upright habit. The glossy, prickly, 2-inch (5 cm) leaves are wavy. Bright red berries are persistent, remaining on the plant during summer, autumn and winter. This hybrid is generally more attractive and hardier than both English and American holly, and bears more berries. Prefers fertile, well-drained, acidic soil in full sun or partial shade. One male will pollinate up to eight females. Tip pruning encourages new growth and maintains density. It is an excellent choice for hedges, foundation plantings and as a lawn highlight. Can be pruned into cones to make sentinels on both sides of a gate or doorway.

Itea virginica
Virginia sweetspire
Zones 6–9

Native to the eastern U.S., this deciduous shrub grows to 5 feet (1.5 m) high and spreads to form a colony. Leaves are oval, dark green and up to 4 inches (10 cm) long, turning purplish red or bright red in autumn. Fragrant white flower clusters bloom during summer. Plants prefer moist, fertile, slightly acidic soils in sun or partial shade. 'Henry's Garnet' flowers profusely and has intense purple-red autumn color.

Jasminum nudiflorum
Winter jasmine
Zones 6–10

Native to China, this early spring-flowering shrub grows to 4 feet (1.2 m) high and up to 7 feet (2.1 m) wide. Its long, arching branches are studded with yellow flowers and resemble forsythia from a distance. It likes to be trained over a wall or secured to a trellis. Since the slender branches root readily in contact with soil, they can form a dense thicket. The branches are bright green and stand out in the winter landscape.

JUNIPERUS

Juniper

Zones 3–9 depending on variety

This is a large group of evergreen, coniferous plants with needle-like foliage, consisting of three main groups: groundcover types, shrub types and trees (see page 188). The groundcovers range from a few inches to 3 feet (91 cm) high; the shrub types are usually slow growing, and in time will make a small tree up to 20 feet (6.1 m). The tree types can grow to 50 feet (15.2 m) or more. Therefore, there is a juniper to fit any landscape use.

Juniperus chinensis
Chinese juniper

Zones 4–9

There are many low-spreading varieties apart from the bushy and pyramidal tree types. Plants enjoy sun to light shade and take most well-drained soils.

Juniperus horizontalis
Creeping juniper

Zones 3–9

Native to North America, this low-spreading, tough evergreen grows to 2 feet (61 cm) high with a spread of up to 8 feet (2.4 m). The long trailing branches form dense mats, and the leaves vary from green to steel blue in color, depending on the variety; many of them have a purplish cast in winter. Creeping junipers prefer a well-drained, stony or sandy, slightly alkaline soil in full sun. This is a popular, mat-forming groundcover which persists in poor situations, including seashore plantings. Invaluable as a slope cover to control erosion, it is also effective for rock gardens and as an edging to foundation plantings.

Kalmia latifolia
Mountain laurel
Zones 4–9

Native to the eastern U.S. and closely related to rhododendron, this broadleaf evergreen grows slowly to 8 feet (2.4 m) high with an upright, bushy habit. In youth, it can be symmetrical and dense; in old age, it becomes open and gnarled with sinuous trunks and limbs. Curious hexagonal-shaped flowers are borne in large showy clusters up to 5 inches (13 cm) across. Colors include white, pink, red, mahogany and purple. The buds are especially attractive, folded like a closed umbrella. The 2- to 5-inch (5 to 13 cm), leathery, dark green leaves are arranged in a whorl. Brown seed capsules last throughout the winter, but are best removed before they develop seeds to encourage more profuse flowering for the next season. Plants prefer cool, moisture-retentive, well-drained, acidic soil in full sun or partial shade. Mulch to keep the soil moist. Use in woodland gardens and massed on slopes.

Kolkwitzia amabilis
Beautybush
Zones 5–8

Native to China, this large, weeping, deciduous shrub grows to 15 feet (4.5 m) high and 10 feet (3 m) wide with a fountainlike habit. Its graceful, tightly packed branches create an avalanche of pale pink tubular blossoms in spring. The dark green leaves are fuzzy and turn a dull red in autumn. The decorative brown bark peels in long strips and flakes on older stems. This easy-to-grow plant prefers well-drained loam soil in full sun or partial shade. It makes a good screen or border plant and likes to be planted along a terrace or trained up a trellis so its branches can cascade elegantly.

Kerria japonica
Japanese kerria

Zones 4–9

Native to China, this spring-flowering, deciduous shrub grows to 8 feet (2.4 m) high and 9 feet (2.7 m) wide with a mounded habit. It is densely branched and twiggy, spreading by suckering. Bright green leaves turn yellow in the autumn. The golden-yellow, single cup-shaped flowers resemble wild yellow roses, though the double-flowered variety 'Pleniflora' tends to be more widely grown. The variegated variety 'Picta' does not grow as large as the species and does not burn in the summer heat. Kerria prefers loamy, well-drained soil of moderate fertility in light shade. Plants are effective massed in woodland gardens in company with azaleas.

Lagerstroemia indica
Crape myrtle

Zones 6–10, depending on variety

At temperatures below –10°F (-23°C), most plants die back to the ground and grow new flowering branches to behave like a herbaceous perennial. Native to China and Korea, this small tree grows to 20 feet (6.1 m) high and from 12 feet (3.6 m) wide, although there are dwarf hybrids that are bushy. Flowers are composed of generous clusters resembling large lilac blooms. These can be 12 inches (31 cm) long in pink, watermelon-red, purple or white flowers. Young leaves are bronze, maturing to medium or dark green with a vivid show of orange, red and yellow autumn color. Attractive, smooth, brownish-gray bark peels to reveal maroon and pinkish marbling. A moist, well-drained soil in full sun is preferred, but dry poor soil, pollution and extreme heat are tolerated. Use as a lawn accent and to create an avenue framing a path. Suitable for planting in containers, it is extremely popular where summers are hot because of its heat and drought resistance. The U.S. National Arboretum has introduced a family of extra-hardy hybrids, which are recommended for foundation plantings and are named after Native American tribes.

Lespedeza thunbergii
Bush clover

Zones 4–7

May die back to the roots in cold climates to perform as a herbaceous perennial. Native to northern China and Japan, this fountainlike shrub grows 6 feet (1.8 m) in a single season. Long, slender flowering stems are so heavy that they arch over, producing a handsome cascading effect. The pea-like trifoliate leaves are bluish-green, and it bears small, rosy-purple, pea-shaped flowers in 6-inch (15 cm) long racemes at the branch tips in late summer. Annual pruning keeps plants bushy and compact; otherwise, the brittle stems are prone to breakage.

Ligustrum x vicaryi
Vicary golden privet
Zones 6–10

Native to Europe, privet is a slow-growing, deciduous shrub that reaches 12 feet (3.6 m) high and 15 feet (4.5 m) wide with a dense, rounded habit. The oval leaves of this hybrid are golden in full sun and yellow-green if planted in a shady area. Inconspicuous white flower clusters bloom in summer. Plants adapt to a variety of soils in full sun or partial shade but the coloring is more effective in sun. Use alone as a specimen foundation accent or in a group to form a hedge. Alternate with a regular green privet to make a "checkered" effect.

Leucothoe fontanesiana
Fountain leucothoe
Zones 4–6

Native to the eastern U.S., this broadleaf evergreen has majestic, long, arching, leathery green leaves which stir with the slightest breeze. Fragrant, white, pendulous flowers bloom in spring with the leaves turning bronze in autumn. Plants prefer a humus-rich, moisture-retentive, well-drained, acidic soil in partial shade. Protect from full sun and wind. Massed, it makes an excellent cover for banks and will cascade over retaining walls. Use along woodland paths, especially in the company of Japanese maples whose russet autumn colors contrast well with the lustrous evergreen leaves of leucothoe. *L. axillaries*, coast leucothoe (zones 6–9), is only slightly less hardy and is also native to the southeastern U.S. This broad-leaf, evergreen shrub grows to 2 feet (61 cm) tall with a dense form and arching stems. Tiny, bell-shaped flowers appear in spring among dark green, shiny leaves. Plants prefer to be placed in semi-shade and are suitable for groundcover.

Lonicera sempervirens
Trumpet honeysuckle
Zones 4–9

Native to the eastern U.S., this deciduous, twining vine reaches 20 feet (6.1 m) high. From late spring through summer, it bears showy, unscented, trumpet-shaped, orange-yellow or scarlet flowers that are arranged in whorls at the ends of slender branches. Oval leaves are bluish-green beneath. 'John Clayton' has yellow flowers and 'Magnifica' has intense red flowers. Related species include *L. periclymenum* (zones 4–8), which has pink and yellow flowers. *L. japonica* 'Halliana' (zones 4–9) has yellow and white flowers and is useful as a groundcover for difficult-to-plant slopes. Prune heavily to keep bushy and allow it to twine up the support as a vine. *L. fragrantissima* (zones 4–8) is early flowering, covering itself with extremely fragrant white flowers on a wide-spreading shrub. Blooms on wood grown the previous year, so should not be pruned in late autumn or early spring or the flower buds will be cut off.

Mahonia aquifolium
Oregon grapeholly
Zones 4–8

Native to the Pacific Northwest, this evergreen shrub has handsome hollylike leaves and yellow flowers followed by blue berries. Plant mahonias in a sheltered spot to avoid burning of the foliage from winter winds. Plants prefer some shade and tolerate most soils with good drainage; however, they do best in a humus, moisture-retentive soil. It spreads by means of underground stolons and soon forms a large clump.

Myrica pensylvanica
Bayberry
Zones 1–8

Native to coastal Newfoundland and the eastern U.S., this unusually hardy, deciduous and semi-evergreen shrub grows to 9 feet (2.7 m) high with stiff, straight, erect branches. Leaves are gray-green and aromatic. The flowers of the two sexes are on different plants, so both male and female plants must be near each other to produce berries. The blooms are greenish and interesting when seen closely but are not effective in the landscape. The berries, used to scent bayberry candles since Colonial times, are first green, then gray and remain on the plants all winter until songbirds eat them.

Nandina domestica
Heavenly bamboo
Zones 6–9

Native to China, this bamboo-like shrub grows to 8 feet (2.4 m) tall with multiple upright stems. Fine-textured, 2-inch (5 cm) long leaves are arranged in threes and concentrated at the top of the plant. Clusters of white flowers bloom in summer, followed by brilliant crimson-red berry clusters that persist through winter months into the following spring. The autumn foliage turns plum red. *Nandina* prefers sandy, well-drained, fertile soil in full sun or partial shade, and spreads by rhizomes. It is useful as a screen, background or foundation planting, and can also be grown as a container plant. Dwarf forms are suitable for massing as a groundcover. The generous berry clusters make beautiful holiday decorations and arrangements.

Osmanthus heterophyllus
Holly osmanthus
Zones 6–9

Native to China, this broadleaf evergreen grows to 10 feet (3 m) high with a similar spread. It is valued for its lustrous, dark green, spiny leaves and dense growth, suitable for a hedge. Heavily scented white flowers bloom in autumn and are hidden by the foliage. Plants prefer a moisture-retentive, well-drained, acidic soil in full sun and will withstand heavy pruning. Similar in appearance to holly, it may be trimmed into cones and topiary shapes.

Pachysandra procumbens (above)
Allegheny spurge

Zones 4–9

Native to the Allegheny Mountains of the eastern U.S., this deciduous groundcover resembles Japanese pachysandra but with larger leaves which are deeply indented. Fragrant white flowers appear in early spring as new leaves emerge from the soil. Plants prefer a moisture-retentive, acid, well-drained, humus-rich soil in partial to full shade. This is an excellent groundcover, spreads by rhizomes and looks especially attractive massed along woodland paths.

Pachysandra terminalis (right)
Japanese pachysandra

Zones 4–8

Native to Japan, this long-lived evergreen groundcover spreads by rhizomes and forms a solid 8-inch (20 cm) high mat, which is uniform in light to deep shade. New light green growth gradually changes to lustrous dark green. Foliage is indented, hiding the cream-colored flowers that appear in spring. It is one of the most popular plants to cover large areas under trees and on slopes.

Paeonia suffruticosa
Tree peony

Zones 5–8

Native to China, this spring-flowering, deciduous shrub grows to 6 feet (1.8 m) high and up to 12 feet (3.6 m) across with multiple trunks and a loose, mounded habit. Beautiful maple-shaped leaves and huge single or double flowers up to 10 inches (25 cm) across make this one of the most spectacular of all flowering shrubs. Color range includes white, yellow, pink, red, crimson, purple and maroon, all with a prominent powdery yellow crest of stamens in the center. Prefers a well-drained, humus-rich soil in a sheltered position. Likes its feet in the shade and its head in the sun, although it will tolerate partial shade. This is a good family of plants to collect and plant throughout the garden as lawn accents, in mixed shrub borders and as foundation plantings. The coveted variety 'Joseph Rock' is white with ruffled petals and maroon petal markings. It was discovered in the grounds of a Chinese monastery by the American plant explorer of the same name.

Parthenocissus quinquefolia
Virginia creeper

Zones 3–9

Native to North America, this deciduous, vigorous vine grows up to 30 feet (9.1 m) tall, attaching itself to walls and other structures by its tendrils. Grown for its beautiful orange to scarlet fall color, the saw-toothed, lustrous green summer leaves are divided into five leaflets. Plants prefer well-drained, moisture-retentive loam soil in full sun or partial shade. In addition to covering walls and arbors, it makes a good weed-suffocating groundcover on slopes.

Parthenocissus tricuspidata
Boston ivy

Zones 4–8

Native to Japan and central China, this fast-growing, deciduous vine is similar to *P. quinquefolia* in all respects except that the glossy 8-inch (20 cm) wide foliage is variable in shape, usually three lobed or divided into three leaflets. Autumn color varies from orange to burgundy. Plants make a dense wall cover, even blanketing a building if not controlled; it is also useful for covering arches and arbors.

Philadelphus coronarius
Mock orange

Zones 5–8

Native to southeastern Europe and Asia Minor, this carefree deciduous shrub grows 10 feet (3 m) tall and just as wide with a rounded habit, although there are several dwarf varieties. The vigorous, erect, dense plants have oval, dark green leaves and a display of extremely fragrant clusters of inch-wide (2.5 cm) white flowers in early summer. Both single and double forms are available. Prefers well-drained, fertile soil in full sun or partial shade, and tolerates dry conditions. Plants should be pruned after flowering to prevent legginess, or the multiple trunks should be thinned and limbed high to accentuate their slender lines. Suitable as a lawn accent, the plants also make good informal screens and windbreaks.

Phyllostachys aureosulcata
Yellow groove bamboo

Zones 6–11

Native to China, this is undoubtedly the most popular of hardy bamboos, principally because of its attractive canes, which are bright yellow, streaked with green. The erect stems grow to 20 feet (6.1 m) high and spread by aggressive underground stolons that can double the planting area each year. Planting them in containers can control this invasive tendency. The leaves are green and willowlike. Highly wind resistant, plants are popular components of roof gardens, and they make good windbreak hedges and screens. Bamboo, in company with weeping willows, is one of the few plants that can immediately convey an Oriental aura. Another hardy bamboo, *P. edulis* (zones 6–10) is valued for its edible young shoots.

Other hardy forms of bamboo include *Fargesii nitida* (zones 4–8), a clumping bamboo good for screening; *Sasa tsuboiana* (zones 4–8), a groundcover bamboo with broad, pointed leaves that lie horizontally; and *Pleioblastus fortunei* (zones 5–8), also suitable for groundcover, particularly the white-striped variegated varieties.

Physocarpus opulifolius
Ninebark

Zones 2–7

Native to eastern and central North America, this tough, multi-stemmed shrub grows to 10 feet (3 m) high and equally wide with an upright, spreading habit. Pinkish-white 2-inch (5 cm) flower clusters appear in summer. Older stems are covered with attractive shaggy bark, which peels off in long fibrous strips. Ninebark (pronounced nini-bark) is a good choice in northern landscapes where many other shrubs won't survive. It makes an effective hedge, screen or windbreak. Prune to control size and form immediately after flowering. Overgrown shrubs can be cut back to the ground in early spring to renew. The variety 'Diabolo' has lobed leaves which are purple-red all season long.

Shrubs

Pieris japonica
Japanese andromeda
Zones 5–8

Native to Japan, this large broadleaf evergreen grows to 12 feet (3.6 m) high, spreading 8 feet (2.4 m) wide. Plants display a bushy habit with spreading branches and lance-like foliage. New leaves are a rich bronze, which change to a lustrous, dark green at maturity. Large drooping clusters of slightly fragrant, white, urn-shaped flowers bloom in early spring. Flower buds add winter appeal, since they are formed the summer prior to flowering. This easy-care shrub prefers a humus-rich, well-drained, acidic soil in full sun or partial shade, sheltered from wind. Prune after flowering to maintain a compact habit. It is effective in shrub borders mixed with other broadleaf evergreens such as azaleas and rhododendrons. A number of pink-flowering varieties are especially appealing as foundation plants, notably 'Dorothy Wyckoff.'

Pinus mugo
Mugo pine
Zones 2–7

Native to central and southern Europe from Spain to the Balkans, this needle-leaf, slow-growing, evergreen shrub grows to 20 feet (6.1 m) tall with a 30-foot (9.1 m) spread. It is usually low spreading or pyramidal in habit. This is a diverse species, and the size of the plant can vary from a low, bushy dwarf to a large shrub. Some of the dwarf varieties are 'Compacta' growing 3 feet (91 cm) tall and 4 feet (1.2 m) wide and *P. mugo* var. *mugo*, which grows 8 feet (2.4 m) high and 10 feet (3 m) wide. Plants prefer moist loam soil in sun or partial shade; it is also suitable for groundcover. Prune dwarf varieties to maintain a dense, cushionlike habit.

Poncirus trifoliata
Hardy orange
Zones 5–9

Native to China, this green-stemmed, thorny, bushy, deciduous shrub grows to 20 feet (6.1 m) high. It bears fragrant, citruslike, white flowers in spring followed by masses of golfball-size yellow fruits that ripen in autumn and smell of lemon-scented soap. The large seeds, resembling lemon pips, germinate readily all around the parent plant in spring. Needs only light tip pruning to maintain a tidy shape. Tolerates poor soil if drainage is good. Useful for container plantings, hedging and in mixed shrub borders.

Potentilla fruticosa
Shrubby cinquefoil
Zones 2–8

Native to Europe and Asia, this small, hardy, deciduous shrub grows to 4 feet (1.2 m) high with equal spread and a dense, rounded habit. The long-stalked, bright green leaves consist of five oval leaflets. The flowers can be creamy white, bright yellow, pink and tangerine, resembling miniature single-flowered roses. Plants bloom intermittently starting in late spring. They are adaptable to a wide range of soils including dry, wet, heavy and sandy soil in full sun or light shade. Good for groundcovers and accents in borders. The pink, tangerine and red flowering varieties tend to be sparse flowering, except in areas with cool moist summers.

Prunus glandulosa
Flowering almond
Zones 4–8

Native to China and Japan, this small, deciduous shrub has an upright and somewhat rounded habit with slender multi-stems splayed out like a fan. The most popular variety, 'Rosea', has lovely 1-inch (2.5 cm) double flowers crowded along the stems like pink powder puffs, which appear in early spring. The foliage is oval and light green with no autumn interest. Plants prefer well-drained, moist, humus-rich soil in full sun. Prune after flowering to increase new stem development. Use in mixed borders, especially close to early-flowering magnolias. Popular for planting in the middle of late daffodil and early tulip displays and in beds of early perennials, such as pansies, to provide a spectacular color highlight.

Pyracantha coccinea
Firethorn
Zones 6–9

This broadleaf evergreen is native to Italy and the Caucasus Mountains and grows to 6 feet (1.8 m) high by 10 feet (3 m) wide with an erect, open habit of stiff, thorny branches. The lustrous, dense, dark green leaves may turn brown during winter in unprotected areas. Profuse white showy flowers, which resemble hawthorn, bloom in spring and have a musty odor. The spectacular, orange-red or yellow fruits persist through the winter. Plants prefer well-drained sandy or loam soil in full sun or partial shade. The fruits are susceptible to fireblight, a bacterium that turns them black as if scorched. Use as an informal hedge or barrier; it is also good to espalier on walls and trellises. 'Mohave' is resistant to scab disease and fireblight.

Rhamnus frangula
Buckthorn
Zones 3–7

Native to Europe, western Asia and North Africa, this large shrub has naturalized in the eastern and midwestern U.S. Flowers are small, green and inconspicuous. 'Columnaris' is upright, creating a tall hedge up to 15 feet (4.5 m) high. The oval green leaves turn red in autumn. 'Asplenifolia' has slender, fernlike leaves.

Shrubs

RHODODENDRON SPECIES AND HYBRIDS

Azaleas and Rhododendrons

Zones 4–9, depending on variety

Botanically, there is no difference between an azalea and a rhododendron, for they are both members of the genus *Rhododendron*, but nurserymen and gardeners like to make a distinction on the basis of appearance. Rhododendrons generally have larger, more leathery leaves than azaleas, and the flowers of rhododendrons are usually larger, borne in dome-shaped trusses at the ends of spreading branches. Azaleas can be sheared to keep them compact, but it is best not to prune rhododendrons. In general, azaleas are more compact and shrublike than rhododendrons, and they are more adaptable to a wide range of conditions, tolerating heat and drought better than most rhododendrons, which prefer to be in a lightly shaded location. Azaleas can be divided into evergreen and deciduous. The Exbury strain of deciduous azaleas is famous for its orange and yellow shades, and also for its strong fragrance. However, they tend to be short-lived where summers are hot and humid, since mostly North American mountain species were used in their parentage.

Wild species of both hardy rhododendrons and azaleas are concentrated in Asia and North America, notably in mountainous areas where swirling mist maintains a cool environment during summer. Throughout the world, there are many good gardens to evaluate rhododendron varieties including Bodnant Gardens (U.K.), the Pukeiti Rhododendron Garden (New Zealand) and the Rhododendron Species Foundation, Washington State (U.S.).

Most azaleas and rhododendrons thrive in a humus-rich, acid soil. Though their nutrient needs are low if they are mulched with an organic material such as leaf mold, shredded leaves or pine needles every year, an annual feeding with an acid fertilizer will generally help improve blooming, especially along house foundations, where soil can be heavily alkaline from building debris. The following are some outstanding species or varieties of azaleas and rhododendron:

Rhododendron arborescens
Sweet or smooth azalea

Zones 5–9

This species is native to the Allegheny mountains of the eastern U.S. It generally grows 8 feet (2.4 m) tall and upright along mountain streams and across cool mountain ridges. Eventually, it becomes wider than high. Plants flower in early summer, making it one of the last azaleas to bloom. The flowers smell like sweet heliotrope and vary in color from white, flushed pink or red to yellow blotched but always have red stamens. Foliage is glossy bright green turning dark red in autumn.

AZALEAS

Rhododendron calendulaceum
Flame azalea

Zones 5–9

This deciduous, fragrant azalea from the Allegheny Mountains of the eastern U.S. grows to 8 feet (2.4 m) tall, in open woods on hills or mountains and in colors ranging from yellow through orange to scarlet. Flowering time is spring. In autumn, the foliage turns yellow to bronze.

Rhododendron periclymenoides
Pinxterbloom azalea

Zones 5–8

A deciduous shrub from the Appalachian Mountains (U.S.) and growing to 5 feet (1.5 m), this azalea resembles a honeysuckle plant with its fragrant, tubular pink or white blooms, which appear in spring before the leaves are fully unfurled. Although it thrives in light shade, it tolerates and looks especially beautiful when planted beside a pond or stream.

Rhododendron prinophyllum
aka *R. roseum*
Roseshell azalea
Zones 3–8

This deciduous azalea, native to the U.S. Appalachian Mountains, resembles *R. periclymenoides* and *R. nudiflorum*. Plants grow to 5 feet (1.5 m) high, its bright pink flowers releasing a clove-like scent.

Rhododendron prunifolium
Plumleaf azalea
Zones 5–9

Native to the U.S. states of Georgia and Alabama, this deciduous shrub grows to 10 feet (3 m) high with orange-red flowers. It is the latest blooming of all azaleas, in midsummer, and one of the most shade tolerant.

Rhododendron schlippenbachii
Royal azalea
Zones 4–8

Beautiful in both spring and autumn, the fragrant 3-inch (8 cm), pale pink, spotted flowers appear just as the leaves are unfolding. In autumn, these leaves turn yellow, orange and crimson. The plants grow upright, yet eventually spread to be wider than they are high. Not demanding of highly acid soil, as are most other azaleas.

Rhododendron vaseyi
Pinkshell azalea
Zones 4–8

Native to the mountains of western North Carolina, this lovely pale pink azalea forms upright plants to 10 feet (3 m) tall. Blooms appear in spring before the leaves unfold with single flowers that may be white or pale pink. They are graceful and give an airy effect. The plant will grow in either moist or dry soils and in full sun as well as light shade.

R. yedoense var. poukhanense
Korean azalea
Zones 5–9

This is a low-spreading, evergreen azalea that is deciduous in cold winters. Plants grow to 6 feet (1.8 m) high, displaying lightly fragrant, single lavender-pink flowers. It blooms in spring with mid-season tulips. Especially beautiful planted with redbuds and pink-flowering crabapples to create a sensational monochromatic pink garden.

AZALEA HYBRIDS

Zones 4–9, depending on variety

Hardy hybrid azaleas are divided between evergreen hybrids from species mostly native to Asia and deciduous hybrids from species mostly native to North America, but also from Asia, in particular *R. molle*. The following are popular:

Exbury hybrids
Zone 5–7

These hybrids, developed by Lord Lionel de Rothschild at his Exbury estate in the U.K. using mostly deciduous North American species, are upright growing types, up to 12 feet (3.6 m) high with russet autumn colors and medium-green summer foliage. The spring-flowering, fragrant flowers are usually funnel shaped, and colors come in all shades of yellow, orange, red and pink. They are similar in appearance to several other deciduous strains including Knap Hill (British) and Ilam (New Zealand). Some of the world's finest collections of Exbury and other deciduous azaleas can be seen at Bodnant (U.K.), Savill Gardens (U.K.), Maple Glen (New Zealand), Trelinnoe Garden (New Zealand) and Stanley Park, Vancouver (Canada). Exbury varieties such as 'Hotspur Red' (reddish-orange), 'Golden Sunset' (yellow) and 'Gibraltar' (orange) are fragrant. Although cold hardy, they are generally short lived where summers are hot and humid.

Gable hybrids

Zones 5–8

These evergreen azaleas were bred for hardiness by Joseph B. Gable in Stewartstown, PA, U.S. The Korean azalea (*R. yedoense* var. *poukhanense*), an extra-hardy, deciduous, evergreen azalea and the evergreen Kaempfer azalea, (*R. kaempferi*) were used as parents for many of this group. The scarlet-red Gable hybrid azalea 'Stewartstonian' and the pink 'Rosebud' are probably the most famous cultivars from Joe Gable. Plants can be kept low and compact by heavy pruning, but left alone they grow tall and erect, their oval pointed leaves turning molten bronze in autumn.

Ghent hybrids
R. x gandavense
Zones 4–8

Ghent azaleas are similar in appearance to Exburies. They are deciduous, grow up to 10 feet (3 m) tall and are of extremely mixed parentage, including the species *R. calendulaceum, luteum, molle, nudiflorum* and *viscosum*. Hardiness and a wide color range rich in yellow, orange and pink are the most important attributes of these hybrids, which grow best in light shade.

Girard hybrids
Zones 6–9

This strain of excellent large-flowered, evergreen azaleas for cold climates originates from Gable crosses. 'Girard's Hot Shot' (a reddish orange) and 'Purple Robe' (a beautiful clear purple) are especially beautiful.

Glenn Dale hybrids
Zones 6–8

Originated from an aggressive breeding program undertaken at the U.S. National Arboretum, this evergreen azalea is hardy to -10°F (-23°C) and some 450 cultivars are available, most with large flowers. The varieties 'Ben Morrison' (a spectacular large-flowering pink and white bicolor) and 'Buccaneer' (an early-flowering reddish orange) are especially good for home landscapes.

Kaempferi hybrids
Torch azalea
Zones 6–9

These are similar to the Kurume hybrids but taller growing and derived from *R. kaempferi*. They are strong growing, becoming tree-like with age. When this happens, it is best to prune away the lower branches to leave a multi-stemmed shrub with an umbrella of flowers that occur in spring. Some of the world's most beautiful azalea gardens, Calloway Gardens, Georgia (U.S.) and Winterthur, Delaware (U.S.) rely heavily on the Kurumes and the Kaempferis, which are planted in lightly shaded woodland and across sunny meadows. Varieties available include 'Fedora' (salmon rose), 'Holland' (large red) and 'Palestrina' (white).

Knap Hill hybrids
Zones 4–8

This group of deciduous, fragrant azaleas was hybridized by Anthony Waterer in England and was continued after his death by Knap Hill Nursery. Parents of the group are *R. molle, calendulaceum, occidentale* and *arborescens*. Knap Hill hybrids are characterized by flowers of large size, like rhododendron, mostly single, but a few with double blooms. In addition to the huge flowers, many cultivars bear them in large trusses. Flower colors range from creamy whites through all shades of pink, red, yellow and orange.

Mollis hybrids
Zones 5–8

These deciduous, fragrant hybrids are derived from mostly Asian species. They are rich in shades of yellow, orange and red, plus white, and grow to 5 feet (1.5 m) high. Most bloom in late spring and bloom clusters can be 5 inches (13 cm) or more in width. Mollis hybrids resemble Exbury and Ghent hybrids, but they are usually not long lived where summers are hot.

North Tisbury hybrids
Zones 6–8, depending on variety

U.S. plant breeder Polly Hill, of Martha's Vineyard, experimented with seeds and cuttings from Japan to produce these hardy, mostly late-blooming, low-growing azaleas suitable for groundcover, trailing over low walls and even growing in hanging baskets. They resemble Kurume hybrid azaleas, but generally they are slow growing and stay below 2 feet (61 cm) in height. Specimens of the dwarf variety 'Michael Hill' have grown just 18 inches (46 cm) high, spreading 4 feet (1.2 m) in 10 years. The cultivar 'Joseph Hill' is a particularly fine dwarf with glowing red flowers, frequently seen planted in rock gardens in light shade.

RHODODENDRONS

Hardy rhododendrons are generally divided into three main categories: hybrids, species and a third class identified as tender vireya rhododendron, mostly from the tropical climate of Indonesia. The following hardy hybrids are popular among home gardeners:

'America'
Zones 5–8

This member of a class known as Iron Clads for their cold hardiness was developed in the U.K. It has dark red flower clusters borne on a mounded plant and develop their best display in full sun. Plants grow to 6 feet (1.8 m) and more with an equal spread, suitable for small gardens and along the house foundation. It is similar to 'Nova Zembla', which is another red Iron Clad rhododendron.

Kurume hybrids
Zones 6–8

This group of evergreen azaleas is derived mostly from an obscure Japanese species, *R. sataense*, from the island of Kyushu. They are compact, twiggy plants, densely foliaged with small glossy leaves. Flowers are borne in incredible profusion. Plants usually are billowing and upright, up to 6 feet (1.8 m) high. Blooms of most are single, ranging in color from white to all shades of pink, red, violet and purple. The variety 'Coral Bells' has small, profuse flowers in pale pink with a deeper pink eye. 'Hinode Giri' has vivid red flowers with a satinlike sheen and is most often used massed to cover sunny slopes. 'Hino Crimson' is a shimmering bright red. All flower in the spring.

'Cynthia'

Zones 6–8

An old favorite, popular in European parks and gardens, that can reach up to 20 feet (6.1 m) high and twice as wide. Dark red flower trusses are borne in such profusion they can almost completely hide the foliage. A particularly large specimen can be seen in the valley garden Bois des Moutiers on the Normandy coast.

'English Roseum'

Zones 5–8

This pink Iron Clad is a common color for rhododendron and is widely used where hardiness is important. A good selection for beginners since it succeeds where other rhododendrons perish, particularly where summer heat and humidity is a problem. Plants grow to 20 feet (6.1 m) high and make a good companion for 'America' and 'Nova Zembla.'

'Nova Zembla'

Zones 5–8

An Iron Clad variety that is similar to 'America' but not such an intense red. A vigorous plant noted for its heat tolerance, growing to 6 feet (1.8 m) high.

'PJM'

Zones 5–8

Though the vivid pink flowers are small, only growing up to 4 inches (10 cm) across, compared to most other hybrids, they are prolific. Since it is one of the earliest flowering and hardiest, it is popular for massing around trees and as a slope cover.

'Scintillation'

Zones 6–8

Developed on Cape Cod (U.S.), it is the best known of the Dexter hybrids. The lightly fragrant, pale pink flowers have maroon spotted yellow throats. The impressive 3-inch (8 cm) wide individual blooms form a large truss of up to 15 flowers. It was almost lost to cultivation after the death of its breeder, Charles Dexter, but a single surviving specimen was discovered in a test planting at the New York Botanical Garden, and increased from cuttings.

RHODODENDRON SPECIES

In general, the hardy species are not as ornamental as the hybrids, although they are used in woodland gardens where a more refined hybrid might look out of character. The following are the most widely grown:

Rhododendron catawbiense
Catawba rhododendron

Zones 4–8

Native to the Allegheny Mountains of the U.S., this large evergreen grows to 10 feet (3 m) high, bearing high-domed trusses of purple-pink flowers in early summer. It is a parent of many Iron Clad rhododendron hybrids including pink 'Roseum Elegans', crimson 'America' and red 'Nova Zembla'.

Rhododendron maximum
Rosebay rhododendron

Zones 4–7

Native to the eastern U.S. from Canada to Georgia, this large evergreen bears light pink flower trusses in midsummer and prefers light shade.

Rhododendron mucronulatum
Korean rhododendron

Zones 4–7

This short-lived, deciduous rhododendron from China and Korea grows up to 6 feet (1.8 m) high and blooms in early spring at the same time as magnolia and forsythia, with which it is often partnered. Single, lavender pink blooms appear before the leaves and are subject to damage by late frost. Heavy shearing after flowering keeps the plant compact, stimulates subsequent flowering and increases the plant's life span.

Rhododendron carolinianum
Carolina rhododendron

Zones 4–8

Native to the Blue Ridge Mountains and Smoky Mountains of the U.S., this billowing evergreen shrub grows to 8 feet (2.4 m) high and just as wide. Pale pink flowers with yellow throats and green spots bloom in late spring.

Shrubs

Rhododendron ponticum
Pontic rhododendron

Zones 6–9

Though native to the mountains of Turkey, this vigorous, self-seeding, evergreen species has become so invasive in Snowdonia and parts of Scotland (U.K.) that parks employ workers to eradicate them. Plants grow to 15 feet (4.5 m) high and bear large trusses of mauve flowers with orange throats. It is useful as a windbreak hedge where they are not likely to become invasive.

Rhododendron yakushimanum
Yak rhododendron

Zones 5–8

Native to Yakushima Island, Japan, the Yaks are slow-growing, mounded, compact, deciduous shrubs with large flower trusses that are variable in color, usually white-tinted pink but sometimes all white and all pink. Plants grow to just 4 feet (1.2 m) high, resent high summer heat and are mostly used in rock gardens where boulders, running water and gravel can create a cool microclimate in summer. 'Mist Maiden' grows the largest flower trusses.

Rhodotypos scandens
Jetbead

Zone 4–8

Native to Japan and central China, this refined, deciduous shrub grows 6 feet (1.8 m) high with an upright spreading habit. They have small, single, white, rose-like flowers, which start to open in late spring and continue blooming intermittently all summer. These are followed by shiny jet-black fruits that stay on all winter. The leaves are dark, serrated and veined, remaining green long after the leaves of most other deciduous shrubs have fallen. Grown as much for its decorative fruits as for its flowers.

Rhus aromatica
Fragrant sumac

Zones 3–9

Native from Canada to the northern parts of Florida and westward to Texas, this rapidly spreading shrub grows to 6 feet (1.8 m) high, creating aggressive colonies by stolons or suckers. Plant on dry banks for erosion control. Small yellow flowers in clusters open before the leaves in early spring, and are followed by red berries. The fragrant foliage turns orange and scarlet in autumn. Prefers sun or light shade and good drainage.

Rhus typhina
Staghorn sumac

Zones 3–8

Native from Canada to Georgia and westward to Iowa, this fast-growing, small tree loses its lower branches so that slender trunks support a fountain of leaves. The young twigs are hairy, like the new horns of a stag, hence the common name. The slender leaves turn red in autumn as the greenish-yellow springtime flowers mature into crimson fruit clusters. The variety 'Laciniata' differs from the species by having the leaflets deeply toothed and divided. Best used at the extremities of a garden where it can be allowed to spread by suckers. Plants prefer full sun and good drainage but tolerate moist soil and light shade.

Ribes alpinum
Alpine currant
Zones 2–7

Native to Europe, this slow-growing, bushy shrub grows to 6 feet (1.8 m) high and has such a densely twiggy habit, it can be used as a hedge. Severe pruning can keep it compact, creating a wall of ivy-shaped leaves that do not turn color in autumn. The spring-blooming, greenish-yellow flower clusters are decorative. Both male and female plants are needed to produce berries, which are decorative in autumn. However, the female plant serves as a host to white pine blister rust, and for this reason, nurseries generally offer only male plants.

Ribes odoratum
Clove currant
Zones 4–6

Native mainly to the midwestern U.S., this short-lived, deciduous shrub grows to 6 feet (1.8 m) high and is bushy and irregular in shape. The yellow flowers are highly fragrant and appear in spring. Black edible berries ripen in late summer, provided plants of both sexes are planted, and the foliage turns scarlet in autumn. Plants prefer full sun and good drainage, and are useful for decorating rock gardens and stream banks.

ROSA

Rose
Zones 2–10, depending on variety

Although hardiness varies among species and hybrids, roses are among the hardiest of ornamental-flowering plants with origins in North America, Europe, the Middle East and Asia. Some roses, particularly those bred in Canada and known as the 'Explorer' series (such as 'Henry Hudson'), are hardy to zone 2. Roses are classified as woody plants. Most grow thorny and shrublike, some growing tall enough to climb high into trees and up trellis. Others are low and spreading, and are capable of making a weed-suffocating groundcover.

Roses have one purpose in life, and that is to bloom. Give them full sun and soil that drains well, and they are capable of generous quantities of bloom. Some pests and diseases, such as aphids, mildew and black spot, can shorten the bloom period by weakening the plant. Some roses give one spectacular burst of bloom in late spring, while others are repeat blooming. This often depends on cool night-time temperatures and adequate irrigation in the absence of rainfall. In areas with warm summers, rose growers often mulch beds with stone to keep the roots cool and prolong the bloom period.

Roses are versatile in the landscape. They combine well with perennials and other flowering shrubs, especially clematis, which will entwine its stems through rose canes to mingle their flowers. Those listed below are the major classes and their landscaping uses are described.

Shrubs

HYBRID TEA ROSES

These are the most popular, principally because they have the largest flowers, usually one to a stem. 'Peace' (a bicolor yellow and pink) and 'Double Delight' (a bicolor yellow and red) are examples of hybrid teas. They grow to 5 feet (1.5 m) high, and even higher in fertile soil. They are commonly used singly as accents or grouped in mixed rose borders.

'Double Delight'
Zones 5–9
Hybridized by Armstrong Roses (U.S.), the 5-inch (13-cm) wide, highly fragrant flowers are unique among bicolored roses. They are carmine red at the petal tips and a creamy yellow toward the high-peaked center. Leaves are dark green on upright canes that grow to 4 feet (1.2 m) high. They are outstanding for garden display in mixed borders and excellent for cutting.

'Mister Lincoln'
Zones 5–9
Hybridized in the U.S. from a cross between 'Chrysler Imperial' and 'Charles Mallerin', the 6-inch (15 cm) wide flowers are one of the finest dark reds in roses with good substance and a high peak, as well as heavy fragrance. Plants grow to 5 feet (1.5 m) high with large, dark green, leathery leaves. Exquisite in flower arrangements, especially picked in bud, and a good accent for mixed borders.

'Peace'
Zones 5–9
The most widely known of all roses, 'Peace' grows to 6 feet (1.8 m) tall and over 2 feet (61 cm) wide, blooming all season with large, 6-inch (15 cm) wide, slightly fragrant flowers. These are yellow with pink petal tips, forming the classic, high-centered hybrid tea shape so valued for cutting. Plants are disease resistant with shiny dark green foliage and thorny canes. Can be used singly as a lawn highlight and also trained flat against a sunny wall or fence. Also consider 'Chicago Peace' with deeper yellow and pink coloring and 'Pink Peace': both are mutations of the original.

'White Masterpiece'
Zones 5–9
Hybridized in the U.S. by Jackson & Perkins, the exhibition-quality, creamy white flowers are large, up to 6 inches (15 cm) across, high centered, sweetly fragrant and accented against dark green, disease-resistant leaves. Use it massed in beds and borders and in all-white gardens.

FLORIBUNDAS

Grow clusters of flowers and are usually smaller than hybrid teas. They tend to be shorter, up to 4 feet (1.2 m) high, and bushier than hybrid teas. Popular examples are 'Iceberg' (white) and 'Impatient' (orange-red).

'Amber Queen'
Zones 5–9
Hybridized in the U.K. by the House of Harkness, plants grow bushy to 3 feet (91 cm) high. Leaves are large, glossy, dark green and coppery red. Plump bronze buds open to shapely, fully double, dusky orange flowers that grow up to 4 inches (10 cm) across and are borne in clusters of up to seven blooms. Best used massed in mixed shrub borders and popular for cutting.

'Betty Prior'

Zones 5–9

This heavy-blooming, bushy rose has a rounded profile with moderate thorns and semi-glossy, medium green leaves. Plants grow to 7 feet (2.1 m) tall and 2 feet (61 cm) wide. Profuse clusters of carmine-pink, single blooms with a light tea-rose fragrance appear in early summer with lighter flowering into autumn. They are highly disease resistant and, in most years, not subject to black spot or powdery mildew. Singly or massed, it creates a bright, showy effect. Use also as a dense, free-flowering hedge.

'Eyepaint'

Zones 5–9

A cross between an unknown seedling and 'Picasso' and introduced by the House of McGredy, New Zealand, plants grow to 4 feet (1.2 m) with a spreading, vigorous growth habit. Thorny canes bear slightly fragrant, magenta-red, single flowers nearly 3 inches (8 cm) across with a white eye and gold crown of stamens among dark green leaves. Best used singly in mixed borders, along walls and fences and atop terraces where the canes can be allowed to cascade.

'Iceberg'

Zones 5–9

The profuse flowering and romantic appeal of its pristine 3-inch (8 cm) white flowers are the main reasons to grow 'Iceberg'. Plants grow to 4 feet (1.2 m) tall with an upright, bushy habit. The abundant clusters of hybrid tea-shaped blooms appear in early summer with all-season repeat flowering. Moderately fragrant, this tough, hardy plant is heat tolerant and disease resistant, except to black spot. It makes an impressive hedge. There is a climbing form that is sensational in "all-white gardens" when trained over arches and arbors.

Shrubs

'Showbiz'
Zones 5–9

Hybridized by Tantau of Germany, the bushy, compact habit and profuse flowering of its camellia-like flowers, which grow to almost 3 inches (8 cm) across, make it the perfect rose for massing. Growing to just 4 feet (1.2 m) high, its blood-red flowers lack fragrance, but the strong flush of color in early summer is followed by another in autumn with moderate repeat bloom in between.

'Sunsprite'
Zones 5–9

A sweet and powerful scent of licorice is emitted from the deep yellow, double flowers that occur in clusters in early summer on a compact, shrubby plant, which grows to 3 feet (91 cm) tall and wide. Plants are disease resistant, robust and moderately thorny with shiny, deep green leaves. Mass in the landscape for maximum effect.

GRANDIFLORA

This designation is only used in the U.S. In other countries, grandifloras are considered to be hybrid teas. They have flowers the size of hybrid teas and are cluster-flowered. All these types are grafted onto a hardy rootstock, usually *R. multiflora*, with a swelling on the stem that shows the union of the two grafts. If suckers spring up from below the graft union, remove them.

'Queen Elizabeth'
Zones 5–9

Though recognized as a hybrid tea in many countries because of its large hybrid tea-shaped blooms, in the U.S., it is known as a grandiflora because the flowers are borne in clusters like a floribunda, but they are larger than a floribunda. They produce 4-inch (10 cm), double pink, moderately fragrant, high-centered flowers. Plants grow to 7 feet (2.1 m) high and 3 feet (91 cm) wide and are disease resistant with shiny, dark green leaves. There is also a climbing form to 14 feet (4.3 m) high. Use singly as a lawn highlight and in mixed shrub borders.

'Sexy Rexy'
Zones 5–9

What 'Iceberg' is in a white floribunda, 'Sexy Rexy' is in pink—an incredibly profuse-blooming rose with good repeat bloom. Introduced by the House of McGredy, New Zealand, plants grow to 5 feet (1.5 m) high and are almost suffocated in double, soft pink, 3-inch (8 cm) wide roses, in large, slightly fragrant clusters against small, light green leaves. Bushy growth to 4 feet (1.2 m) high makes it suitable for planting singly in mixed borders and for massing.

CLIMBERS

They have long, vigorous canes suitable for tying to supports, since they cannot climb unaided. The popular 'Blaze' (crimson) and 'Mermaid' (yellow, single-flowered) are both capable of extending their canes 20 feet (6.1 m) and more.

'America'

Zones 5–9

All-season bloom, together with 4-inch (10 cm), double, coral-pink, strongly fragrant flowers are reasons to grow this tall plant. The upright canes are strong and vigorous, and grow up to 12 feet (3.6 m) tall. Attractive, medium green, disease-resistant foliage makes this a favorite to train up a trellis, wall or arbor.

'American Pillar'

Zones 6–9

Flowering over a four-week period in early summer, this old garden rose produces large sprays of 2-inch (5 cm) deep single pink flowers with a white eye. Plants grow to 20 feet (6.1 m) tall, producing long, moderately thorny canes and leathery, dark green leaves. It is a favorite for covering high arches and arbors. Birds enjoy the bright red hips in autumn.

'Blaze'

Zones 5–9

This repeat-flowering rose is a first-rate performer, growing quickly to 12 feet (3.6 m) tall. Producing prolific clusters of rich red 3-inch (8 cm) blooms in midsummer, its flowering can be so profuse that the blooms hide the foliage. A remarkably disease-free and vigorous plant, it is sometimes known by its original name, 'Paul's Scarlet Improved'. Use over arches and arbors. Pruned, it makes a spectacular hedge. Flower clusters are splendid for instant bouquets.

'Dortmund'

Zones 4–9

This upright, vigorous climber produces very thorny canes to 12 feet (3.6 m) tall with dark green and shiny foliage. Large 3-inch (8 cm) clusters of bright red, ruffled flowers with white eyes and gold stamens appear in early summer and exude an apple-like fragrance, followed by large orange-red hips. Plants have excellent disease resistance and are suitable for training up arches and arbors, also for cascading over terraces. Good repeat bloomer.

Shrubs

'Zéphirine Drouhin'
Zones 6–9

Classified as a Bourbon rose and introduced from France in 1868, plants grow to 8 feet (2.4 m) high and are covered in highly fragrant pink flowers up to 4 inches (10 cm) across. The swirling petals give it an old-fashioned appearance, and the smooth stems allow it to be grown close to benches where it will not snag clothing.

SHRUB ROSES

These include many old garden roses, ranging in height from 3 to 6 feet (91 cm to 1.8 m). They are bushy and dense enough to create a good hedge. Examples are 'Bonica' (shell pink) and the popular 'Flower Carpet' series, suitable for low hedging and slope cover.

'Abraham Darby'
Zones 6–9

Introduced by English rosarian David Austin, this is one of his most popular colors in a series of modern roses deliberately bred for an old-fashioned appearance. The 5-inch (13 cm) wide, fragrant flowers are a soft apricot with yellow tints and a swirling petal pattern. Plants grow to 6 feet (1.8 m) high and 4 feet (1.2 m) wide. They are extremely thorny, and are everblooming from early summer to autumn frost. Other popular roses from David Austin include 'Graham Thomas' (yellow), 'Mary Rose' (pink) and 'Othello' (red).

'Ballerina'
Zones 5–9

Developed by the house of Bentall (U.K.) and classified as a hybrid musk rose, the vigorous plants grow arching, lightly thorny canes bearing small, glossy green leaves. Lightly fragrant pink flowers, little more than 1 inch (2.5 cm) wide, have white centers, which are displayed in generous clusters. Heavy bloom occurs in early summer with some repeat bloom into autumn. Popular for grafting to create a weeping rose standard; it is also ideal for decorating mixed borders as a single background specimen, growing to 4 feet (1.2 m) high and 6 feet (1.8 m) wide.

'New Dawn'
Zones 5–9

This upright, rampant grower reaches 15 feet (4.5 m) tall and 8 feet (2.4 m) wide. Generous quantities of soft, shell-pink, loosely double, 3-inch (8 cm) flowers are borne in early summer, emitting a sweet fragrance. Stems are long enough for cutting. It is popular for arbors and arches, also as a hedge with regular pruning. The canes are only moderately thorny, and the disease-resistant leaves are an attractive shiny green.

'Belle de Crécy'
Zones 3–9

Introduced from France in 1829 and classified as a Gallica, this is one of the most popular of old garden roses, valued for its fruity fragrance and swirling dusky violet-pink petal pattern around a button center. Vigorous, disease-resistant, arching canes create a dense bush up to 5 feet (1.5 m) high. Prickly canes bear dark green leaves. Perfect for cottage gardens surrounded by perennials. One flower will fill a room with fragrance.

'Bonica'
Zones 4–9

This repeat-blooming shrub rose is exceptionally hardy and disease resistant, blooming all summer long with abundant scentless, medium pink flower clusters. The plant grows to 5 feet (1.5 m) high and wide with orange-red hips. This is one of the best of a series of shrub roses called 'Meidiland', which were developed in France. Other good varieties include 'Meidiland Red' and 'Meidiland Scarlet'. All are useful as a flowering hedge.

Shrubs

'Cécile Brunner'
Shrub/Polyantha
Zones 5–9

Introduced from France, this dwarf polyantha rose is small in stature with a tidy habit and suitable for small or large gardens. It bears perfectly formed, tiny, light pink buds which are lightly fragrant on a bushy, rounded, spreading shrub growing to 3 feet (91 cm) high and wide. Foliage is dark green, dense and nearly thorn-free.

'Champlain'
Zones 3–9

Hybridized in Canada and introduced by the Department of Agriculture, Canada, this unusually hardy, dense and bushy rose grows to 4 feet (1.2 m) high. Prickly canes bear small pale green leaves. Flowers are a dark, lightly fragrant, double rosy-red and are borne in clusters. Mostly used as a background highlight or hedge.

'Cardinal de Richelieu'
Zones 4–9

Introduced from France in 1840 and classified as a Gallica, it is actually a cross between a Gallica and China rose. Unique among old garden roses for its purple, 2-inch (5 cm) wide, double flowers with button centers and a fruity fragrance. Bushy and compact plants grow to 4 feet (1.2 m) high. The smooth canes bear small, glossy, dark green leaves. Spectacular partnered with 'La Reine Victoria' in floral arrangements and also in cottage gardens.

'Charles de Mills'
Shrub/Gallica
Zones 4–8

This old garden rose was probably bred in Europe in the 19th century. Plants grow to 5 feet (1.5 m) tall and 4 feet (1.2 m) wide, bearing magenta 3-inch (8 cm) blooms with a slight fragrance. The 200 petals of the flowers are extraordinary in number and arrangement. Thick, erect canes produce toothed, glossy and dark green leaves. The plant is disease resistant with a long life and makes an attractive hedge.

'Carefree Beauty'
Zones 4–9

Superb disease resistance, excellent all-season bloom and winter hardiness are all attractions of this upright, spreading shrub rose. Plants grow to 6 feet (1.8 m) high and 4 feet (1.2 m) wide, blooming summer through autumn with loosely formed, long-stemmed clusters of moderately fragrant, rosy-pink, semi-double flowers. Good for cutting and can be used for hedges and screens, massed and as a specimen.

'Flower Carpet'
Zones 4–9

A very popular rose for massing to create a slope cover or dense hedge, on account of its heavy bloom production and disease resistance. The original 'Flower Carpet' is a semi-double carmine pink, up to 3 inches (8 cm) across and repeat blooming on plants 3 feet (91 cm) high. Subsequent additions include white, red, yellow and other colors.

'Frau Dagmar Hartopp'
Shrub/Hybrid Rugosa
Zones 3–8

This Danish hybrid is an extremely hardy, repeat-blooming, rugosa shrub rose that grows up to 4 feet (1.2 m) high and wide. It bears intensely fragrant, 3-inch (8 cm), pale pink blooms from early summer until frost. Autumn leaf coloring is also outstanding, the foliage turning from dark green to deep reddish purple and then to rich gold. Large orange-red hips enhance these colors. It is a good plant for problem areas such as near a hot driveway or at seashore locations. It also makes a short, impenetrable hedge.

'Hansa'
Shrub/Hybrid Rugosa
Zones 2–9

Introduced from Holland in 1905, this vigorous shrub rose has a dense, spreading habit with glossy, serrated, deeply veined leaves and large, mauve-red, fragrant, double flowers up to 5 inches (13 cm) across. These appear in late spring and summer. Large, cherry-size, red fruits ripen in late summer and persist into autumn. Plants are valued for hedging and erosion control, especially in sandy coastal gardens.

'Harrison's Yellow'
Shrub/Old garden rose
Zones 3–9

Introduced in 1830 from the garden of Mr. G. F. Harrison (sometimes spelled Harison), who lived in what is now midtown Manhattan, New York. It is believed to be a natural cross between the Austrian briar rose (*R. foetida*) and the Scotch briar rose (*R. spinosissima*). The arching, thorny canes grow to 7 feet (2.1 m) high and are studded with double pale yellow flowers up to 2 inches (5 cm) across in spring. A good disease-resistant rose to grow up a trellis, against a wall and to arch over low fences. The flowers have a yeasty fragrance and make good companions for late-flowering tulips and early-flowering bearded irises.

'Henry Hudson'
Zones 2–8

Developed by Felicitas Svejda, of Canada, and introduced by the Canadian Department of Agriculture in 1976, this hybrid rugosa rose is one of a group of extra hardy roses called the 'Explorer' series, all with names of Canadian explorers. Plants grow to 5 feet (1.5 m) high and bear dark green, leathery, veined leaves. The flowers grow in clusters and are white and semi-double with golden-yellow centers up to 3 inches (8 cm) wide. They are fragrant, bloom all summer and finish the season with an attractive display of red hips. Used mainly for hedging, especially in coastal gardens, because of its rugosa parentage and salt tolerance.

'Knockout'

Zones 5–9

Hybridized in the U.S., the cherry blooms are 3 inches (8 cm) across with an almost fluorescent sheen to the petals. These sweetly scented, semi-double flowers are highlighted by dark green foliage, which is followed by orange hips in autumn. Plants are disease resistant, grow to 3 feet (91 cm) high and are perfect for massing or as a low hedge. Repeat flowering all season.

'La Reine Victoria'

Zones 4–9

Introduced from France in 1872, this old garden rose is classified a Bourbon and derived from crosses between China roses and Damask roses. The exquisite, cupped double flowers form almost a sphere of shell pink, up to 3 inches (8 cm) across. The thorny canes grow to 6 feet (1.8 m) high and are best displayed espaliered against a high wall or fence. Its perfume is an enchanting apple fragrance. An essential component of any cottage garden or old garden rose collection.

'Madame Hardy'

Shrub/Hybrid Damask

Zones 4–9

This old garden rose grows to 6 feet (1.8 m) tall and 5 feet (1.5 m) wide, flowering in summer with no repeat bloom. The 3-inch (8 cm) white blooms of the classic old rose form have a sweet, musky fragrance with a hint of lemon. The lush flowers contain up to 200 petals and grow in clusters. Plants are upright and bushy with moderately thorny canes. Long living and disease resistant, it makes a lovely, tall hedge.

'Sally Holmes'

Shrub/Climber

Zones 5–9

Vigorous canes bear abundant clusters of slightly fragrant, single white blooms that can be mistaken for a rhododendron from a distance. Plants grow to 12 feet (3.6 m) tall and 6 feet (1.8 m) wide. Best used to cascade over a terrace or trained as a climber. Individual blooms are 3 inches (8 cm) across, but the clusters can be 8 inches (20 cm) wide.

'Tuscany Superb'

Shrub/Gallica

Zones 4–8

Probably bred in Europe in the 19th century, this old garden rose grows 4 feet (1.2 m) tall and wide. The 4-inch (10 cm) wide, fragrant blooms are the color of dark wine or mulberry. The thick, erect canes have disease-resistant, dark green leaves. Makes an attractive hedge or shrub accent.

MINIATURES

Bushy and cushion shaped, they are usually not more than 2 feet (61 cm) high, although there are climbing miniatures. Use them as edging, massed to make a groundcover, in rock gardens spilling over rock ledges and also in containers.

'Jeanne Lajoie'

Miniature Climber

Zones 5–9

Late spring flowering, the masses of pink, 1-inch (2.5 cm), double blossoms occur singly and in clusters on vigorous, well-branched canes. Plants can grow to 8 feet (2.4 m) tall, creating a pillar of blooms. The glossy, dark green foliage is disease resistant. Plant against a trellis or allow it to sprawl as a slope cover. It is also useful as a hedge.

Orange Honey
Miniature

Zones 4–9

Striking, yellow-orange, double, high-centered, fragrant blooms cover this plant, which grows to 16 inches (41 cm) tall and flowers in early summer. The foliage is dull green on moderately thorny canes. Plants form a bushy, spreading shrub that is repeat blooming. Use massed as a colorful groundcover, as a low hedge and singly in a rock garden to cascade over rock ledges. Excellent for growing in containers and edging garden paths.

Shrubs

SPECIES ROSES

Rosa eglanteria
Sweetbriar rose
Zones 5–9

Native to England, this disease-free species rose grows to 10 feet (3 m) tall and 8 feet (2.4 m) wide, bearing clusters of fragrant small flowers with five pink petals and prominent yellow stamens. It blooms in early summer with no repeat bloom. Upon being crushed, the foliage smells of green apples, and the upright, arching canes are extremely thorny. It makes a good barrier or privacy hedge.

Rosa gallica
Apothecary
Zones 4–8

Both disease resistant and winter hardy, this old garden rose is usually grown as a feature of herb gardens, since its fragrant petals are used in potpourris. Its deep pink, semi-double flowers measure 3 inches (8 cm) across and appear in early summer. Its fragrance intensifies after drying. Plants are mounded and upright with bristly canes. Can be used as a background for mixed borders.

Rosa glauca aka *R. rubrifolia*
Red leaf rose
Zones 2–8

This species rose is indigenous to high elevation areas of Europe. The small, serrated leaves are a blue-green attached to red stems, and the branch tips are red. The fragrant 1-inch (2.5 cm), five-petalled flowers are pink with white centers, occurring in late spring. Plants grow to 6 feet (1.8 m) high and are almost devoid of thorns. Usually used as a background in perennial gardens and as a curiosity in rose collections.

Rosa foetida
Austrian Copper 'Bicolor'
Zones 3–9

This is a natural mutation of a species rose indigenous to Persia but cultivated for centuries in Europe, especially Austria. The original species displays five yellow petals up to 2 inches (5 cm) across. 'Bicolor' is a copper-red with a yellow center and a yellow reverse, a unique color in roses. Plants are thorny, and the long canes grow to 8 feet (2.4 m) high, arching out like a fountain. The small, dull green leaves invariably discolor from disease (usually black spot) and drop to the ground soon after blooming in spring. In spite of its hardiness, therefore, it is not long lived. The flower fragrance is sickly-sweet.

Rosa moyesii
Moyes rose
Zones 4–9
This vigorous species rose is native to China. Growing to 13 feet (3.9 m) high, plants produce long, thorny canes with small, dull green leaves. The rose-red, five-petalled, slightly fragrant flowers measure up to 2 inches (5 cm) across with a circle of yellow stamens in the center. Bright red hips follow the early summer blooms. They are a good component of berry gardens and as background for perennial gardens.

Rosa rugosa
Beach rose
Zones 2–9
Native to Japan but naturalized along the temperate coasts, plants thrive in harsh seaside conditions, even up to the shoreline. It also adds both fragrance and beauty to a garden. Magenta-pink flower buds of five to 12 petals appear from spring to frost. The plant grows to 6 feet (1.8 m) tall and wide with dark green, wrinkled, leathery foliage, which turns yellow in autumn. Large, round hips measuring an inch (2.5 cm) in diameter are edible and are used in preserves.

Rosa spinosissima
Scotch rose
Zones 4–9

This tough, hardy rose has attractive, non-recurring, small, creamy white flowers, which bloom profusely in late spring with a light but sweet scent. These are followed by purple or black 1-inch (2.5 cm) hips, which are sometimes used as holiday decorations. Tolerates dry, windy sites such as coastal gardens. In exposed locations, it grows shorter than its usual 4 feet (1.2 m) height, thus making a low, thorny groundcover.

TREE ROSES

Also called rose standards, they are grafts involving a straight rose trunk up to 5 feet (1.5 m) high and a top-knot of another variety, usually a hybrid tea or floribunda but can also be a species, shrub rose or miniature.

'The Fairy'
Tree/Polyantha
Zones 4–9

This rose with miniature blossoms is a favorite with gardeners because it is a tough, disease-resistant and hardy plant despite its delicate appearance. Bushy and compact, it grows to 4 feet (1.2 m) high and wide. Small, light pink, non-fragrant flowers are borne in summer in large clusters and make handsome bouquets. It does well in pots and as an attractive, ever-blooming hedge. 'The Fairy' is also a popular rose for grafting onto a trunk to create a tree form or rose standard.

SALIX

Willows
Zones 2–9, depending on variety

Hardy willows have been revered in art more than any other woody plant, especially the weeping willows (Trees, see page 199). Shrubby willows, such as pussy willows, have also been immortalized in art, most notably the pollarded willows painted by Van Gogh and Monet. When pollarded (all branches cut back to the trunk to force new growth), the plant produces an explosion of slender new branches called whips or whithies, which are used for basket weaving.

Salix discolor
Pussy willow
Zones 2–9

Native to the eastern U.S., this large, fast-growing shrub grows to 20 feet (6.1 m) tall and thrives in full sun and moist soil, although plants tolerate a wide range of soils. The "pussies" (immature flowers) are smoky-white and emerge in early spring along slender, whiplike branches, which are used for indoor arrangements. The plant usually has multi-trunks but can be trained to a single main stem to form a small tree. The removal of stems from the crown after flowering forces an explosion of new growth in summer, thus creating a pollard form, valued as a lawn or foundation accent. Several other willows are valued for their hardiness, including the following:

Salix integra 'Hakuro Nishiki'
Japanese dappled willow
Zones 3–10

Native to Japan, this wide-spreading shrub grows to 10 feet (3 m) high with a rounded habit. The juvenile foliage exhibits green and white variegation in the spring with a touch of pink. The variegation lasts several months. This stunning willow may be trained as a standard and grown in a container.

Sambucus nigra 'Black Beauty'
European elder

Zones 5–6

This large, multi-stemmed, deciduous shrub grows to 20 feet (6.1 m) tall and is valued for its almost black foliage in spring and masses of flat-topped pink flower clusters. Over the summer, the dark foliage changes to a dark green. Plants demand full sun and a moisture-retentive, humus-rich soil. They are difficult to grow without copious irrigation where summers are hot and humid.

Sambucus racemosa 'Plumosa Aurea'
European red elder

Zones 3–6

This elderberry has deeply cut, golden yellow leaves. The coloration is not lost during the summer months, and it should be considered where a large, bushy, yellow-leaved plant is desired. Flowers are white and borne in spring in flat clusters. The leaves are sharply serrated. Prefers full sun and good drainage.

Sarcococca hookeriana var. humilis
Sweetbox

Zones 5–8

Native to the Himalayas and China, this broad-leaf evergreen is low growing, seldom more than 30 inches (75 cm) high, with a spread to 8 feet (2.4 m) or more by means of rhizomes. However, shearing around the sides easily controls it. The leaves are a lustrous dark green with very fragrant, small white flowers early in the spring. Sweet box should be sited where the fragrance of the flowers can be appreciated. It makes an excellent evergreen groundcover or foundation plant in sun or light to deep shade. The variety 'Humilis' is hardy to zone 4.

Schizophragma hydrangeoides
Japanese hydrangea vine

Zones 6–9

Native to Japan and Korea, this woody vine resembles climbing hydrangea and climbs by holdfast aerial roots up to 30 feet (9.1 m) tall. The large, oval, serrated leaves are dark green. Broad, flat clusters of white flowers appear summer to autumn. 'Moonlight' has blue-green leaves with a silvery cast. 'Roseum' has pink in its flowers. Best grown against a wall, fence or large tree in soil that drains well in sun or part shade. It is usually a better choice for covering walls than English ivy on account of its generous floral display.

Shrubs

Stephanandra incisa 'Crispa'
Cut-leaf stephanandra

Zones 4–7

Native to eastern Asia, this variety grows to 3 feet (91 cm) high, as opposed to 6 feet (1.8 m) for the species. It is a thicket-forming shrub with arching shoots; handsome, dissected, crinkly foliage; and a low-spreading groundcover habit. The plant becomes slightly mounded in the middle but prostrate at the edges. Give it full sun or light shade and good drainage. Can be used to create a low hedge.

Symphoricarpos albus
Snowberry

Zones 3–7

Native to North America, this upright or spreading shrub grows to 6 feet (1.8 m) tall, depending on variety. The leaves are oval and dull green with pink flowers in spring followed by white fruit from late summer to winter. *S. a.* var. *laevigatus* bears more and bigger fruit than the species. Best fruit production is in full sun, but the plant tolerates poor soil, urban air, shade and neglect. A related species, *S. x chenaultii* (zones 4–7) has red berries that are white on the underside. The autumn berry display is highly ornamental. *S. orbiculatus*, Indian currant or coralberry (zones 3–7), is native to North America. This upright shrub grows to 3 feet (91 cm) high and is suitable for erosion control. Fruits are coral-red, ripening in autumn.

Skimmia japonica
Japanese skimmia

Zones 6–9

Native to Japan, this broadleaf evergreen shrub grows to 5 feet (1.5 m) high with a similar spread and a mounded, dense habit. The flower sexes are on separate plants. One male plant can pollinate a dozen female plants for berry production. Purple-red flower buds open to sweetly scented, creamy white flowers in spring, followed by festive, bright red berry clusters on female plants. The oblong, smooth leaves are green above and lighter green below. Plants prefer well-drained, humus-rich, acidic soil in partial shade. Skimmia can be grown in tubs for patio and courtyard decoration. It is also popular as a bonsai subject.

SYRINGA

Lilacs

Zones 3–7, depending on variety

One of the most uplifting sights in nature is to travel a country road in spring and see a neglected old lilac in full bloom by the foundation of a deserted dwelling, while the rest of the property has reverted to wilderness. Such survivors show not only the toughness and longevity of lilacs, but also the high regard in which they are held. Faithfully, they seem to shrug off all kinds of stress from pests, climate extremes and impoverished soil, although they prefer slightly alkaline or neutral soil in full sun with good drainage. They are grown for their beautiful fragrant blooms composed of four-petalled flower clusters 6 inches (15 cm) long and even larger in certain hybrids. Most grow upright, suckering at the base to produce a large shrub. The foliage is spear shaped and in summer usually becomes infected with powdery mildew. Scale and borers can also weaken them. It is important

Spiraea japonica
Japanese spirea

Zones 4–8

There are many varieties of this low, bushy, deciduous shrub. It grows quickly to 5 feet (1.5 m) high and wide in sun and soil with good drainage. Grown chiefly for its showy, late spring, pink to rose-red flower clusters and sharply indented foliage, it usually displays colorful yellow foliage in autumn. Popular as an accent in mixed borders and foundation plantings. 'Anthony Waterer' grows to 4 feet (1.2 m) with carmine-pink flowers that bloom for most of the summer. 'Goldflame' has arresting yellow-orange foliage in spring, which fades to yellow-green in summer and flames to orange in the autumn. 'Bumalda' grows less than 3 feet (91 cm) high and is hardy to zone 3.

to know whether hybrids have been grafted onto common lilac or privet. Avoid privet because they will sucker constantly. It is also possible that the privet will eventually take over the lilac.

Syringa vulgaris
Common lilac

Zones 4–8

Native to eastern Europe, this suckering, spreading, large shrub has heart-shaped to oval leaves and grows to 20 feet (6.1 m) high. It bears very fragrant single or double flowers in dense conical panicles up to 8 inches (20 cm) long in spring. There are many outstanding hybrid varieties such as 'Charles Joly' (double dark purple), 'Maréchal Foch' (carmine pink), 'Mont Blanc' (white), 'Primrose' (pale yellow) and 'Sensation' (single purple with white edges). It is virtually indestructible.

Syringa 'Miss Kim'
Miss Kim lilac

Zones 5–8.

Native to Korea and northern China, this compact, mound-shaped plant covers itself in late spring with erect panicles of pale lilac-blue flowers. Plants grow to 8 feet (2.4 m) high by 10 feet (3 m) wide. The leaves may turn purple in autumn. *S. meyeri* 'Palibin', Meyer lilac (zones 4–7), is native to Korea with a compact, rounded shrub that grows to 6 feet (1.8 m) tall. It produces oval leaves and bears fragrant bluish-pink or lavender-pink flowers in small panicles up to 3 inches (8 cm) long in late spring and early summer.

Tamarix ramosissima
Tamarix

Zones 3–8

Native to southeastern Europe and central Asia, this deciduous, fast-growing, spreading shrub reaches 15 feet (4.5 m) high with a loose, open, weeping habit and attractive, bright green, feathery foliage. It has airy clusters of tiny pale pink flowers that bloom in late spring. Plants prefer well-drained, acidic soil in full sun and tolerate sandy soil and seashore conditions. Although it is not long lived, tamarix is suitable for mixed borders to produce a misty quality. Several plants are used as accents in Monet's garden at intervals along perennial borders.

Taxus cuspidata
Japanese yew

Zones 4–7

Native to Japan, Korea and Manchuria, this fast-growing, hardy, needle evergreen is variable in size, according to variety. Plants can grow to 50 feet (15.2 m) high with a 25-foot (7.6 m) spread and an upright habit. Leaves form a distinct V-shaped pattern as they lie flat in two rows along the stem. Stem bark is reddish-brown and flakes off with age. Oval, poisonous, red berries appear in autumn. Plants prefer well-drained loam soil in full sun or part shade. The tall varieties make good accents as sentinels at doorways and garden entrances, also valuable as a hedge. Dwarf spreading kinds can be sheared into mounds.

Shrubs

Viburnum
Viburnum

Zones 2–9, depending on variety

This large plant family of 150 species or more has many forms. Some have flat, white flower clusters resembling lace-cap hydrangeas, and others have snowball-size, globular flower heads. Almost all have the bonus of decorative berry clusters in autumn. These berries are relished by songbirds and may be red, yellow, blue or black depending on variety. Indigenous to both the European and North American continents, the hardy varieties are generally easy to grow in full sun or light shade, and although most prefer good drainage, some tolerate boggy soil. Most are evergreen in mild winter areas, but tend to be deciduous in harsh winters. The leaf coloration of the North American species in particular can be exceptional. Although floral color is limited to white or pale pink, the propensity of bloom can be astonishing, especially among sterile flower forms, which sacrifice berries for increased flower production. For best berry production among non-sterile kinds, plant viburnums in groups to ensure cross-pollination. Flowering times vary from early spring to early summer depending on the variety. They are outstanding in shrub borders and at the edges of woodland. In many display gardens, such as Winterthur, Delaware, viburnums sweep across an entire hillside in company with rhododendrons, which then extends into woodland beside a stream and a romantic bridge. The following are the most ornamental:

Viburnum dilatatum
Linden viburnum

Zones 3–8

This is the one to grow if you desire an avalanche of beautiful deep red berry clusters in autumn. Native to China and Japan, tubular white flowers form domed clusters up to 5 inches (13 cm) across. The broadly oval-shaped leaves are dark green, serrated and deeply veined, turning shades of orange-red to burgundy in autumn. Plants grow to 10 feet (3 m) high. 'Iroquois' is an exceptionally generous berry producer.

Viburnum x burkwoodii
Burkwood viburnum

Zones 4–8

This dense, twiggy, evergreen shrub grows to 8 feet (2.4 m) high with fragrant white, pink-tinged, domed flowers in spring. Elliptical red berries follow and last into the winter months. Leaves are dark green, glossy, oval and toothed. 'Mohawk' is resistant to bacterial leaf spot and powdery mildew.

Viburnum carlesii
Koreanspice viburnum

Zones 5–8

Native to Korea and Japan, this is a parent of the Burkwood hybrid viburnum, and therefore is similar in appearance. Not as vigorous or free flowering, but it is grown mainly for its fragrant, domed, white flowers in spring. Plants grow to 8 feet (2.4 m) high.

Viburnum opulus 'Sterile'
European snowball bush

Zones 4–8

The conventional species is known as the Guilder rose and bears flat, white flower clusters that resemble miniature white hydrangea, followed by red berries. The 'Sterile' selection is probably the most widely planted of all viburnums, on account of its robust growth and snow-white, globular flowers that bend the branches with their weight in spring. Since the flowers are sterile, they do not bear berries but compensate with extraordinary flowering potential. The maple-shaped leaves turn shades of yellow and red in autumn.

Viburnum plicatum 'Plicatum'
Japanese snowball bush

Zones 6–8

This variety is hardly distinguishable from the European snowball bush except for its leaf shape, which is spear shaped and serrated. It is also spring flowering. There is a beautiful pale pink selection 'Roseum'.

Viburnum plicatum 'Tomentosum'
Doublefile viburnum

Zones 4–8

Easily identified in late spring with its sweeping, slender branches studded with 3-inch (8 cm) wide white flowers resembling miniature hydrangeas, and heart-shaped, toothed green leaves that are deeply veined. Generous red berry clusters follow in autumn. The variety 'Lanarth' is the most free flowering of all on account of its sterile flower clusters, although it bears no berries. Sensational planted among red-flowering rhododendrons so their blossoms mingle.

Viburnum rhytidophyllum
Leatherleaf viburnum

Zones 6–8

Though not as free flowering as other viburnum, this has handsome leaves, which are dark green, spear shaped, deeply veined and serrated. The flower clusters are white, nodding and up to 8 inches (20 cm) across. These are followed in autumn with black oval berries.

Viburnum setigerum
Tea viburnum

Zones 5–7

Narrowly upright in form and sometimes leggy, this shrub has arching branches with large, shiny, dark green leaves [to 4 inches (10 cm) long] that turn yellow, orange and red in autumn. The fragrant, white, fertile flowers are borne in flat 2-inch (5 cm) diameter clusters in late spring. The berries are reddish-orange; they turn translucent with the first frost and then brown.

Viburnum trilobum
Cranberry viburnum

Zones 2–7

The hardiest viburnum for garden display, this is a popular variety for enriching wildlife habitat on account of its edible red berries and tolerance of moist soil. Although the flat, white flower clusters are generally not as showy as other viburnum, the orange-red berries that ripen in autumn are extremely decorative and relished by songbirds. The three-pronged, dark green leaves are maple shaped and turn yellow to red in autumn. Native to North America, plants form a dense shrub up to 15 feet (4.5 m) high, suitable for creating an informal, billowing hedge.

Vinca minor
Periwinkle

Zones 3–9

Native to Europe, plants have naturalized across North America, especially in woodland, where light shade encourages it to spread across the ground to immense distances. Plants have smooth, shiny, dark green, evergreen, oblong leaves and slender, ground-hugging stems that knit together to create an attractive weed-suffocating groundcover. Plants remain low at no more than 6 inches (15 cm) high. Blue, starlike 1-inch (2.5 cm) flowers appear in early spring and continue into summer. Although sometimes slow to get established, plants can grow fast, especially in moisture-retentive, organic-rich soil. 'Alba' is an attractive white mutation, and several variegated forms are available with leaves margined white. Use wherever you might use English ivy as a groundcover. A less hardy but closely related species is *V. major* (zones 6–9), which has larger flowers. A variegated form, 'Elegantissima', has larger variegated foliage and is often used as a curtain draped from window box plantings, hanging baskets and over terraces.

Vitex agnus-castus
Chaste tree

Zones 6–9

Chaste tree can be grown as a large, deciduous, multi-stemmed shrub or small tree up to 20 feet (6.1 m) tall. Valued for its beautiful, cut-leaved foliage and light violet-blue flowers. These plants start to bloom in midsummer and continue into autumn. In harsh winters, plants will die back to the ground, but since blooms form on new wood, this is not a disadvantage. If cut back to the ground after flowering, the plant rarely grows much more than 4 feet (1.2 m) high in gardens with a short season. Its vigorous upright growth results in almost vertical branches. Provide full sun and good drainage. 'Silver Spire' produces white flowers.

Weigela florida
Weigela

Zones 4–8

Native to Asia, this billowing, deciduous shrub is greatly under-used in gardens. Its profuse flowering follows the main azalea displays of spring, and they are often mistaken for an azalea from a distance. Valued for masses of trumpet-shaped flowers in mostly shades of pink and red, there are also varieties with bronze and silver-variegated foliage to create a tapestry effect in the landscape even when the plants are not in bloom. Plants are easy to grow in most well-drained soils in full sun or light shade. Growth habit is upright to 6 feet (1.8 m), spreading to 12 feet (3.6 m). The sheer weight of the flowers makes the side branches arch and bend to the ground. The leaves are spear shaped, usually dark green turning dull brown in autumn. Prune mature plants after flowering to maintain an attractive mounded shape. Best used in mixed borders, as a foundation accent and as a dense informal hedge. 'Bristol Ruby' is a popular hybrid with ruby-red flowers. 'Wine & Roses' bears rosy-pink flowers and dark bronze foliage.

WISTERIA

Wisteria

Zones 5–10, depending on variety

One of the world's most widely published spring garden scenes is Claude Monet's Japanese bridge covered in wisteria. Across a corner of his water lily garden is a canopy of Japanese wisteria in two colors—white and blue. The white is slightly later flowering and creates the effect of a lace curtain. He planted another blue wisteria along a footpath bordering his pond, so that the spent flowers could drop to briefly color the path blue, and also cast exquisite reflections on the surface of his pond. It is believed that Monet was inspired to create the wisteria canopy for his bridge from descriptions of a wisteria canopy extending 60 feet (18.3 m) above a stone zig-zag bridge in the Sento Imperial Palace Garden in Kyoto, Japan.

A common problem in gardens with harsh winters, especially in zones 5 and 6, is the failure of wisteria to bloom. This will happen if the soil lacks phosphorus. More often, it happens when a warming trend in spring causes the flower buds to partially open, and then an unexpected freeze kills the embryo. This is called "bud blast" and bloom is lost for that season.

Described here are three types of wisteria—the Japanese, Chinese and American—all with pendant flower clusters that hang like slender bunches of grapes. The Japanese and Chinese are so similar in appearance, it is hard to tell them apart, except that the Chinese flowers are not as impressive as the Japanese; they are generally shorter in length, not as fragrant and later flowering by a week. The American wisteria is similar in appearance to the Chinese, but the flowers are half their length, a paler blue, and later flowering by another week.

Care must be taken when planting any of these wisteria, for they will grow up to 10 feet (3 m) in a season, thus becoming invasive and even strangling the trees on which they are climbing. Moreover, the heavy vines can become so dense and suffocating, they will quickly rot wooden structures. Therefore, consider threading them through more durable stone balustrades and up metal supports. Give them all full sun and good drainage for best flowering performance.

Azaleas are good to plant near wisteria, for azaleas will provide flowers from the ground to eye level with the wisteria extending its floral display high into the sky, thus filling one's entire field of vision with color.

Wisteria floribunda
Japanese wisteria

Zones 5–10

Indigenous to Japan and the subject of numerous Japanese silk-screen prints, the Japanese wisteria is the one to grow when you want flower clusters dripping through the slats of overhead arbors. The compound bright green leaves are composed of slender, spear-shaped leaflets. The strong, twining stems will climb 30 feet (9.1 m) and more. These are draped in flower clusters up to 20 inches (50 cm) in length that can create a curtain of color in shades of blue, pink and white, followed by brittle pods containing beanlike seeds. Plants can be trained to a tree form—a single main trunk with a top-knot of flowering branches draped over an umbrella of wire supports.

Wisteria sinensis
Chinese wisteria

Zones 5–10

Indigenous to China, it produces vines identical to the Japanese wisteria but with shorter flower clusters, up to 12 inches (31 cm) long. 'Black Dragon' has unusual dark purple flowers. There are also white and double-flowered forms. Earlier flowering than American wisteria and later flowering than Japanese wisteria, Chinese wisteria is often entwined with both of these to achieve flushes of color from spring through summer.

Wisteria frutescens
American wisteria

It is indigenous to North America, mostly from Virginia to Texas. Although it will also grow to 30 feet (9.1 m), it tends to be less vigorous than the Asian species. The flower clusters are smaller, up to 6 inches (15 cm) long, and it is later blooming than the Asian. It still presents a generous floral effect from late spring to midsummer and can be used up a trellis and over arches in the same way as the Asian species.

Trees

In the entire plant kingdom, nothing seems to evoke awe and admiration more than trees. The thought of a 300-year-old oak falling victim to a developer's chainsaw will rally whole neighborhoods into saving the tree.

What is it about trees that evoke such feelings? Partly, it seems that trees are natural landmarks and memorials. Because their life span can be greater than humans', they carry their associations from one generation to the next. But mostly, it is a matter of beauty—the ability of trees to significantly improve the quality of our surroundings, whether it is a blizzard of pink cherry blossoms in spring or the pencil-straight trunk and lofty lime-green canopy of a tulip tree.

The famous American landscape architect, Thomas Church, explained it well in his book The Education of a Gardener when he wrote: "Never underestimate the value of a handsome tree. Protect it. Build your house and garden compositions around it, for it offers you shade, shadow, pattern against the sky, protection over your house, a ceiling over your terrace."

Trees can be planted singly to create a lawn accent, or grouped to create a wooded lot to improve the value of a house. They can also be used as a woodlot or wildlife sanctuary, as a small decorative grove, as a windbreak and for skyline interest. Trees add character to a landscape. They are the most dominant plants in the landscape, and will help to identify a garden theme or region. Willows are associated with Japanese gardens, and ginkgo with Chinese. White birch and Japanese pines can evoke a mountainous setting. Lombardy poplars are appropriate for a vineyard or Italian garden, while bald cypresses are appropriate for a swamp or bog garden. English oak and English yew can evoke memories of English stately homes.

ABIES

Firs

Zones 2–7, depending on species and variety

Abies balsamea
Balsam fir

Zones 2–6

Native to high elevations of the northeastern U.S., this dense, columnar, needle evergreen grows to 70 feet (21.3 m) high, its branches extending at an oblique angle. The needles are 1 inch (2.5 cm), blue-green and fragrant. The violet-purple cones are up to 3 inches (8 cm) long. It is handsome as a single specimen or planted as a grove for windbreak, also popular as a Christmas tree. Give it full sun and good drainage. Plants struggle where summers are hot and humid.

Abies concolor
White fir

Zones 3–7

Native to mountain regions of the west and southwestern U.S., this needle evergreen grows to 70 feet (21.3 m) high. Its bluish-green appearance and attractive, spire-like, columnar shape make it a popular tree to silhouette against the skyline and for planting as a windbreak. Plants prefer sandy loam in full sun, though tolerate a wide range of soils with good drainage.

Abies koreana
Korean fir

Zones 5–7

Native to Korea, this is a slow-growing, compact pyramidal tree, which seldom grows over 30 feet (9.1 m) tall. Its shiny, dark green needles are forward curving to reveal the silver underneath, thus creating a frosted or shimmering appearance. Cones are reddish, turning bluish-purple when mature and are borne on young trees. Requires full sun and good drainage.

LEFT: A pair of Norway spruce contrast with white oak and tulip trees in a woodland garden.

Trees

ACER

Maples

Zones 4–9, depending on variety

Totaling perhaps 150 species worldwide, maples can be a blessing and a curse, depending on the species or variety. Many are simply too big for small gardens, but they make wonderful skyline trees, especially those like sugar maple that can display brilliant orange or red leaf color in autumn. At the other extreme in terms of size, the slower-growing, more compact Japanese maples are highly valued. The mature specimens of these small ornamental trees command the highest prices at auction for their strong autumn leaf color. Norway maple and box elder maple can be invasive, and though special selections of these are desirable, the wild forms are best avoided.

There are many different kinds of maples from tall shade trees to midsize and even small and shrublike ones. Maples do well in full sun or light shade but this varies from species to species. The soil should be fertile and high in organic matter to retain moisture, but well drained.

Acer campestre
Hedge maple

Zones 5–8

This deciduous, medium-sized tree forms a dense rounded shape and grows up to 30 feet (9.1 m) tall with equal spread. Its low-branching habit and tolerance of heavy pruning make it popular as a hedge.

Acer ginnala aka *A. tataricum* subsp. *ginnala*
Amur maple

Zones 2–8

This hardiest of maples can withstand temperatures as low as -50°F (-46°C). It is often used as a substitute for *A. palmatum* and *A. japonicum* in brutally cold climates. Plants grow to 25 feet (7.6 m) high with an equal or greater spread. It has three-lobed, toothed leaves which attain a striking red fall color. Clusters of small, fragrant, yellowish flowers in early spring are followed by handsome, bright red, winged seeds. Give it full sun and good drainage.

Acer griseum
Paperbark maple

Zones 4–8

Native to China, this deciduous, small tree grows slowly to 30 feet (9.1 m) high and wide. It is popular for its orange-brown bark, which peels and curls in papery strips. Usually grown as a lawn accent with bulbs such as crocus naturalized around its trunk. Give it sun or light shade and good drainage.

Acer japonicum
Fullmoon maple

Zones 5–7

This highly desirable landscape tree is similar to *A. palmatum*, except that it tends to grow taller [to 30 feet (9.1 m) and equally wide] and the sharply divided, toothed leaves are not as fleecy and lacy as those of *A. palmatum*. Autumn leaf coloration is equally dramatic.

Acer palmatum
Japanese maple

Zones 5–9, depending on variety

Surely there is no tree more valued for decorative effect in a home landscape than the Japanese maples (*A. palmatum* and *A. japonicum*). *A. palmatum*, in general, is more widely grown than *A. japonicum*, which it resembles closely. A slow-growing, easy-care, hardy, deciduous tree native to Japan, hundreds of varieties of *A. palmatum* are available. Growing to 25 feet (7.6 m) high, they have four seasons of interest, even in a wintry landscape.

Botanically, *A. palmatum* has been divided into nondissected and dissected types, which refer to the leaf shape. Nondissected varieties have the normal five-fingered maple-leaf shape with a serrated edge; but in the dissected types, the fingered parts of the leaf are cut more deeply, becoming lace-like and giving the plant a more refined appearance.

The nondissected varieties are used mostly for bold accents in the landscape, especially when planted among evergreens and to line driveways. The dissected kinds generally do not grow more than 10 feet (3 m) high. They are sensational in planters used to decorate a deck or patio, as sentinels beside the entrance to a house, as accents in a rock garden, beside water features and as bonsai subjects. The branches often display a layered effect, and they are especially beautiful when planted along a flight of steps or at the top of a retaining wall, where their pliable, outspreading branches can drape over the wall.

drains well. Though plants prefer full sun, they tolerate light shade. Mulch around the base to discourage competition from weeds, and protect new plantings during the first year from winter winds by erecting a burlap windbreak. Good companion plants include hostas and ferns, rhododendrons and azaleas.

Although most Japanese maples can be left to create a natural mounded habit with no pruning needed to maintain a pleasing outline, the Japanese like to prune away low branches so the snaking silhouette of multiple trunks can be seen. The effect of this lower-branch pruning is especially beautiful when it frames a nearby decorative element, such as a bench or a boulder, and even more so when several Japanese maples with different leaf colorations are planted together and pruned so it's possible to see through them. The overhead canopy of green and bronze leaves then presents a kaleidoscope of color when backlit, not only in spring and summer, but also in autumn when the leaves turn to various shades of russet.

Acer pensylvanicum
Moosewood
Zones 3–7
Native to the eastern U.S., this small, upright tree has a broad crown and grows up to 20 feet (6.1 m) tall and 15 feet (4.5 m) wide. The most striking feature is its green and white striped bark. Give it full sun or light shade and good drainage.

Acer platanoides
Norway maple
Zones 4–8
Native to Norway, plants grow to 50 feet (15.2 m) tall with a very dense, rounded crown. Plants have good yellow autumn color and pollution tolerance. Once widely recommended as a street tree but now out of favor because of its voracious roots and invasive self-sown seedlings. 'Crimson King' has purple leaves. It is slower growing and more compact than the species. 'Drummondii' has attractive variegated leaves. Provide all these with full sun and good drainage.

Though green and bronze are the most familiar leaf colors, there are yellow and red-leafed varieties, and also a green-leafed kind with coral-red juvenile branches that stand out in the landscape during winter.

In spring, the leaves of the green-foliaged kinds are almost iridescent in their brightness, fully opening to a darker green and creating a foliage canopy in summer that is dense, cushionlike and soothing in appearance. But the best visual sensation occurs in autumn when the leaves turn golden or crimson, depending on the variety. Even after the leaves have dropped and the bare branches are exposed, the tight knit of branches can create a delicate tracery that is accentuated by a fresh fall of snow, which creates a fleecy effect.

Japanese maples can be highly variable in habit and appearance. The popular purple-leafed nondissected variety, 'Bloodgood', will grow to be 20 feet (6.1 m) tall and equally wide, sending up multiple sinuous trunks that have a charcoal gray, polished appearance, especially after a shower of rain.

The variety 'Waterfall' has more finely dissected foliage with a mature height of only 10 feet (3 m). It is aptly named, for the closely spaced, overlapping leaves create a weeping, billowing effect like a waterfall with a heavy flow.

Insects and diseases are surprisingly few in Japanese maples; they tolerate high heat and drought and a wide range of soils except wet soil, where they are susceptible to root-rot diseases.

Transplant young trees balled and burlapped into acid soil that

Acer rubrum
Red maple
Zones 3–9

Native to swamps of North America, this pyramidal, deciduous tree grows quickly to 60 feet (18.3 m) tall. The dark green leaves are three-cornered and turn a brilliant orange or red in the autumn. 'October Glory' and 'Red Sunset' have blazing red leaves. Plants prefer full sun and good drainage, but tolerate boggy soil and light shade.

Acer saccharum
Sugar maple
Zones 4–8

Native to the eastern U.S., plants grow moderately to 60 feet (18.3 m) high and an equal spread. Renowned for its spectacular autumn color from yellow and orange to deep red and scarlet. It needs room to reach full size. Though several maples can be tapped for their sap to make maple syrup, the sugar maple yields the best quality.

Aesculus hippocastanum
Common horse chestnut
Zones 4–7

Native to Europe, this large tree needs ample room to grow, as it attains 70 feet (21.3 m) in height and up to 70 feet (21.3 m) in width. A dense canopy of large, five-fingered, serrated leaves makes underplanting difficult. Flowers are produced in late spring and are known as "candles", arranged in conical clusters up to 12 inches (31 cm) long in mostly white, but also pink. Golf-ball size, spiny green fruits mature in autumn, containing inedible brown nuts called "buckeyes" in the U.S. and "conkers" in the U.K. Not a tree for small gardens, but good for parks and skyline plantings. Plants prefer full sun and good drainage.

Aesculus x carnea
Red horse chestnut
Zones 3–8

This cross between *A. hippocastanum* and *A. pavia* grows to 40 feet (12.2 m) high, displaying rose-red flowers in late spring. A billowing appearance and drought tolerance make this an ideal lawn accent, and also to line a driveway. Handsome even when not in bloom on account of its large palmate leaves.

Albizia julibrissin
Silk tree, Mimosa
Zones 6–11

Native to China, this fast-growing, short-lived, deciduous tree adds a tropical accent to gardens owing to its lacy foliage and pink flowers arranged in clusters that cover the tree in summer and resemble an upturned shaving brush. These are followed by flat, black bean pods. Plants are tolerant of poor soil and hot, dry summers. Give them full sun and good drainage. Useful as a lawn accent since the airy foliage casts light shade, allowing grass to grow up to the trunk. 'Summer Chocolate' has unusual bronze foliage.

Amelanchier arborea
Serviceberry

Zones 4–9

Native to North America, this deciduous, small tree grows 25 feet (7.6 m) high with a variable spread and rounded habit. It provides interest in all seasons: showy clusters of white hawthornlike flowers appearing in mid- to early spring; small, edible, purplish-black, round fruits ripen in June; medium to dark green leaves turn yellow, orange and red in the autumn; and a tracery of winter branches and twigs occurs in the winter. Plants prefer well-drained, moist, acidic soil in full sun or partial shade. Commonly found in nature at the edge of woodland, in hedgerows and along stream banks. *A. canadensis*, shadblow serviceberry (zones 3–8), is more erect and upright with small red fruit relished by songbirds.

Aralia elata
Japanese angelica tree

Zones 3–9

Native to northeast Asia, this deciduous, small tree grows to 30 feet (9.1 m) high by 15 feet (4.5 m) wide with a layered arrangement of leaves. In summer, it displays showy white flower clusters up to 18 inches (46 cm) across and interesting large leaves composed of serrated, spear-shaped leaflets resembling a massive wisteria. Plants perform best in well-drained, humus-rich, fertile soils and good drainage. There are several interesting variegated forms with white leaf margins. The stems and branches are spiny. A North American species, *A. spinosa*, Hercules club (zones 4–9), is similar but less hardy; it suckers vigorously and is spinier.

BETULA

Birches

Zones 2–9, depending on species and variety

The family of birches has 60 species worldwide, of which *B. papyrifera*, white birch, canoe birch or paper birch (zones 2–8), is one of the hardiest of trees, native to North America, including Alaska. Birches popular in gardens are mostly grown for their pale bark, which can be honey-colored, as in the river birch, and white, as in the Himalayan and canoe birches.

Betula nigra
River birch

Zones 4–9

Native to riverbanks of the northeastern U.S., the wild forms have shaggy gray bark, but the mutation known as 'Heritage' is far more desirable. Not only does it grow up to 5 feet (1.5 m) a year, it has flaking bark that peels off in orange segments revealing underneath a smooth, honey-colored trunk with tints of pink. Though plants prefer boggy soil, they will tolerate dry soil once established in full sun or light shade. Grows to 40 feet (12.2 m) high and 15 feet (4.5 m) wide. The spear-shaped, serrated leaves turn buttercup-yellow in autumn. Greenish-yellow pendant catkins appear in spring before the leaves are fully unfurled. Useful as a lawn specimen and planted in groves. Can be grown as a single or multi-stemmed specimen.

Betula papyrifera
Canoe birch, Paper birch, White birch
Zones 2–8
Native mostly to New England, the bark is a ghostly white flecked with black. Unfortunately, where summers are hot and humid, plants can suffer from heat stress and pest problems and are generally short lived. Especially beautiful planted along streams and lakes among evergreens to create exquisite reflections. Also valued for its yellow autumn leaf color.

Betula pendula
European silver birch
Zones 2–8
Though the silvery white bark is decorative when young, it darkens to black with age. The weeping forms are especially beautiful. The arching habit creates a beautiful drapery of leaves, which are golden yellow in autumn. Since the mature height is 80 feet (24.4 m) and 60 feet (18.3 m) wide, it needs room. Splendid as a lawn accent, it also makes a visually exciting skyline tree.

Betula utilis aka B. jacquemontii
Himalayan birch
Zones 6–8
The acknowledged hardiness of this extremely handsome white birch is not a true indicator of its range, since it becomes stressed where summers are hot and humid. The finest specimens tend to grow in cool coastal or high elevation conditions. Varieties 'Grayswood Ghost' and 'Jermyns' with shining white bark are outstanding, especially in woodland gardens where the white can create a startling contrast to other trees with darker bark.

Carpinus betulus
European hornbeam
Zones 5–7
This relatively small shade tree grows to 40 feet (12.2 m) high with a dense pyramidal form. Handsome, furrowed, gray bark and very dark green, sawtooth-edged leaves have good autumn color before turning parchment brown and hanging on late in the season. Give it full sun or light shade and good drainage. 'Fastigiata' is the commonly grown variety. Its almost vertical branches make a good tall hedge. *C. caroliniana*, ironwood (zones 3–7), is native to the northeastern U.S. and similar in appearance to the European hornbeam but hardier.

Carya species
Hickory, Pecan
See Fruit & Nuts, page 216.

Castanea mollissima
Chinese chestnut
Zones 4–8
This deciduous, vigorous, spreading tree is native to China, growing to 70 feet (21.3 m) tall and wide. It has toothed, glossy, mid-green leaves up to 8 inches (20 cm) long with panicles of white flowers in summer. These have a musty odor and are followed by spiny nut cases with edible nuts. Mostly grown as a lawn accent to replace the almost extinct American chestnut, *C. dentata*, which is susceptible to chestnut blight.

Catalpa bignonioides
Southern catalpa
Zones 5–9
Native to the southeastern U.S., this deciduous, broad-leaved tree grows to 50 feet (15.2 m) high and wide. White flowers with maroon throats are borne in conspicuous clusters in late spring, followed by long beanlike seedpods. Plants prefer fertile, well-drained soils in full sun. The golden-leafed form, 'Aurea', is frequently used as a lawn accent by pollarding annually to control its height. This type of pruning encourages extremely large, heart-shaped leaves.

Cedrus atlantica glauca
Blue Atlas cedar

Zones 6–9

Native to the Atlas Mountains in North Africa, this handsome evergreen conifer displays beautiful blue needles, forming a pyramid shape and growing to 60 feet (18.3 m) high and equally wide. Pliable branches shed heavy loads of snow. It makes a good skyline tree and a magnificent lawn accent, but it requires too much space for small gardens. Plants prefer a well-drained soil in sun or partial shade. It is the variety 'Pendula' that is more widely grown in gardens, since its weeping branches can be espaliered against a wall to grow long distances.

Cedrus libani
Cedar of Lebanon

Zones 5–7

Native to Asia Minor, this massive evergreen grows to 60 feet (18.3 m) and more with a spread of up to 100 feet (30.5 m). From a distance, the tree looks black because its needles are such a dark green. Mostly associated with historic estates and large parks, it makes a wonderful skyline accent. Give it full sun and good drainage.

Celtis occidentalis
Hackberry

Zones 3–9

Native to the eastern U.S., this coarse, rugged-looking, widely adapted, fast-growing, deciduous tree reaches 60 feet (18.3 m) high with an upright, rounded habit. Similar in appearance to the pest-prone American elm, it is a good choice for impoverished soil in full sun. Their orange-red to dark purple berries are relished by songbirds. Useful to line driveways, property boundaries and for skyline effect.

Cercidiphyllum japonicum
Katsura tree
Zones 5–8

Native to China and Japan, this spreading, deciduous tree grows to 60 feet (18.3 m) tall and is usually multi-trunked with a pyramidal growth habit. It likes a moisture-retentive soil in sun to part shade. The foliage is heart shaped, bluish-green in the summer and an orange-yellow in the autumn with an odor of burnt sugar when ready to fall.

Cercis canadensis
American redbud
Zones 4–9

Native to the eastern U.S., this has been described as the most beautiful of native American trees after dogwood. The short-lived small tree grows to 30 feet (9.1 m) high in sun to light shade with an open form and very dark bark. Rosy-pink, pea-like flowers are produced in early spring before the leaves unfurl and seem to grow directly from the trunk and branches. In severe winter areas, redbuds should be transplanted only in early spring so that plentiful natural rainfall can help the roots grow quickly. Use as a lawn accent, as sentinels to a driveway and along woodland paths. Makes a good companion to dogwood and azaleas. 'Forest Pansy' is a strikingly beautiful purple-foliaged form, the new foliage even more intense than the old.

C. *chinensis*, Chinese redbud (zones 5–9), is a similar species and native to China. This shrubby tree has multiple stems, growing to 20 feet (6.1 m) high. C. *siliquastrum*, Judas tree (zones 6–9), is native to the Mediterranean and is identical in many respects to the American redbud but not as hardy.

CHAMAECYPARIS

False cypress
Zones 4–9, depending on species

False cypress can be distinguished from arborvitae by the white x's on the undersides of the leaves. There are many varieties and cultivars, dwarf and variegated forms, as well as full-size, upright specimens that grow to 80 feet (24.4 m) tall. All are descended from five species; the best four are listed below. They are tolerant of alkaline soils but are best grown in well-drained, slightly acidic, moisture-retentive soil in full sun.

Chamaecyparis lawsoniana
Lawson cypress
Zones 5–9

Native to the western U.S., this fast-growing species has a narrowly columnar habit to about 60 feet (18.3 m) tall. There are blue-green forms including 'Allumii', slow growing to 30 feet (9.1 m) and 'Ellwoodii', dense, compact growth to 8 feet (2.4 m). Golden-leafed forms include 'Golden King', 'Lutea', and 'Stewartii', all conical to 30 feet (9.1 m) or more.

Chamaecyparis nootkatensis
Alaska cedar
Zones 4–7

In the wild, this is a pyramidal tree to 80 feet (24.4 m), coarser than Lawson cypress and with standing poorer soil. Its most desirable form is the weeping 'Pendula', slow growing to 10 feet (3 m).

Chamaecyparis obtusa
Hinoki false cypress
Zones 5–8

The foliage of this popular evergreen is considered the most beautiful of any conifer, for the needles are splayed out like a fan on tightly grouped branches that present a swirling motion. In the wild, the pyramidal tree grows to 70 feet (21.3 m) high, but there are numerous selections that grow shorter, even dwarf. The foliage color ranges from gold to green and blue. The two most important small garden varieties are 'Gracilis', a slender form growing to 20 feet (6.1 m) high and 'Nana Gracilis', a miniature of 'Gracilis' growing to 4 feet (1.2 m) high. Hinoki cypresses need a sunny spot protected from wind, which causes tip burn, in a fertile, humus-rich, acid soil with good drainage. Mulch to help retain soil moisture.

Chamaecyparis pisifera
Sawara false cypress
Zones 4–8

Native to Japan, numerous varieties are suitable for small gardens. 'Boulevard' has silvery blue-green foliage; 'Filifera' has drooping, threadlike, green foliage; and 'Filifera Aurea' has yellow foliage. All grow to 8 feet (2.4 m), present a cone shape and are especially desirable as hedges, often alternated to create a checkered design.

Chionanthus retusus
Chinese fringe tree
Zones 6–9

Leaves and flower clusters are shorter than in the American fringe tree. Leaves are more oval in form and the flowers appear a few days later than the American. Otherwise similar in appearance, except for its tendency to grow as a big, multi-stemmed shrub up to 20 feet (6.1 m) high.

Chionanthus virginicus
Fringe tree
Zones 4–9

Native to North America, fringe trees are handsome, dioecious (male and female on separate trees), small trees with large, spear-shaped leaves resembling a magnolia. These turn yellow in autumn. The frothy, fringe-like, fragrant, white flowers that appear in late spring are enchanting. Plants grow to 20 feet (6.1 m) high and a similar spread, suitable for small gardens. They are excellent companions to rhododendron, particularly at the edge of woodland. Give them a moisture-retentive, fertile, acid soil in sun or partial shade. The flowers of the male trees are showier, although the females produce dark blue berries relished by songbirds.

Cladrastis lutea
Yellowwood
Zones 4–8

Native to the eastern U.S., this elegant medium-sized tree grows a billowing leaf canopy up to 50 feet (15.2 m) high and an equal spread. Low branches sweep to the ground, creating a broad, rounded crown draped with white, wisteria-like, pendant flowers. These appear in early summer giving the tree an airy, shimmering appearance. A bonus is its brilliant yellow autumn foliage. Give it full sun and good drainage. Pruning should be done in summer, since cuts made in winter or spring bleed profusely. Also, trees may not bloom until 10 years of age.

CORNUS

Dogwoods

Zones 3–9, depending on species

Hardy dogwoods are among the most beautiful trees nature created with the mass flowering of the common American dogwood in white and shades of pink being a highlight of many spring gardens. Described here are the most desirable for small gardens.

Cornus alternifolia
Pagoda dogwood, Wedding cake dogwood

Zones 3–7

This North American native is best appreciated as a single specimen on a hillside where its distinctive layered branches can be fully appreciated, especially the variegated varieties with white edging to the green leaves. The white flowers are displayed in flat clusters along gray branches in late spring, followed by reddish-purple foliage and blue berry clusters in autumn. Plants grow to 25 feet (7.6 m) high and prefer sun or partial shade in soil with good drainage. Use as an avenue along a driveway as well as a lawn accent.

Cornus florida
Flowering dogwood

Zones 3–9

This is one of the most beautiful flowering trees for gardens with sharp winters and long, hot summers—a combination that produces the best flowering, particularly in the land of its birth, the eastern U.S. Unfortunately, periods of drought can weaken American dogwoods, allowing a blight disease to kill them. In maritime climates, such as the U.K. and New Zealand, cool summers will drastically reduce the flowering display. The 3-inch (8 cm) wide flowers are mostly white and shades of pink. The horizontal branches bend to create a curtain of bloom before the broadly oval leaves are fully unfurled. These turn shades of red in autumn, accompanied by small, oval red berries. Plants thrive in sun or partial shade, prefer good drainage and acid soil. They are the perfect accompaniment to azaleas. Use as a lawn accent or foundation highlight, and also to line a driveway, in groves at the edge of woodland and as an under-story planting beneath tall trees such as maples and oaks.

Cornus kousa
Kousa dogwood

Zones 5–8

This native of Asian woodland was propelled into prominence after a blight disease began to kill off American dogwoods all along the northeast coast of North America. Though the Korean flowers in late spring, a good three weeks later than the American, the Korean is disease resistant. Plants grow to 25 feet (7.6 m) high with an equal spread, mostly in an upright, billowing form with branches and trunk that are mottled. The dark green, spear-shaped, smooth leaves turn russet colors in autumn, when decorative, edible, cherry-size orange or red fruit ripen all along the branches. Plants prefer full sun and good drainage. Though mostly white flowering and four-petalled, a series of hybrids using the Korean dogwood as a parent has extended the color range to pink. Called the Stellar hybrids, the variety 'Stellar Pink' bears large dusky-pink flowers. Use as a lawn highlight, in groves, as an avenue to line a driveway and at the edge of woodland.

CRATAEGUS

Hawthorn

Zones 3–8

There are more than 100 different species of hawthorn native to North America. They are popular for their pretty flower clusters and showy fruit in the autumn, but they are susceptible to fireblight, cedar-apple rust, aphids and scale. Extensive hybridizing has been done with European species to produce superior varieties. Listed below are a few of the more popular species:

Crataegus laevigata aka *oxyacantha*
European or English hawthorn
Zones 5–9

Some of the most beautiful and venerable trees in nature are the European or English hawthorn, shaped into stunted, sinuous forms on desolate heaths and cliff-tops where little else will grow. This medium-sized, deciduous, thorny tree grows to 25 feet (7.6 m) high and 20 feet (6.1 m) wide with 2-inch (5 cm), toothed, lobed leaves; although the leaves are lacking good autumn color. It is best known through its varieties: 'Paul's Scarlet' (clusters of double rose to red flowers) and 'Crimson Cloud' aka 'Superba' (bright red single flowers with white centers and vivid red fruit).

Cornus mas
Cornelian dogwood
Zones 5–9

This Asian native grows to be a billowing small tree up to 20 feet (6.1 m) high and equally wide and is covered with greenish-yellow flower clusters in early spring, before the spear-shaped green leaves appear. Flowering coincides with forsythia. Edible, bright red, ornamental fruits ripen in autumn. Give the plants full sun or light shade. Plants are suitable for planting at the edge of woodland and as lawn accents, especially underplanted with early-flowering bulbs such as crocus and Siberian squill.

Crataegus phaenopyrum
Washington hawthorn
Zones 3–8

Native to the eastern U.S., this small, spreading, deciduous tree grows to 25 feet (7.6 m) tall with an upright, rounded habit. It bears an abundance of white blossoms in spring and brilliant red berry displays in autumn. Plants prefer fertile loam soil in full sun. They make an excellent lawn highlight and can be pruned heavily to create an attractive flowering hedge. The sharp thorns on the branches deter intruders. A related species, *C. viridis* (especially the variety 'Winter King'), is valued for its extra-heavy red berry display that persists into winter. There are more than 100 different species of hawthorn native to North America. Extensive hybridizing has been done with European species to produce superior varieties.

Trees

Cryptomeria japonica
Japanese cedar

Zones 6–8

Native to Japan, this handsome evergreen conifer has its needles arranged in dense spirals, giving it such a refined appearance that plants can be used as lawn highlights. Plants grow to 60 feet (18.3 m) tall with a pyramidal habit in sun to light shade. A rich, moisture-retentive, acid soil is preferred, as they do not tolerate drought. Beautiful reddish-brown bark peels off in strips. Sensational planted in groves, to line driveways and as a tall hedge.

Davidia involucrata
Dove tree

Zones 6–8

Native to China, this deciduous, pyramidal, small tree grows to 30 feet (9.1 m) tall. Resembling a magnolia in leaf with broad, spear-shaped, serrated, green leaves, it is coveted for its grace and highly unusual flowers. These are actually large white bracts that tremble in the slightest breeze, looking like a tree full of doves or fluttering handkerchiefs, hence its other common name, handkerchief tree. These can be 6 inches (15 cm) long and 4 inches (10 cm) wide with a black button center. Plants prefer a moisture-retentive soil with good drainage in sun or light shade. Protect from wind. Useful as a lawn accent, especially one with a high hedge or wall to dissipate winter winds.

Diospyros
Persimmon

See Fruit & Nuts, page 216.

Elaeagnus angustifolia
Russian olive

Zones 2–9

This fast-growing, small, deciduous tree grows to 20 feet (6.1 m) high and equally wide with narrow, willowlike, 2-inch (5 cm), silvery gray leaves. Very fragrant, yellowish flowers are borne in early summer, followed by berrylike fruit attractive to birds. Can take a wide range of conditions: heat, cold, drought and impoverished soil. Mostly used as an informal hedge or windbreak, and to add a silvery highlight in the landscape.

Fagus grandifolia aka *F. americana*
American beech

Zones 3–9

Native to northeastern North America, this robust, wide-spreading, deciduous tree is similar in appearance to the European beech but two zones hardier. The serrated, spear-shaped leaves turn golden in autumn. Plants grow to 80 feet (24.4 m) high and equally wide. A good skyline tree and a wonderful lawn accent with its dove-gray bark, providing there is space for it. It is also suitable for avenue plantings.

Fagus sylvatica
European beech
Zones 4–7

Native to Europe, this large, deciduous tree grows to 90 feet (27.4 m) with an equal spread. Bright green oval leaves are serrated and have prominent leaf veins, changing to parchment brown in autumn. Inconspicuous green flowers are followed by small, nutlike seed capsules, which are enjoyed by squirrels. The beech is slow growing with a massive, smooth, dove-gray trunk. It prefers deep loam soil in full sun and good drainage. Too large for small gardens, it makes a magnificent lawn highlight and skyline tree. Plants can be trained and pruned to make an arbor for a tunnel effect and also to create a dense hedge. There is the majestic weeping form 'Pendula' and the purple-leafed form 'Riversii' that make especially beautiful lawn accents. Variegated selections include 'Aurea-Variegata' with leaves margined yellow and 'Roseo-Marginata', a tricolor with purple leaves margined pink and white.

Franklinia alatamaha
Franklin tree
Zones 6–9

Native to Georgia, U.S., this small, deciduous tree is now extinct in the wild owing to a devastating root disease introduced when southern U.S. plantations began planting cotton. Plants usually grow to 20 feet (6.1 m) high in humus-rich, well-drained, acidic to neutral soil in full sun. Glossy, 6-inch (15-cm) long, mid to dark green leaves resemble a magnolia. Fragrant, camellia-like, white flowers up to 3 inches (8 cm) wide with yellow stamens are borne in late summer and early autumn, at the same time as the leaves start turning a brilliant orange color. Best used as a lawn accent and along the house foundation.

FRAXINUS

Ash

Zones 3–9, depending on species

Ash trees in general are mostly recommended for parks and large estates, since they can grow too tall and wide for small gardens. Described here are two from North America and one from Europe.

Fraxinus americana
White ash
Zones 6–9

Native to the northeastern U.S. and Canada, these large, deciduous trees grow to 80 feet (24.4 m) and more with a similar spread. The smooth, spear-shaped leaflets are borne in groups of seven, turning mostly yellow in autumn. Inconspicuous flowers produce bunches of winged seeds that can be a nuisance by being blown some distance from the tree, to germinate where they are not wanted. Plants prefer full sun and moisture-retentive soil with good drainage. Special selections chosen for intense autumn color are suitable for skyline effect, such as the orange-red 'Skyline', which is seedless.

Fraxinus excelsior
European ash

Zones 5–9

Native to Europe, plants are similar in appearance to the green ash, but the spear-shaped, serrated leaflets are borne in groups of seven to 11. Prefers full sun and limestone soil, though it tolerates a wide range of soil conditions where drainage is good. It is suitable for use as a skyline tree and wherever it has room to spread, such as a golf course. The variety 'Aurea' has especially beautiful golden yellow autumn foliage.

Fraxinus pennsylvanica
Green ash

Zones 3–9

Native to the northeastern U.S. and Canada, this large billowing tree is similar in appearance to the white ash, except the spear-shaped leaflets are serrated and borne in fives. Generally not as shapely as the white ash, plants grow to 60 feet (18.3 m) and more with a similar spread. Though prolific along streams in its native habitat, the green ash tolerates a wide range of soils including dry soil and summer heat. The green ash species is as invasive as the white ash; however, the variety 'Marshall's Seedless' is sterile. Not recommended for home gardens but suitable for golf courses, parks, city streets and shopping malls.

Ginkgo biloba
Maidenhair tree
Zones 3–9

Native to China, this deciduous, large tree grows slowly to 80 feet (24.4 m) tall with an upright, pyramidal habit. The female becomes more wide spreading than the male with age. The fan-shaped leaves turn golden-yellow in autumn. Prefers sandy loam soil in full sun. Male trees are more desirable than females, since the females develop yellowish plumlike fruits that are malodorous. The male form of this tree is a popular street tree and lawn highlight. 'Autumn Gold' is a male selection with a good spreading habit and bright golden autumn color. 'Fastigiata' has a columnar habit. 'Pendula' has somewhat weeping or pendulous branches.

Gleditsia triacanthos var. *inermis*
Thornless honeylocust
Zones 4–9

Native to the eastern U.S., this tall, deciduous, spreading tree has extremely fine, textured foliage that casts filtered shade. Rare in large trees, the graceful leaf arrangement allows shade-tolerant turfgrass and part-shade perennials to grow underneath. Greenish flower clusters occur in summer. The gray trunks have a basket-weave pattern, and the compound leaves turn yellow in autumn. Plants grow to 70 feet (21.3 m) high and more with a mounded canopy. They prefer deep soil with good drainage in full sun and adapt to adverse conditions such as heat and drought. Useful as lawn accents, for skyline effects and casting cool, light shade over decks and patios. Two popular varieties are 'Shademaster' (more upright and faster growing) and 'Sunburst' (golden-yellow new foliage in spring).

Gymnocladus dioica
Kentucky coffee tree
Zones 5–9

Native to the eastern U.S., this dioecious (separate male and female trees), deciduous, large tree grows to 70 feet (21.3 m) tall and up to 50 feet (15.2 m) wide with deep, bluish-green, compound summer foliage resembling wisteria. Greenish white flower clusters are borne in summer, followed by knobby brown bean pods. Plants prefer full sun and a deep soil. Largely trouble-free and tolerant of hot, dry summers. Use as a lawn accent and for skyline effect. Called coffee tree because early colonists to North America brewed a coffee-flavored drink from its beans, which have since proven to be carcinogenic.

Halesia carolina aka *H. tetraptera*
Silver bell
Zones 5–8

Native to the eastern U.S., this small, deciduous tree grows to 40 feet (12.2 m) with an upright, spreading habit. Beautiful pendant, bell-shaped, white flowers crowd the branches in spring. Oval, dark green leaves change to lime-green in autumn. Plants prefer fertile, humus-rich, acid soil in sun or partial shade. Makes a beautiful lawn highlight, also effective planted in woodland gardens. A related species, *H. monticola*, mountain silverbell (zones 4–8), also native to North America, is much taller growing to 100 feet (30.5 m) and unsuitable for small gardens. It is slightly hardier than Carolina silverbell.

Ilex aquifolium
English holly
Zones 6–9

Generally displays a more attractive form than American holly with glossy, darker green leaves and richer berry display, but otherwise similar in height and habit of growth, although it is not as hardy.

Ilex opaca
American holly
Zones 5–9

Native to North America, this broad-leafed evergreen tree grows slowly to 50 feet (15.2 m) high, forming a pyramidal shape of spiny dark green leaves. Bright red berries in autumn and winter follow inconspicuous white flowers in early summer. Plants prefer a moist sandy or acid loam soil in sun or part shade. One male plant is needed for every six females in order to produce berries. American holly makes a good evergreen lawn highlight and windbreak hedge. The branches can be heavily pruned to make a dense impenetrable hedge. 'Jersey Knight' (male) and 'Jersey Princess' (female) both display handsome dark green leaves more attractive than the yellow-green coloring of the species.

Juglans
Walnut
See Fruit & Nuts, page 217.

Juniperus virginiana
Eastern red cedar
Zones 3–9

Native to North America, this large evergreen conifer grows to 50 feet (15.2 m) tall with a variable columnar to broad-spreading habit. The brown bark peels in shreds on a fluted trunk with radiating branches. Needles are gray-green, and blue berries occur in late summer. Plants are suitable for windbreaks, skyline effects and lining avenues.

Koelreuteria paniculata
Goldenrain tree
Zones 5–9

Native to China and Korea, this wide-spreading small tree grows to 30 feet (9.1 m) tall and is one of the few yellow-flowering trees. Though individually small, they are borne in early summer (mid-July) in large, shimmering clusters up to 3 feet (91 cm) across. The fruits that follow are tan-colored, bladderlike pods that persist into winter. Plants prefer full sun, tolerate a wide range of soils and are also heat and drought tolerant. A good street tree, it makes a handsome lawn accent.

Laburnum x watereri
Golden chain tree
Zones 5–7

This is a vigorous, free-flowering hybrid of two European laburnum species, *L. alpinum* and *L. anagyroides*. It has larger flowers [in clusters up to 10 inches (25 cm) long] of a deeper yellow and a denser habit of growth than either parent. Plants grow to 15 feet (4.5 m) tall with an upright habit and oval, pointed, green leaves arranged in threes. Prefers moist loam soil with good drainage in sun or light shade. Pliable branches allow it to be trained over arches to create a flowering tunnel, as seen at Bodnant Garden (U.K.). Makes a beautiful lawn accent and an avenue along a driveway. The variety 'Vossii', raised in Holland, has extra-long flowers, up to 2 feet (61 cm) long.

Larix decidua
Larch
Zones 4–6

Native to Europe, this deciduous conifer grows to 70 feet (21.3 m) tall and 30 feet (9.1 m) wide with a pyramidal habit. Plants prefer sun to light shade in a moisture-retentive, well-drained soil. 'Fastigiata' is a beautiful columnar form. The branches of 'Pendula' are weeping and look especially attractive in autumn when the needles turn golden. *L. laricina*, tamarack (zones 2–8), is one of the hardiest conifers. It is found growing across North America and even Alaska in swamps and bogs.

Liriodendron tulipifera
Tulip tree
Zones 4–9

Native to North America, this tall, fast-growing, deciduous tree has trunks as straight as telephone poles and large, bright green, almost square leaves. Plants grow to 100 feet (30.5 m) tall by 40 feet (12.2 m) wide. It prefers deep acid loam soil in full sun and should be planted in early spring so spring rains can encourage its long taproot to grow deeply. Beautiful, tuliplike, yellow flowers the size of teacups occur after 10 years. Leaves change to butter yellow in autumn. This tree is a good lawn highlight, capable of growing up to 6 feet (1.8 m) a year in its juvenile years. A particularly beautiful variegated selection is 'Aureo-marginatum' with leaves margined yellow.

Liquidambar styraciflua
Sweet gum
Zones 5–9

Native to North America, this large, fast-growing, deciduous, shade tree grows to 60 feet (18.3 m), developing an attractive pyramidal shape. The glossy-green, star-shaped leaves turn yellow and reddish tones in autumn. Hard, brown, spiny seed cases hang from the tree in winter. Give it good drainage in full sun. Sweet gum is a superb lawn highlight and a good street tree. Numerous named varieties are available; some are selected for their exceptional autumn coloring including 'Burgundy', which displays deep reddish purple hues. A seedless variety 'Rotundiloba' with more rounded leaves has been developed to avoid the spiny seed cases from littering lawns and driveways, and 'Albomarginata' has white-edged leaves.

Maclura pomifera
Osage orange
Zones 5–9

This rot-resistant tree can grow to 60 feet (18.3 m) tall, forming a vigorous, dense growth habit of many branches and twigs with heavy thorns. All of these characteristics make it good for informal hedging and as an avenue along a driveway. Leaves are glossy and change to yellow in autumn. Grapefruit-size knobby fruits ripen in autumn. They are decorative and fragrant. Since male and female flowers are borne in spring on separate plants, it is necessary to have a male tree for pollination.

MAGNOLIA

Magnolia

Zones 4–10, depending on species

Magnolias comprise 100 species and are mostly native to China. They are grown primarily for their flowers, but some species, such as North America's *M. grandiflora*, have beautiful evergreen foliage. Blooms of the Chinese varieties are large and mostly white, various shades of pink, pinkish-lavender or reddish to purple, depending on variety. Flowers are followed by oddly-shaped seedpods that split open to reveal bright red, bean-size seeds. Magnolias have no autumn foliage color, but the velvety buds that become apparent during winter are interesting to watch as they swell in preparation to burst open during an early spring warming trend to flower prolifically on bare limbs well ahead of the foliage.

Magnolia 'Elizabeth'

Zones 6–9

A hybrid between *M. acuminata cordata* and *M. denudata*, this deciduous magnolia grows to 40 feet (12.2 m) high and 20 feet (6.1 m) wide with fragrant, pale yellow flowers up to 7 inches (18 cm) wide.

Magnolia 'Girls' hybrids

Zones 6–9, depending on variety

This series of Asian magnolias, all with girls' names, has been developed at the U.S. National Arboretum. All have flowers in shades ranging from pink 'Pinkie' to red-purple 'Ann' and deep purple 'Ricki'. All produce masses of flowers ahead of the leaves and have the appearance of billowing large shrubs, rather than small trees. Plants prefer sun or light shade in moisture-retentive soil with good drainage. Spectacular as a lawn accent and espaliered along walls. In zone 6 gardens, provide protection from winter winds with a burlap windbreak until plants are established.

Magnolia grandiflora

Southern magnolia

Zones 6–9

Native to the southeastern U.S., this magnificent broadleaved, evergreen tree grows to 80 feet (24.4 m) high and 40 (12.2 m) or more feet across. Varieties such as 'Edith Bogue' and 'Bracken's Brown Beauty' must be chosen for zone 6 gardens. The handsome, glossy, green, leathery leaves have brown, feltlike undersides, creating a perfect foil for the huge, waxy, white flowers up to 10 inches (25 cm) across. Summer flowering. Useful to line driveways and espaliered against a wall. As a lawn highlight, it should be sheltered from high winds.

Magnolia hybrid 'Leonard Messel'

Zones 5–9

A hybrid between *M. kobus* and *M. stellata* 'Rosea' raised in an English garden. When this magnificent large shrub, or small tree, is in full flower it displays lovely rosy-pink blooms. Early spring flowering.

Magnolia x soulangiana

Saucer magnolia

Zones 5–9

This spectacular hybrid grows to 25 feet (7.6 m) tall and has spring-blooming, large, goblet-shaped, fragrant flowers, which are usually white suffused with pink. The blooms are susceptible to damage by late frosts.

Magnolia stellata
Star magnolia
Zones 5–9

When grown in a sheltered place, this will be one of the first magnolias to flower in early spring. It blooms when just a few feet high, often growing several main stems like a shrub but can also mature into a dense, rounded, small tree. The 5-inch (13 cm) wide flowers are white, double, star shaped and fragrant with the outsides of the petals sometimes tinged pink. Leaves are smaller and narrower than most other magnolias and often display a yellow or bronze autumn color.

Magnolia virginiana
Sweetbay magnolia
Zones 5–9

This highly fragrant North American magnolia grows to 60 feet (18.3 m) where winters are mild, but usually no more than 25 feet (7.6 m) and shrublike where winters are severe. In late spring, 3-inch (8 cm), fragrant, cream-colored, cupped flowers appear and continue sporadically until midsummer. Evergreen where winters are mild, this magnolia is deciduous at the branch tips in colder regions. Leaves are glossy on top and have a grayish cast beneath. Plants thrive in swampy locations and in moist soil, but will tolerate soils with good drainage if mulched to preserve soil moisture.

MALUS

Crabapple
Zones 2–9, depending on variety

The plant family Malus includes apples and the smaller fruited crabapples. The ornamental crabapples are described here, while the apples are discussed under Fruit & Nuts, see page 211. Most crabapples grow to 25 feet (7.6 m) tall and are valued not only for their profusion of white, pink or rose-colored flowers in spring, but also for their decorative red or yellow fruit in autumn. There are hundreds of cultivars, but many of the older varieties have severe pest and disease problems resulting in defoliation early in the season.

Malus sargentii
Sargent crabapple
Zones 5–8

This shrubby crabapple branches low to the ground, often with such a tight knit of branches that there is no discernible main trunk. Plants grow to 8 feet (2.4 m) high and often twice as wide and are covered in white blossoms in spring before the leaves unfurl. The blossoms are followed by clusters of marble-size fruit that turn yellow and then red when completely ripe; they are relished by songbirds. Native to China, it does not harbor cedar apple rust disease, likes full sun and tolerates most soils with good drainage. An excellent lawn accent.

Malus hybrid 'Red Jade'
Zones 5–8

This is the perfect crabapple as a lawn accent for small gardens, since the habit is compact and weeping. Flowers are deep pink in spring, followed by deep red fruit in autumn, which cover the fountain of slender branches from top to toe. Plants grow to 15 feet (4.5 m) high and equally wide. They are also suitable for growing in a container. If you have space for only one crabapple, make it this one.

Metasequoia glyptostroboides
Dawn redwood

Zones 5–8

Native to China, this deciduous conifer grows quickly [up to 5 feet (1.5 m) a year] to 100 feet (30.5 m) and more with a spire-like habit. The bark is reddish brown and the fluted trunk is buttressed, giving the tree a prehistoric appearance. The dark green needles turn russet brown in autumn. Plants prefer a moist, loam acid soil in full sun. Though good drainage is preferred, it is also suited to moist soil beside lakes, ponds and streams. Use as a windbreak, to create an eerie grove and as a tall lawn highlight. This species was thought to be extinct until 1940, when a stand of about five trees was discovered growing wild in China along the Yangtze River by an American expedition.

Nyssa sylvatica
Sour gum

Zones 5–9

This deciduous, pyramidal tree, native to the eastern U.S., grows slowly to 50 feet (15.2 m) high by 30 feet (9.1 m) wide in acid soil. Give it full sun and good drainage, although moist soils are also suitable. The autumn foliage is brilliant orange or scarlet. It makes an excellent skyline tree. Must be planted as early as possible in spring in order for its long taproot to grow deep during spring rainfall.

Oxydendrum arboreum
Sourwood

Zones 4–9

Native to North America, this deciduous, pyramidal tree grows to 30 feet (9.1 m) high, has gracefully curved branches, large oval green leaves and attractive clusters of white flowers blooming in late summer. The leaves turn yellow, red or purple in autumn. Give it full sun and good drainage. It makes an excellent lawn highlight and is also a good house foundation plant.

Parrotia persica
Persian parrotia

Zones 5–8

Native to Iran, this deciduous, medium-sized tree grows to 40 feet (12.2 m) high and 30 feet (9.1 m) wide with a rounded, oval habit. Plants prefer slightly acid, well-drained soil in sun. Brilliant autumn color and beautiful exfoliating bark are distinctive features. This is a tough, adaptable tree suitable for planting as a lawn accent and along the house foundation.

Paulownia tomentosa
Empress tree

Zones 6–9

Native to China and root hardy to zone 5, this fast-growing, deciduous tree grows up to 60 feet (18.3 m) high at the rate of 8 feet (2.4 m) a year. It has large, bright green, heart-shaped leaves that appear in spring after the ornamental, lavender-blue, foxglove-like flowers. Plants tolerate a wide range of soils, heat and drought. If the tree is cut back annually, it will grow giant-sized leaves up to 2 feet (61 cm) long, but flower production is thereby inhibited. Useful as a lawn highlight and to create an avenue.

Phellodendron amurense
Amur cork tree
Zones 3–7

Native to northeast Asia, this deciduous, broad-spreading tree grows to 45 feet (13.7 m) high by 50 feet (15.2 m) wide. At maturity, it displays a picturesque flat-topped form and interesting corky bark. The female form should be avoided because of its messy black, berry-size fruits and strong odor. The lance-like leaflets are grouped in sets of seven or more, turning yellow in autumn. Useful for skyline effect.

Picea glauca var. albertiana 'Conica'
Dwarf Alberta spruce
Zones 3–6

This is one of the most popular of dwarf evergreen conifers, developing a dense, cone-shaped, bushy habit in rock gardens, foundation plantings and containers. It rarely grows more than 1 or 2 inches (2.5 to 5 cm) each year. Give it full sun and good drainage. Plants are used mostly as an accent and as a low, slow-growing hedge.

Picea pungens 'Glauca' (TOP RIGHT)
Blue spruce
Zones 2–7

Native to Colorado, this popular evergreen conifer grows slowly to 100 feet (30.5 m) or more. It produces a beautiful conical shape and blue, needle-like foliage. Plants prefer a fertile, moisture-retentive loam soil in full sun, although it is tolerant of heat and drought. Spectacular as a lawn highlight and tall windbreak hedge, this selection is a variety of the green-foliaged Colorado spruce. Many compact and dwarf forms are available, such as 'Hoopsii' and 'Montgomery', which have a slower-growing, mounded shape popular for edging walks and decorating rock gardens.

Pinus mugo
See Shrubs, page 142.

Pinus strobus
Eastern white pine
Zones 3–8

Native to North America, this fast-growing evergreen grows to 80 feet (24.4 m) in a pyramidal habit. Its soft-textured appearance is a result of the long, blue-green needles and makes it popular as a tall windbreak. Plants tolerate a wide range of acid soil conditions including dry and moist soils. Prefers full sun but tolerates light shade. Many dwarf varieties have been developed that are suitable for rock gardens and small spaces such as foundation plantings. A weeping form, 'Pendula', has long, arching branches that sweep to the ground. Some other beautiful species of hardy pine are *P. aristata*, bristlecone pine (zones 4–7); *P. bungeana*, lacebark pine (zones 4–8); *P. cembra*, Swiss stone pine (zones 4–7); *P. densiflora*, Japanese red pine (zones 3–7); *P. parviflora*, Japanese white pine (zones 4–7); *P. sylvestris*, Scots pine (zones 2–8;) *P. thunbergiana*, Japanese black pine (zones 5–7); and *P. wallichiana*, Himalayan white pine (zones 5–7).

Trees

Platanus x acerifolia
London plane tree
Zones 5–8

This massive hybrid of *P. orientalis* and *P. occidentalis* grows to 100 feet (30.5 m) tall and 80 feet (24.4 m) wide with a pyramidal form in sun to light shade. Plants prefer a fertile, moisture-retentive, well-drained soil. They are grown for their imposing stature and handsome marbled bronze and olive green bark. The large leaves resemble a maple. Although too large for most gardens, they make good street trees and skyline accents. The variety 'Bloodgood' has good resistance to anthracnose and powdery mildew. The golf-ball-size, hairy, brown fruits can be messy.

Platanus occidentalis
American sycamore
Zones 5–8

Native to the eastern U.S., this species grows up to 80 feet (24.4. m) tall making it slightly shorter than the London plane tree. Where the London plane tree is tolerant of a wide range of soil conditions and climate, the American sycamore prefers a moist soil. Good for planting beside water features, especially rivers and streams where it can be given room to spread.

Populus hybrid
Hybrid poplar
Zones 4–9

Hybrids of species native to North America and Europe, these fast-growing, deciduous trees grow in poor soils where other trees perish. They like full sun and tolerate high heat and humidity. Developed to re-forest impoverished soils as a result of strip mining, they are good lawn accents and skyline trees. These poplars are mostly upright and spire-like in habit with pointed, oval, green leaves that shimmer and shine with a silvery sheen in the slightest breeze. Use them for a property boundary, windbreak or avenue along a driveway—wherever a tall, fast-growing tree is needed for screening and erosion control. Keep clear of pipes and drains because of its vigorous root system. 'Androscoggin' is the most widely available of the hybrids recommended for home landscapes.

PRUNUS SPECIES AND HYBRIDS

Ornamental cherries
Zones 2–9, depending on variety

"I am of the humble opinion there are to be found among the cherries some of the most lovely trees in the world: and in making this statement I do not exclude the tropics." So wrote the late Captain Collingwood ("Cherry") Ingram, the world's leading authority on ornamental cherries, in his book *Ornamental Cherries* (Country Life). He included in this assessment the spectacular blue jacaranda trees of Brazil and the orange-red flamboyant trees of the Caribbean, describing them as "vulgar, a trifle tawdry." The wild cherries, *P. sargentii*, *P. serrulata* and *P. x subhirtella* have a refined charm when in bloom, and a delicacy of color and form that appeals to a gardener's aesthetic sense in a way that the others never can. I would add to this list of pre-eminent flowering cherries *P. yedoense*, since their spring flowering on the slopes of Mt. Yoshino, Japan, is undoubtedly the most beautiful flowering tree display in all of nature. Indeed, so highly rated is the Yoshino cherry that many cities and parks are planted with them exclusively, including Washington D.C., where thousands of tourists flock to see their mass flowering, which usually occurs in March.

This very large plant family includes peaches, plums, cherries, almonds and apricots, all listed in the chapter on fruits, page 211. The most popular ornamental prunus species include the following:

Prunus x blireiana
Blireiana plum
Zones 6–8

This rounded, densely branched, small tree blooms in spring, growing to 20 feet (6.1 m) high and equally wide. Flowers are light pink, double and an inch (2.5 cm) in diameter and are set against red-purple leaves. Small, edible fruits the same color as the leaves are borne later in the season. This hybrid stays in flower longer than many of the other flowering plums.

Prunus cerasifera
Cherry plum
Zones 5–9

A small tree, it is sometimes grown as a shrub with several stems rising from the ground. Dense, twiggy and thorny, the leaves are light green and flowers are white or pale pink, appearing in early spring. Fruits are yellow or red, about an inch (2.5 cm) in diameter and delicious to eat. This species is not as popular as its purple-leaved forms described below. *P. cerasifera* 'Newport' (zones 4–8) has purple leaves, light bronze-purple when young, and pale pink to white flowers, growing to 12 feet (3.6 m) high. 'Thundercloud' is similar to 'Newport', except it grows a little taller and a little broader to 15 feet (4.5 m) tall.

Prunus 'Hally Jolivette'

Zones 6–8

This is a stunning cross involving two of the most beautiful Japanese cherries, *P.* x *yedoense* and *P.* x *subhirtella*. This densely branched, rounded, small tree [usually less than 12 feet (3.6 m) high] has pink buds and double white flowers over a long period in early spring at the same time as daffodils.

Prunus sargentii

Sargent's cherry

Zones 4–7

"If I am right in believing this to be the most lovely of all cherries, further praise is hardly needed," wrote Collingwood Ingram. It is an upright, spreading tree attaining 60 feet (18.3 m) in height. The flowers are small, barely 1 inch (2.5 cm) across, pale pink and arranged in fours all along the branch tips. Small, oval, red fruit follow the flowers. Leaves, oblong and serrated, start off red and turn green. It is among the first cherry trees to turn color in autumn, usually a rich orange or red. Plants have been known to withstand freezing down to -23°F (-30°C) without injury. In full flower, it presents a blizzard of bloom.

Trees

Prunus serrulata
Japanese flowering cherry
Zones 5–8

A wide spreading tree that usually grows with the main trunk divided into several trunks just a few feet above ground level. It has handsome red bark and single white flowers appearing in spring. There are many varieties, one of the most popular being 'Kwanzan', which is one of the main varieties used around the Tidal Basin in Washington D.C. Growing to 18 feet (5.5 m) tall, the young leaves are copper-red· and flowers are deep pink and double, nearly 3 inches (8 cm) in diameter.

Prunus x subhirtella
Higan cherry
Zones 6–8

Probably the most widely planted of all cherries, this is also one of the earliest of the Oriental-type cherries to bloom. The light pink, single flowers appear in early spring, before the leaves appear, with the first daffodil displays. Sometimes the flowering is so profuse that the blossoms practically hide the branches of the tree. *P. x s.* 'Autumnalis' (autumn Higan cherry) has semi-double, pale pink flowers that appear in spring, and sometimes in autumn. 'Pendula' (weeping Higan cherry) displays long slender leaves that stay green far into autumn. The slender pendulous branches make this a picturesque accent during the entire year. Plants grow to 25 feet (7.6 m) wide and high. The most common form has single, mauve-pink flowers that appear before the leaves, creating a flowering fountain. There is also a double-flowered form.

Prunus x yedoensis
Yoshino cherry
Zones 5–9

This hybrid between *P. x subhirtella* and *P. speciosa*, discovered in Japan as a cultivated tree, is the main flowering cherry planted around the Tidal Basin, Washington D.C. Plants grow to 30 feet (9.1 m) high and 40 wide and are covered in fragrant white flowers in early spring. There is also an especially beautiful weeping form.

Pseudolarix kaempferi aka amabilis
Golden larch

Zones 5–9

Native to southeast China, this deciduous, coniferous tree grows to 50 feet (15.2 m) tall by 40 feet (12.2 m) wide with a pyramidal, wide-spreading habit. Plants prefer acid, well-drained soil in sun to light shade. Makes a good skyline accent. Foliage turns orange in autumn.

Pseudotsuga menziesii
Douglas fir

Zones 5–7

Native to Colorado and the Pacific Northwest, this tall, spire-like, needled evergreen is long lived in soil with good drainage. Plants make good Christmas trees and can grow to 300 feet (91.4 m) in acid, fertile soil with full sun. One tree makes a good lawn highlight; several will create a windbreak. The variety 'Glauca', Rocky Mountain Douglas fir (zones 4–6), is more widely adapted, hardier and slower growing.

Pterostyrax hispida
Fragrant epaulette tree

Zones 5–8

Native to Japan, this small deciduous tree grows to 20 feet (6.1 m) high with a spread of 10 feet (3 m) and an open spreading habit. The attractive spear-shaped leaves are light green with gray green beneath. Creamy white, fringed, lightly fragrant flowers in drooping clusters are borne in late spring or early summer, followed by long-lasting, small, yellow, cylindrical fruits which are attractive on bare winter branches.

Pyrus calleryana 'Bradford'
Bradford pear

Zones 4–8

Native to China, this is a handsome, deciduous tree for all seasons: beautiful white blossoms in early spring; dark green leaves during summer; gorgeous orange leaves in autumn; and an attractive wintry silhouette when it loses its leaves. Plants tolerate a wide range of soils, pollution and fireblight disease, which is so common to other ornamental pears. Useful for lining a driveway and as a street tree. Although the 'Bradford' pear is itself a variety of *P. calleryana*, it is prone to wind damage. 'Aristocrat' (pyramidal form) and 'Chanticleer' (upright form) are more wind resistant.

Pyrus salicifolia 'Silver Frost'
Willow-leaved pear

Zones 5–9

Native to southern Europe, Iran and Turkey, this spreading, deciduous tree has pendent shoots and willowlike, gray, felted leaves. In spring, creamy white flowers are decorative, followed by pear-shaped green fruit. Very popular as a lawn accent.

QUERCUS

Oaks

Zones 2–10, depending on variety

Surely the common concept of oak trees are the champion oaks of old England, which survive for hundreds of years and eventually grow gnarled and hollow with age. Oaks are distinguished by fruiting bodies called acorns, consisting of an oval or round nut seated in a rough-textured cup, maturing in autumn. Although most large oaks are generally unsuitable for small gardens, a number of them are better proportioned for confined spaces including the North American pin oak, so-called because its leaves are not scalloped but sharply indented. The following hardy oaks are good for gardens:

Quercus alba
White oak
Zones 3–9

This North American native is a long-lived, handsome tree suitable for skyline effect and for creating a wooded lot. Plants grow to 100 feet (30.5 m) high with a spread of 80 feet (24.4 m).

Quercus macrocarpa
Bur oak
Zones 2–8

Similar to white oak in appearance and stature, plants are hardier and produce a golf-ball-size acorn almost completely enclosed by a scaly cup with a fibrous lip.

Quercus palustris
Pin oak
Zones 4–8

Native to North America, this fast-growing oak [up to 3 feet (91 cm) a year] grows to a mature height of 60 feet (18.3 m) with a beautiful pyramidal habit. Dark green, sharply indented leaves turn parchment brown in the fall and persist on the tree through the winter. Tolerates a wide range of acid soil conditions including swampy soil. This oak makes a good lawn highlight and street tree; it is especially popular for lining a driveway. A related variety, *Q. coccinea* (scarlet oak) is almost identical in appearance to the pin oak, but has beautiful red autumn leaf coloring.

Quercus phellos
Willow oak
Zones 5–9

Distinct among oaks because of its slender, willowlike leaves, plants grow to 60 feet (18.3 m) high and 40 feet (12.2 m) wide with a domed shape. Native to the eastern U.S., the leaves change to shades of yellow and red in autumn. Makes a good lawn highlight and avenue for a driveway.

Quercus robur
English oak
Zones 4–8

Native to Europe, plants grow to 100 feet (30.5 m) high and 60 feet (18.3 m) wide. Useful for skyline effect and parkland. The variety 'Fastigiata' has upright branches resembling a poplar and is suitable for tall hedging and planting as sentinels along a house foundation. Poor autumn color compared to hardy North American species.

Robinia pseudoacacia
Black locust
Zones 4–9

Native to the eastern U.S., this fast-growing, suckering, broadly columnar tree with spiny shoots has oval, dark green leaflets, growing up to 12 inches (31 cm) long that average about 15 to a leaf cluster. Plants grow to 80 feet (24.4 m) tall with a spread of 35 feet (10.7 m). In late spring and early summer, fragrant white flowers are borne in pendent 8-inch (20 cm) clusters. Grow in full sun in a moisture-retentive but well-drained soil. Shelter from strong winds, as the branches are brittle. 'Frisia' is an exceedingly beautiful, graceful tree with golden-yellow foliage, which is yellow-green in summer, then turning orange-yellow in autumn.

Salix alba 'Tristis' aka S. x chrysocoma
Weeping willow
Zones 2–9

A hybrid between species native to North America and China, this magnificent, billowing, deciduous tree is fast growing to 100 feet (30.5 m) and equally wide. The yellow branch coloring intensifies in early spring just before the leaves emerge. Plant away from the house, at the edge of a property and along stream banks or pond margins, where its majestic presence can be best admired. The vigorous root system can interfere with sewer lines and drains. Many other willows have a weeping habit including forms of *S. alba*, white willow (zones 2–8) and *S. babylonica*, Babylon weeping willow (zones 3–8). A new hybrid willow *S.* 'Golden Curls' (zones 5–8) from Australia uses *S. matsudana* 'Tortuosa' (corkscrew willow) and *S. alba tristis* (golden weeping willow) in its parentage and grows at the astonishing rate of 12 feet (3.6 m) a year. It is useful as a windbreak, has an upright habit and resembles a poplar.

Sassafras albidum
Sassafras
Zones 5–8

Native to the eastern U.S., this tenacious, small, deciduous tree grows quickly to 25 feet (7.6 m) high, although it can grow to 50 feet (15.2 m). Its furrowed trunk and gnarled, outstretched branches produce a dramatic winter silhouette. The autumn color can be yellow, orange, scarlet and purple, all on the same tree.

The roots were once used by colonists to make tea and root beer, but the tree's volatile oil, safrole, is now considered to be carcinogenic. Useful planted in hedgerows and as a skyline accent.

Sciadopitys verticillata
Japanese umbrella pine
Zones 5–9

Native to Japan, this conical, very slow-growing, symmetrical evergreen grows to 70 feet (21.3 m) tall. The glossy, needle-like leaves are borne in whorls at the shoot tips like the spokes of an umbrella. Plants prefer a well-drained, slightly acidic, moisture-retentive soil in full sun or part shade. Useful as a windbreak and skyline accent.

Trees

Sequoiadendron giganteum
Hardy giant sequoia
Zones 6–8

A giant conifer native to the High Sierras of California, this is a big tree, unsuitable for most gardens, but often planted for skyline effect and bonsai. Plants can grow to 300 feet (91.4 m) high, creating a thick, straight, reddish-brown bark and a pyramidal shape. It is a zone hardier than its relative, the giant California coastal redwood *S. sempervirens*, and more tolerant of dry soil.

Sophora japonica
Japanese pagoda tree
Zones 4–9

Native to China and Korea, this rounded, deciduous tree grows quickly to 75 feet (22.9 m) tall and equally wide. Plants prefer full sun and well-drained soil. It bears creamy-white, slightly fragrant flower clusters in midsummer, although blooming often does not occur until after 10 years. The spear-shaped leaflets are arranged in groups of seven or more, creating an airy canopy. It grows under many adverse conditions and makes a good lawn tree, since turf will grow right up to its trunk. 'Pendula' is a beautiful weeping form.

Sorbus americana
American mountain ash
Zone 3–8

This native of the northeastern U.S. and Canada is similar in appearance to *S. aucuparia* but a zone hardier and more tolerant of hot, dry summers. In autumn, leaves turn all shades of yellow and red.

Sorbus aucuparia
European mountain ash
Zones 4–7

Though susceptible to the ravages of fireblight disease, a virus infection that turns berries black and causes early defoliation, this deciduous tree is good for late summer, scarlet-red berry displays; some varieties are yellow, pink and apricot. The leaves are composed of sets of up to 15 serrated, spear-shaped leaflets. The small white flowers, borne in flat clusters in spring, are also ornamental. Good lawn highlight and rarely needs pruning. Naturally forms a tidy, upright, oval outline and strong single trunk.

Staphylea trifolia
Bladdernut

Zones 3–8

Native to North America, this upright, suckering, small tree grows to 15 feet (4.5 m) high. In early spring, it bears abundant, bell-shaped, greenish white flowers in nodding clusters followed by pale green, bladderlike fruit. The trifoliate leaves turn dull yellow in autumn. Plants prefer full sun or light shade and a moisture-retentive, well-drained soil. Useful as a lawn highlight.

Stewartia pseudocamellia
Japanese stewartia

Zones 5–8

This pyramidal Japanese species grows to 30 feet (9.1 m) high and 20 feet (6.1 m) wide. Its cup-shaped white flowers resemble a camellia. Unlike camellias, the flowers are slightly fragrant and appear in early summer when few other trees are blooming. The spear-shaped, serrated, bright green leaves turn shades of orange, red and purple in the autumn. The exfoliating bark reveals a camouflage pattern of orange, green and gray, which provides all-season interest. Plants prefer acid soil and grow best in moisture-retentive soil, but dislike intense heat and drought unless light shade can be provided during the heat of the day. Outstanding as a lawn accent. *S. sinensis*, Chinese stewartia (zones 5–8), is similar in appearance but with 2-inch (5 cm), fragrant, white flowers.

Styrax japonicus
Japanese snowbell

Zones 6–8

Native to Japan, this deciduous plant sometimes grows as a tree and sometimes as a wide-spreading, large shrub with a flat top up to 30 feet (9.1 m) high. Room must be allowed for the width, which may be twice the height when the plant is mature. White bell-like flowers appear in spring, hanging conspicuously from the undersides of the branches and beneath the dark green leaves. Plants prefer a moist but well-drained soil in sun or partial shade. It is especially beautiful planted on a hillside, so that the rows of numerous flowers can be best appreciated. *S. obassia*, fragrant snowbell (zones 6–8), has ascending branches rather than horizontal ones.

Syringa reticulata
Japanese tree lilac

Zones 4–7

Native to Japan, this upright, billowing, deciduous shrub grows to 30 feet (9.1 m) tall. Leaves are lance shaped and sharply pointed up to 6 inches (15 cm) long. Plants bear fragrant creamy white flowers in large showy panicles to 8 inches (20 cm) long in early summer. Useful as a street tree and lawn accent. Provide full sun and well-drained, slightly acid soil.

Taxodium distichum
Swamp cypress

Zones 5–10

Native to the southeastern U.S., this pyramidal, deciduous conifer grows 70 feet (21.3 m) tall in moisture-retentive soil or standing water in full sun. Develops knobby growths called "knees" in waterlogged sites. Foliage turns an orange-brown in the fall. The trunk is buttressed near the base on mature specimens. Useful as a skyline accent. Suitable for planting beside lakes and as a highlight in bog gardens.

Trees

Taxus cuspidata
Japanese yew
Zones 4–7

Native to Japan, Korea and Manchuria, this fast-growing evergreen tree or large shrub can grow to 50 feet (15.2 m) high and spread 25 feet (7.6 m) wide with an upright habit. Plants are mostly multi-stemmed with dark green needles, forming a distinct V-shaped pattern as they lie flat in two rows along the stem. The stem bark is usually reddish brown and flakes off with age. Oval red berries appear in autumn. Prefers well-drained loam soil in full sun or part shade but is tolerant of drought. Tall varieties make good accents as sentinels to doorways and garden entrances; it is also valuable as a hedge. Dwarf, spreading kinds can be sheared into mounds.

Thuja occidentalis
American arborvitae
Zones 3–7

Native to the eastern U.S., this slender evergreen tree can grow to 60 feet (18.3 m) high and 15 feet (4.5 m) wide, although there are also dwarf globular, conical and cylindrical varieties. Juvenile foliage is needle-like, and mature foliage is in flat sprays. Although suitable as a lawn highlight and foundation accent, it is most often used as a tall hedge and windbreak.

Tilia americana
American linden
Zones 3–8

Native to North America, this pyramidal, deciduous tree grows to 80 feet (24.4 m) high by 60 feet (18.3 m) wide. Give it fertile, well-drained soil in sun or partial shade. It is a stately symmetrical tree with a clean straight trunk. *T. cordata*, littleleaf linden (zones 4–7), is shorter and more suitable for small gardens. 'Greenspire' is a vigorous grower with a conical habit to 50 feet (15.2 m) tall. Makes a good street tree and lawn accent.

Tsuga canadensis
Canadian hemlock

Zones 3–8

Native to North America, this tall, slow-growing, pyramidal, needle evergreen grows up to 100 feet (30.5 m) tall. Its fine needles give it a soft appearance. Small brown cones hang from the branch tips. Plants prefer humus-rich, acid soil in sun or partial shade. Makes a good lawn highlight, an excellent windbreak and a superb hedge, since it tolerates severe pruning. *T. canadensis* 'Sargentii', Sargent's weeping hemlock (zones 3–7), is more suitable for small gardens. This variety grows 4 feet (1.2 m) high and twice as wide with a low spreading habit.

Ulmus americana
American elm

Zones 3–9

Native to the U.S., this vase-shaped, deciduous tree grows to 80 feet (24.4 m) tall. It has been so devastated by Dutch elm disease as to be almost extinct in the U.S.. Better disease-resistant alternatives are *U. parvifolia*, Chinese elm (zones 4–9), especially the variety 'Golden Ray', which has golden, spear-shaped, serrated foliage.

Ulmus glabra 'Camperdownii' aka 'Horizontalis'
Camperdown elm

Zones 4–6

This splendid weeping, deciduous tree has been described as the most beautiful tree that nature ever created, especially in flower. These widely spreading plants are usually grafted about 6 feet (1.8 m) high on the understock and generally grow to 20 feet (6.1 m) tall with pendulous, twisted branches that reach to the ground, thus making a tent of shade. Leaves are serrated to 8 inches (20 cm) long. Tiny pinkish flowers are produced in early spring followed by clustered, winged green fruit. Outstanding as a lawn specimen.

Viburnum prunifolium
Blackhaw viburnum

Zones 3–9

Native to North America, this deciduous, small tree grows to 15 feet (4.5 m) tall with a rounded form in sun to part shade. It has attractive, flat corymbs of white flowers in late spring followed by black edible berries in late summer. For more Viburnum: Shrubs, see page 168.

Zelkova serrata
Japanese zelkova

Zones 5–8

Native to Japan, this deciduous, stiffly vase-shaped, disease-resistant tree grows to 80 feet (24.4 m) tall, displaying serrated, spear-shaped leaves similar in appearance to a beech. It is now widely used as a street tree replacement for the almost extinct American elm, since its form is somewhat similar. Give it full sun and good drainage.

Vegetables, Fruits & Nuts

Edible plants, such as annual and perennial vegetables, orchard fruits and nuts, can be soft-stemmed, herbaceous (such as asparagus) or woody (such as apples). Since the cultivation of these categories is different, they are listed here separately. Medicinal and culinary herbs are listed on page 45.

Hardy Annual Vegetables

Annual vegetables can be classified as "cool season" and "warm season." Cool season vegetables, such as spinach and lettuce, thrive when nights are cool, generally in spring and autumn. They will tolerate frost, but usually succumb to frozen soil. Because of their frost tolerance, they are usually direct-seeded or transplanted into the garden several weeks before the last expected spring frost date in your area, allowing them to mature before hot summer temperatures cause them to bolt to seed.

A second crop of cool season vegetables is normally possible in autumn, when cool night temperatures return. The timing of this second crop is critical and varies according to whether the vegetable matures quickly (like leaf lettuce), or requires time (like Brussels sprouts). For quick maturing vegetables, planting can be done in late summer or early autumn, as soon as night-time temperatures turn cool. For longer maturing vegetables, midsummer planting may be desirable.

The following is a list of cool season vegetables with appropriate comments concerning their hardiness:

Arugula (aka Roquette)
An early salad green, it takes 20 days to first harvest. Direct-sow seeds in early spring. Seedlings will tolerate mild frosts. Mature plants will survive severe frost in autumn and winter.

Broad Beans (aka Fava beans)
Pre-germinate seeds for early spring sowing. Shell beans ready to harvest in 85 days for eating cooked. Seed may also be direct-sown, since seedlings tolerate mild frost. Mature plants will survive mild frost in autumn and winter.

LEFT: Harvest of hardy summer fruits and berries, including raspberries, blueberries, plums, apricots and peaches.

Beets
Root crop ready to harvest in 55 days for eating cooked. Direct-seed three weeks before last spring frost date, since seedlings tolerate mild frosts. Mature plants will survive severe frost in autumn and winter.

Vegetables, Fruits & Nuts

Broccoli

Transplant four-week old seedlings three weeks before last spring frost date. Edible heads ready to harvest in 50 days for eating fresh or cooked. Mature plants will survive mild frosts in autumn and winter.

Brussels sprouts

Transplant five-week old seedlings three weeks before last spring frost date and in late summer for autumn/winter harvest. Edible, cabbage-flavored sprouts ready to harvest in 100 days for eating cooked. Mature plants will survive heavy frosts in autumn and winter.

Cabbage

Transplant four-week old seedlings three weeks before last spring frost date and in late summer for autumn/winter harvest. Edible heads of early varieties ready to harvest in 65 days for eating cooked. Mature plants will survive severe frosts in autumn and winter, especially winter hardy varieties like 'January King.'

Carrots

Direct-seed three weeks before last spring frost date and again in late summer for autumn/winter harvest. Root crop ready to harvest in 70 days for eating fresh or cooked. Mature plants will survive severe frosts in autumn and winter.

Cauliflower

Transplant four-week old seedlings three weeks before last spring frost date and in late summer for autumn/winter harvest. Edible heads ready to harvest in 60 days for eating fresh or cooked. Mature plants will survive severe frosts in autumn and winter if the leaves are tied up over the curd to protect it.

Chard (aka Silverbeet and Swiss chard)

Direct-seed three weeks before last spring frost date and in late summer for autumn/winter harvest. Spring sowings will also remain productive until winter freezes. Edible leaves ready to harvest in 60 days as salad greens or as a spinach substitute when cooked. The more the outer leaves are harvested, the more new inner leaves will continue to grow until killed by severe freezing.

Celery

Transplant four-week-old seedlings three weeks before last spring frost date. Edible stalks ready to harvest in 80 days for eating fresh or cooked. Mature plants will tolerate mild frost in autumn, especially if soil is heaped up around the stalks.

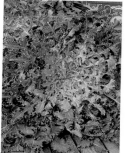

Endive

Direct-seed three weeks before last spring frost date and again in late summer for autumn harvest. Harvest edible leaves as salad greens in 40 days. Mature plants will survive mild frosts in autumn and winter.

Celeriac

Transplant four-week-old seedlings three weeks before last spring frost date. Edible root ready to harvest in 100 days. Tastes like celery when cooked. Mature plants will survive severe frost in autumn and winter.

Kale

Direct-seed or transplant three-week-old seedlings three weeks before last spring frost date. Early varieties like 'Red Russian' are ready to harvest as cooked greens in 50 days. Mature plants will survive severe frosts in autumn and winter.

Corn Salad (aka Mache)

Direct-seed three weeks before last spring frost date and again in late summer for autumn harvest. The oval green leaves are delicious as a salad green, ready to harvest in 50 days. Mature plants will survive mild frosts in autumn and winter.

Kohlrabi

Direct-seed or transplant three-week-old seedlings three weeks before last spring frost date. The bulbous stem tastes like turnip when steamed or boiled, ready to harvest when the size of a tennis ball, usually within 50 days. Mature plants will survive mild frosts in autumn and winter.

Cress

Direct-seed three weeks before last spring frost date. Spicy leaves ready to harvest in 10 days as a salad green. Mature plants will survive mild frosts in autumn and winter.

Leeks

Direct-seed or transplant four-week-old seedlings three weeks before last spring frost date and in late summer for autumn/winter harvest. Edible as a cooked onion-flavored side dish with ready-to-harvest stalks in 100 days. Mature plants will survive severe frost in autumn and winter, especially if straw is piled up against the stalks.

Lettuce

Direct-seed loose-leaf kinds three weeks before last spring frost date. Transplant three-week old seedlings of head varieties three weeks before last spring frost date and again in late summer for autumn harvests. Harvest loose-leaf lettuce in 50 days; head lettuce in 60 days as a salad green. Mature plants will survive mild frosts in autumn and winter.

Mustard Greens

Direct-seed or transplant three-week old seedlings three weeks before last spring frost date. Leaves ready to harvest in 50 days as cooked greens. Mature plants will survive severe frost in autumn and winter.

Onions

Transplant four-week-old seedlings four weeks before last spring frost date, or plant "sets" (bulbs). The bulbous base is ready to harvest in 90 days, sliced as a garnish or cooked. Mature plants will survive mild frosts in autumn and winter.

Parsnips

Direct-seed three weeks before last spring frost date and in late summer for autumn/winter harvest. The white, carrot-shaped roots are ready to harvest in 90 days as a cooked side dish. Mature plants will survive severe frosts, especially if straw is heaped against the leaf stalks.

Peas

Pre-germinate seed or direct-seed three weeks before last spring frost date. Early varieties are ready to harvest in 65 days. Choose between shell peas (with inedible pods), edible-pod peas (also called snow peas) with flat pods and snap peas (with plump edible pods). Mature plants will tolerate mild frosts in autumn.

Radicchio

Direct-seed or transplant three-week old seedlings three weeks before last spring frost date. Edible heads ready to harvest in 60 days as a salad green. Mature plants will survive mild frosts in autumn and spring.

Radish

Direct-seed three weeks before last spring frost date. Early varieties are ready to harvest in 25 days; the round, red or white roots are delicious eaten fresh or mixed into salads. Mature plants of large-rooted varieties, such as 'Round Black' and 'Daikon', will tolerate mild frosts in autumn and winter.

Romanesco

Transplant four-week-old seedlings three weeks before last frost date and again in late summer for autumn harvest. Edible heads ready to harvest in 80 days either fresh or cooked like broccoli. Mature plants will survive mild frosts in autumn and winter, especially if the leaves are tied up over the heads for protection.

Rutabaga (aka Swede)

Direct-seed three weeks before last spring frost date. Harvest the turniplike roots in 100 days for use as a cooked side dish. Mature plants will survive severe frosts in autumn and winter.

Shallots

Transplant four-week-old seedlings three weeks before last spring frost date or plant "sets" (bulbs). The copper-skinned, swollen stem resembles an onion, ready to harvest in 100 days, sliced and diced as a garnish for meat dishes and also pickled and cooked. Mature plants will tolerate mild frosts in autumn.

Spinach

Direct-seed four weeks before last spring frost date and again in late summer for autumn/winter harvest. Ready to harvest in 45 days, eaten fresh as a salad green or cooked. Mature plants will survive severe frosts in autumn and winter, especially varieties like 'Bloomsdale Long Standing.'

Turnip

Direct-seed three weeks before last spring frost date and again in late summer for autumn/winter harvest. The round roots are best eaten cooked as a vegetable side dish. Early varieties such as 'Tokyo Cross' are ready to harvest in 40 days. The tops are edible as cooked greens. Mature plants will survive severe frosts in autumn and winter.

Hardy Perennial Vegetables

Hardy perennial vegetables as listed below need a special area of the garden so they can stay undisturbed from year to year, usually around the perimeter of a kitchen garden, against a south facing wall or fence. A liquid soil feed or a granular fertilizer raked into the upper soil surface is advisable in spring and autumn before new growth occurs. Additionally, or alternatively, garden compost can be applied to the soil surface and raked in to keep the soil nourished.

Armoracia rusticana
Horseradish
Zones 4–8

Native to southeastern Europe, this bog-tolerant, hardy perennial vegetable grows to 3 feet (91 cm) high with a clump-forming, upright habit. Large, dark green, paddle-shaped leaves with wavy edges rise erect from deep, thick taproots. Small white flowers appear in clusters among the leaves in summer. Best confined to a special corner as plants can become invasive. It is propagated from root cuttings in spring and prefers a fertile, moisture-retentive loam soil in full sun. The white taproots are uprooted from the soil, washed clean, dried and shredded to release the hot, pungent aroma that flavors condiments and sauces for beef, pork and seafood.

Vegetables, Fruits & Nuts

Asparagus officinalis
Asparagus
Zones 4–8

This long-lived perennial vegetable has been developed from wild plants growing in the U.K. fens and other wetlands of Europe. Domesticated varieties are grown for their edible young spears that appear in early spring from fleshy roots that spread out like the tentacles of an octopus under the soil. The spears grow quickly and are best harvested when they are 6 to 8 inches (15 to 20 cm) long, before the succulent tip opens out to display fibrous, ferny leaves. Plants can be male or female, the males generally producing the thickest and most succulent stalks. Females bear red berries in autumn when the leaves turn straw colored, and the roots become dormant after frost.

Plants prefer full sun and fertile soil with good drainage. The variety 'Jersey King' is an all male, growing spears as thick as a man's thumb. 'Purple Passion' has purple spears producing spears as thick as two thumbs. If forcing pots are upturned over an asparagus clump, the exclusion of light will produce "blanching." Though this reduces the nutritional value, it improves tenderness. Blanched asparagus spears are valued by gourmet cooks.

Propagation is by seed or year-old roots. When planting from roots, it is best to dig a trench up to 6 inches (15 cm) deep and splay the roots out over a mound of soil in the bottom, spaced at least 2 feet (61 cm) apart and 2 feet (61 cm) between rows. From seed, a light harvest can be made the third season. From roots, a light harvest can be made the second season. Stop harvesting by midsummer to allow sufficient foliage to mature for next season's crop.

Helianthus tuberosus
Jerusalem artichoke
Zones 4–9

Native to the northeastern U.S. and Canada, this perennial sunflower is grown for its edible tubers. Plants grow to 10 feet (3 m) high, topped in late summer by clusters of yellow daisylike flowers with black centers. Although the tubers are edible, no more than one tuber should be consumed during a meal, since they are a purgative. Plant rhizomes at least 2 feet (61 cm) apart, 3 inches (8 cm) deep, in full sun and soil with good drainage.

Nasturtium officinale
Watercress
Zones 6–9

This delicious, vitamin-rich, perennial salad crop is best grown in shallow, running water. Rosettes of dark green, rounded leaves float on the water and remain productive all year, even during winter. Plants prefer a sandy soil. Best grown from seed sown into permanently moist soil three weeks before the last spring frost date and then transplant. If stems grow tall and outgrow their allotted space (usually after flowering), the stems can be cut back to force new juvenile growth.

Rheum x hybridum
Rhubarb
Zones 6–10

Valued for its edible stalks, I never saw rhubarb so big and healthy as in the walled vegetable garden at Cawdor Castle, Scotland, where vigorous clumps produce leaves up to 10 feet (3 m) tall. The head gardener informed me that the secret was cow manure, which he considered more beneficial than stable manure. Native to China, the broad, green, wavy leaves are poisonous, but the thick red stalks are succulent and delicious when cooked and sweetened with sugar, honey or maple syrup. Rhubarb prefers a fertile, humus-rich, well-drained soil in full sun with regular watering. Harlow Carr Gardens, Yorkshire, has one of the largest collections of rhubarb varieties in the world. Some of the best commercially available varieties include 'MacDonald' with bright red stems and 'Victoria' producing mostly green stems tinged red. If flower heads form (these are usually large, creamy white and held high above the foliage), they should be removed to concentrate the plant's energy into the root.

Rumex scutatus
Sorrel

Zones 3–10

This hardy perennial is grown for its edible greens. The spear-shaped leaves have a bittersweet flavor suitable for mixed salads and for making soup. Direct-sow seed or transplant "starts" three weeks before last spring frost date, harvesting leaves in 60 days. When plants start to flower in midsummer, cut the stems back to the ground to force new juvenile growth. This also prevents the plants from self-seeding and becoming an invasive weed. Plants will often endure into winter months or go dormant to sprout again in spring. Harvest the side leaves until plants are well established.

Hardy Fruits and Nuts

Fruits and nuts can be soft-stemmed (herbaceous) or woody. Smaller fruits like herbaceous strawberries and woody currants are usually grown in wide beds or a special area called the "Soft Fruit Garden," where space-saving methods of cultivation can be employed. For example, woody blueberries, currants and gooseberries can be grown as a hedge, while vining grapes and hardy kiwi vines can be grown over an arbor or along a fence. Blackberry canes can be fanned out flat against a sunny wall or trellis.

Woody plants like apples and peaches can take up a lot of space if grown as an orchard. Some trees will need 10-foot (3 m) spacing, but there are special dwarf varieties that can be planted closer together even in containers. Another space-saving idea is to grow fruit trees with pliable branches as espalier with their limbs trained to grow sideways along a sunny wall or fence.

Apples
Malus pumila aka M. x domestica
Zones 3–9, depending on variety

It was long believed that the domesticated apple was a hybrid of several species of uncertain origin, but recent DNA testing and exploration has shown that all domesticated orchard apples are descended from a single species native to Asia. There are dwarf, semi-dwarf and standard varieties, which refer to the height of the plants. These produce mostly red, yellow or green fruits. Dwarfs can be grown in tubs and wherever space is limited, generally staying below 10 feet (3 m). Semi-dwarf trees generally stay below 15 feet (4.5 m) and are most suitable for planting to create a fruiting hedge. Standard apple trees grow to 20 feet (6.1 m) or more. Unless you have a neighbor with apple trees, grow more than one variety since apples like to be cross-pollinated by another apple variety (although crabapples will also serve as pollinators). Apple trees bloom in spring, followed by crisp fruit that ripens in late summer and autumn. They will produce a vast number of branches to the detriment of fruit size, unless pruned each season after fruiting. To save space, apple trees may be trained to create espaliers, usually with selected branches stretched along a wire for support. They can be trained over an arbor to form a tunnel and as "cordons" (ropes) along rails to form a living fence along pathways. A strain of fastigiated apple trees from Europe called 'Colonnade' grows narrow and tall, allowing four trees to be grown in the space normally occupied by one apple tree.

Apricot
Prunus armeniaca
Zones 5–10, depending on variety

Although apricots are relatively hardy small trees bearing delicious golden-orange fruits the size of a small peach, they have a tendency to flower before the last frosts of spring; therefore the unfolding of recently pollinated flowers are highly susceptible to winterkill. The variety 'Goldcot' (zones 5–7) is recommended for northern gardens because it is late flowering, so the fruit is less susceptible to frost damage. Ripening in midsummer, plants prefer full sun and good drainage. To save space, they can be trained against a wall. Plants grow to 15 feet (4.5 m) high. Propagate by grafting and cuttings.

Blackberries
Rubus fruticosus
Zones 4–8, depending on variety

Resembling rose bushes, these bushy plants are widely distributed throughout the Northern Hemisphere. They have arching canes that can be extremely thorny, though there are thornless varieties. Plants grow to 6 feet (1.8 m) high and equally wide, bearing white or pink flowers resembling a wild rose. The thimble-size fruits ripen in late summer, to be eaten fresh or baked into pies and jams. Blackberries have been crossed with raspberries and other bramble fruits to create a range of hybrids including tayberries and loganberries, all similar in appearance. Train the plants along a fence to save space, or plant to form a hedge, spacing plants 6 feet (1.8 m) apart. They demand full sun and a fertile, well-drained soil. Propagate by rooted cuttings.

Blueberries
Vaccinium corymbosum
Zones 2–9

Native to North America, the bushy, deciduous plant known as the highbush blueberry produces small, bell-shaped, white flowers in spring and clusters of marble-size blueberries by midsummer. These are sweet and good for eating fresh, and they make delicious pie filling. Given an acid soil with good drainage and full sun, they are carefree plants, although they generally need netting to protect the crop from being eaten by birds. Propagate by rooted cuttings. There are two main hardy kinds in commerce: highbush blueberries growing to 8 feet (2.4 m) and *V. angustifolium*, lowbush blueberries (zones 3–9), growing to 18 inches (46 cm) and suitable for groundcover. By spacing the highbush blueberries 4 feet (1.2 m) apart, it is possible to create a fruiting hedge.

Cherries
Prunus avium
Zones 3–9

The main parent of domesticated sweet cherries is a deciduous tree native to Asia. The mostly bright red fruit ripens in early summer. However, there are numerous other species from Europe, Asia and North America with varying degrees of usefulness as a dessert fruit. These include *P. cerasus*, sour cherry (zones 3–9), mostly used for pie fillings and the bushy, extremely hardy *P. pumila*, sand cherry (zones 2–9). Plants of sweet and sour cherries can grow to 30 feet (9.1 m) high, but heavy pruning can keep them low growing, and there are dwarf varieties for small gardens. Flowers are usually white and pollinated by bees. Protect the resulting fruit from bird damage by netting. Give cherries full sun and good drainage. Planting two varieties improves pollination. Hardiness in many cherries is achieved by grafting a special fruit stock onto a hardy root stock. The graft union is a swelling just above the soil line. If the root portion sends up shoots, these should be pruned away to leave only the fruit stock to bear fruit. 'Stella' is a strain of cherry developed in Canada with extra large fruit and extra heavy yields. There is also a true dwarf form, 'Compact Stella'. Propagate from rooted cuttings and grafting.

Chestnut, Chinese
Castanea mollissima
Zones 4–8

Native to China, decorative in the landscape because of its generous white flower clusters in summer; they produce edible nuts, which ripen in autumn. Widely grown in the U.S., where it has replaced the disease-susceptible American chestnut (*C. americana*). Plants grow to 40 feet (12.2 m) high and equally wide. The leaves are lance-like and serrated. The nuts are brown and enclosed in a prickly seed case. The flowers have a musty odor. Widely used as a lawn accent.

Chestnut, Spanish
Castanea sativa
Zones 5–9

Native to Europe, this is a handsome, large tree reaching to 100 feet (30.5 m) high. It is widely seen in Europe but scarce elsewhere. Generally, the nuts are larger than the Chinese chestnut. Makes a good skyline accent. When planting for nut production, choose named varieties or hybrids.

Currants
Ribes rubrum
Zones 3–7

Currants produce edible berries in large clusters on bushy plants up to 5 feet (1.5 m) high. Although the red currant is the most popular color, black and white fruiting varieties are available. When fully ripe, they have a tart-sweet flavor. They can be eaten fresh but are best enjoyed as a pie filling and jam. Plants should be spaced at least 3 feet (91 cm) apart in a fertile, well-drained soil in full sun. After the third year, prune the plants back to the soil line to force new juvenile growth. Propagate by taking tip cuttings—bending a cane to the soil, scraping the bark about 8 inches (20 cm) from the tip and burying it in the soil until it roots itself. Currants are closely related to gooseberries and harbor a disease that can kill white pine. They tend to decline quickly where summers are hot.

Elderberry
Sambucus canadensis
Zones 3–8

This multi-stemmed, much branching shrub is native to North America, producing large white flower clusters in summer, followed by an abundance of black berries mostly used for making pie filling, wine and jam. In the autumn, the plant's serrated leaves turn orange and burgundy. There are bronze-leaf and golden leaf forms that can be highly ornamental. Elderberries prefer a moisture-retentive soil and full sun. 'Nova', growing to 8 feet (2.4 m) high, has been selected for its extra-large flower trusses and fruit clusters. Propagate by cuttings.

Filbert, American or hazelnut
Corylus americana
Zones 4–9
Native to the eastern U.S. and Canada, this deciduous, multi-stemmed shrub or small tree grows to 10 feet (3 m) high. Yellow catkins appear in spring ahead of the beechlike leaves, then marble-size nuts in hard shells. Useful as a hedge.

Filbert, Turkish or hazelnut
Corylus colurna
Zones 4–7
Native to Turkey, plants can grow to 50 feet (15.2 m) high, usually forming a short trunk before branching. The yellow catkins are shorter and less conspicuous than the American filbert, and the leaves are more ivy shaped. Nut size and quality is better than the American filbert.

Gooseberries
Ribes uva-crispa
Zones 3–9, depending on variety
Although wild gooseberries found in North America remain tart, the varieties grown for berry production in gardens will taste sweet when fully ripe. The hardiest are the Finnish varieties of 'Hinnomaki Red' and 'Hinnomaki Yellow'; they produce marble-size fruit. 'Invicta', from England, produces fruit the size of a quail's egg. Plants are usually thorny, growing bushy to 3 feet (91 cm) and more. They like full sun and good drainage, but are short lived in areas with hot and humid summers, usually declining after three seasons. Propagate by layers and cuttings. Like currants, they harbor a disease that can kill white pine.

Grapes
Vitis vinifera
Zones 6–9
These vigorous, vining, woody plants can grow to heights of 15 feet (4.5 m) and more, unless rigorously pruned each year in autumn after the bunches of marble-size fruit have been harvested. In home gardens, grape vines are best grown over an arbor or along a section of strong fence. Varieties have different degrees of hardiness, although the hardiest are usually grafts of European varieties onto hardier North American rootstocks. Basically, there are dessert grapes for eating fresh and wine grapes for pressing to make wine. An all-American species, *V. rotundifolia*, muscadine grapes (zones 5–9), have purple fruit and a musky flavor. *V. labrusca* (the American fox grape) includes the famous variety 'Concord' (zones 5–8). An even hardier North American native is *V. riparia*, frost grape (zones 2–8). The variety 'Brant' has sweet black fruit. Dessert grapes can have tender skins and some are seedless. Others may be "slipskins," meaning they have tough skins but juicy, sweet interiors. Fruit color can be red, black (usually a dark, dusky blue) or white, and it's good to plant all three kinds over an arbor for decorative effect. Grape leaves are ivy shaped, turning russet colors in autumn. Propagation is mostly from rooted cuttings.

Kiwi, Hardy
Actinidia arguta

Zones 5–9, depending on variety

Although most people think of kiwi fruit as a tender fruit known as Chinese gooseberry and New Zealand kiwi, there are several hardy varieties bearing smaller but equally delicious fruit. Collectively known as hardy kiwis, these strong-growing vines differ from the more familiar New Zealand kiwi mostly from the size of their fruit, which generally have the shape and appearance of a date. Borne in generous clusters, they ripen in autumn when the green fruits turn brown and sweet. Up to 100 pounds of fruit can be harvested from a mature vine. Plants require good drainage and full sun, preferably with protection from cold winds. They are ideal for growing up walls and over pergolas, spacing plants at least 10 feet (3 m) apart. Plant one male vine for every six females. Propagate by cuttings.

Mulberry
Morus alba

Zones 4–10, depending on variety

Native to China, this relatively small tree grows up to 20 feet (6.1 m) high. In midsummer it produces such prodigious quantities of fruit the size and color of blackberries that they should not be planted near patios, walkways and driveways, where the ripe fruit can cause stains. Plants prefer full sun and good drainage. The large, serrated, heart-shaped leaves turn yellow in autumn. A particularly desirable variety is 'Pendula', the weeping mulberry, which can be grown in a container and kept compact by pruning. 'Illinois Everbearing' is the hardiest, to zone 4. Varieties sold by nurseries are normally self-pollinating. Propagate by cuttings.

Paw Paw
Asimina triloba

Zones 6–8

Grows to 30 feet (9.1 m) tall, generally pyramid shaped when grown alone. Leaves are oval and somewhat drooping with an unpleasant odor when crushed. Fruits are 3 to 5 inches (8 to 13 cm) long and ripen yellow in autumn. The flavor of the soft custardlike flesh is somewhat like that of a banana. Maroon-colored, cup-shaped, nodding flowers attract flies for pollination. Cross-pollination with another tree is needed to set fruit.

Peaches
Prunus persica

Zones 5–10

The hardiness of peaches depends on warm, sunny summers and in its northern limit, shelter from late frost that can damage pollinated flowers and newly set fruit. Planting against a wall so the branches are splayed out as an espalier is recommended. Nectarines are a mutation of peaches and were once commonly called "fuzzless peaches." Their cultural needs are the same, and one will pollinate the other. Give peaches and nectarines full sun and good drainage. Many pests and diseases afflict peaches unless a spray program is used. Borers are worms that will burrow into young trees unless the trunk is wrapped and leaf curl will cause defoliation and fruit drop, but can be controlled by spraying. Dwarf varieties are available for growing in containers to save space. Traditional peaches will grow to 20 feet (6.1 m) high with an equal spread. Propagate by cuttings and grafting.

Vegetables, Fruits & Nuts

Pecans
Carya illinoiensis
Zones 6–11, depending on variety

Native to the southern and central U.S. and related to walnuts, these tall, handsome trees produce hard-shelled nuts that are tough to crack unless special "papershell" varieties are grown. These brown, oval nuts ripen inside green nut cases that split open in autumn when the nuts are ripe. Plants will grow to 100 feet (30.5 m) high and 70 feet (21.3 m) wide, but can be kept short and compact by pruning. The spear-shaped leaves turn a beautiful golden yellow in autumn. Give them full sun and good drainage, and plant two trees for maximum nut production. Varieties are available for specific zones so check with local growers before planting.

Persimmon, American
Diospyros virginiana
Zones 5–9

Most persimmons are not hardy in regions colder than zone 8, including the more desirable Japanese persimmons. The American persimmon grows into a handsome, large, deciduous tree up to 70 feet (21.3 m) high with male and female flowers usually borne on separate trees. The golf-ball-size fruits open a pale orange in late summer and are highly astringent until after autumn frost. The variety 'John Rick' is grown for its desirable eating qualities.

Plums
Prunus x domestica
Zones 5–9

The two most commonly grown plums are the European and the Japanese (*P. salicina*). European plums include the blue-black skinned damson plum, while Japanese varieties can be blue-black, red and yellow skinned. The Japanese are a little less hardy (zones 6–10), but generally more desirable as a dessert fruit for its extra-large size and sweetness. Give plums full sun and good drainage. Propagate by cuttings. Plants grow to 30 feet (9.1 m) high, but can be trained to create space-saving espaliers through rigorous pruning. Recommended varieties include 'Stanley' (European), 'Shiro' and 'Red Heart' (Japanese).

Pears
Pyrus communis
Zones 2–9

Closely related to apples and native to Eurasia, pears can tolerate some shade, although for maximum yields, they prefer full sun and a fertile, well-drained soil. The French are particularly skillful at producing pear varieties, and many have French names such as the russet-colored 'Bosc' and yellow-skinned 'Beurre d'Anjou'. In recent years, *P. pyrifolia*, Asian pears (zones 4–9), have gained in popularity, mainly because they are sweeter than standard pear varieties, and they are much more expensive at the grocery counter. The variety 'Hosui' is particularly desirable for its globe shape and bronze skin. The heart-shaped leaves of Asian pears turn russet colors in fall, while the slender, spear-shaped leaves of standard pears have drab fall coloring. As with apples, there are dwarf, semi-dwarf and standard varieties of pears.

Raspberries
Rubus idaeus
Zones 4–8

Although red raspberries are the most widely grown, black and yellow are popular. Classified as bramble fruits because of their thorny canes and kinship to blackberries, the thimble-size fruits grow in clusters on erect stems that are best tied to supports to prevent the arching canes from bending to touch the ground. Ripening usually occurs in midsummer, although new "everbearer" varieties such as 'Heritage' will crop first on the old part of the cane, and again in autumn on the new part. Best planted from year-old roots in spring or fall, they require full sun and good drainage. Grow them as a "patch" in a circle or square of soil with the roots spaced 18 inches (46 cm) apart. In this manner, the canes tend to be self-supporting. Grown in rows, it is best to plant them against a wall or fence. Plants produce underground runners that can double the size of the planting each year. Prune canes to within 12 inches (31 cm) of the soil after fruiting in autumn, except with everbearers, which can be tip-pruned only to preserve old wood for early summer fruiting.

Strawberries
Fragaria x *ananassa*
Zones 3–10

The garden strawberry is a hybrid from crosses between *F. chiloense* (the North American beach strawberry) and *F. vesca* (the European woodland strawberry). Garden strawberries can be classified as June-bearers (or spring-bearers), which crop for three weeks in June in the Northern Hemisphere; everbearers, which crop in spring and autumn; and day-neutrals, which crop in spring, summer and autumn. Give strawberries a sandy, well-drained, fertile soil in full sun. From a spring planting of year-old roots, it is essential to remove all flowers until midsummer to concentrate the plant's energy into producing a healthy root system. Therefore, in the second season, plants can produce high yields and berries of the largest size. Mulch around the plants with straw or other material to keep the fruit from touching bare soil, since this will cause rot. Cover plants with netting if birds and foraging animals are a nuisance. It is most important to apply a high-phosphorus fertilizer at the start of the growing season, since phosphorus is responsible for flowering and fruit formation. Liquid foliar fertilizers are especially beneficial if applied in a 1-2-1 ratio of nutrients (for example, 10% nitrogen-20% phosphorus-10% potash). To save space, strawberries can be grown in containers.

Walnut, English
Juglans regia
Zones 4–10, depending on variety

Native to southeastern Europe and Asia, these large, dome-shaped, spreading, deciduous trees can grow to 80 feet (24.4 m) high and almost as wide. The edible nut meat is inside a brown shell about the size of a golf ball. This turns black in autumn when ripe. The oily consistency of the nut case can badly stain skin and clothing. Many varieties are zone specific, so check with local growers before planting. The 'Carpathian' strain tends to be hardiest. Plants need full sun and good drainage. Be aware also that the roots of walnuts emit a poison from their roots called juglone, which can be toxic to ornamental plants such as azaleas and rhododendrons. Of three kinds of walnut grown commercially, the English is the most desirable. The other two are *J. nigra*, black walnut (zones 4–10), and *J. cinerea*, butternut walnut (zones 4–9), both of North American origin. These are generally undesirable as garden plants, since the oily black nut cases make a mess. The nut shells are tough to crack open, and the amount of nut meat is small compared to the English walnut.

Botanical Name Index

Common Name Index

About the Author

Born and educated in England, Derek Fell is a widely published garden writer and garden photographer, now living in the United States. Author of more than 100 garden books and calendars, he has won more awards from the Garden Writers Association of America than any other person. A consultant to the White House on garden design during the Ford Administration, Fell's award-winning books include *Great Gardens of New Zealand* (Bateman), *Van Gogh's Gardens* (Simon & Schuster), *550 Home Landscaping Ideas* (Simon & Schuster), *Deerfield Garden – An American Garden through Four Seasons* (Pidcock Press) and *A Photographer's Garden* (Kodak). His articles about gardens and garden design have appeared in publications worldwide, including *Architectural Digest* (USA), *The Garden* (the magazine of the Royal Horticultural Society, Great Britain), and *The New Zealand Gardener*.

Married, with three children, Fell cultivates an award-winning garden at historic Cedaridge Farm, Pennsylvania.

For more information about Derek Fell's writing and photography awards, visit www.derekfell.net.

Acknowledgments

An encyclopedic knowledge of hardy plants comes only from many years of gardening and interaction with other gardeners in various hardiness zones, too many for me to acknowledge individually. However, I do wish to thank Joan Haas, my office manager, for her assistance. A member of the Hardy Plants Society, she not only helped me to select the featured plants, but also assisted with the research, photo selection and proof-checking needed to bring the book into print.

Thanks also to my wife, Carolyn, garden designer, for helping me to grow and evaluate for hardiness many of the plants featured in this book.